Research & Education Association

Verbal Review for the SAT

The Staff of Research & Education Association

Research & Education Association
Visit our website at
www.rea.com

Research & Education Association
61 Ethel Road West
Piscataway, New Jersey 08854
E-mail: info@rea.com

VERBAL REVIEW FOR THE SAT

Printed in the United States of America

Library of Congress Control Number 2005931095

International Standard Book Number 0-7386-0085-7

CONTENTS

ABOUT RESEARCH & EDUCATION ASSOCIATION

Founded in 1959, Research & Education Association is dedicated to publishing the finest and most effective educational materials—including software, study guides, and test preps—for students in middle school, high school, college, graduate school, and beyond.

REA's Test Preparation series includes books and software for all academic levels in almost all disciplines. Research & Education Association publishes test preps for students who have not yet entered high school, as well as high school students preparing to enter college. Students from countries around the world seeking to attend college in the United States will find the assistance they need in REA's publications. For college students seeking advanced degrees, REA publishes test preps for many major graduate school admission examinations in a wide variety of disciplines, including engineering, law, and medicine. Students at every level, in every field, with every ambition can find what they are looking for among REA's publications.

REA's practice tests are always based upon the most recently administered exams, and include every type of question that can be expected on the actual exams.

REA's publications and educational materials are highly regarded and continually receive an unprecedented amount of praise from professionals, instructors, librarians, parents, and students. Our authors are as diverse as the fields represented in the books we publish. They are well-known in their respective disciplines and serve on the faculties of prestigious high schools, colleges, and universities throughout the United States and Canada.

We invite you to visit us at *www.rea.com* to find out how "REA is making the world smarter."

ACKNOWLEDGMENTS

In addition to our authors, we would like to thank Larry B. Kling, Vice President, Editorial, for his overall direction; Pam Weston, Vice President, Publishing, for setting the quality standards for production integrity and managing the publication to completion; Christine Reilley, Senior Editor, for project management and preflight editorial review; Stacey Farkas, Senior Editor, and Jeanne Audino, Senior Editor, for editorial contributions; Diane Goldschmidt, Associate Editor, for post-production quality assurance; Edward Bonny, Copywriter, for editorial contributions; Christine Saul, Senior Graphic Artist, for designing the cover; Jeremy Rech, Graphic Artist, for interior design; and Jeff LoBalbo, Senior Graphic Artist, for post-production file mapping.

We also gratefully acknowledge the team at Publication Services for page composition.

THE NEW 3 R'S: READING, WRITING, AND REASONING

GETTING THE MOST OUT OF YOUR VERBAL REVIEW

What's all the buzz about the new SAT Reasoning Test? For starters, the dreaded Analogies Section has been dropped, while short reading passages and a student-produced essay have been added. To be sure, the test has changed significantly. We know that the verbal part of the test looms as one of the most difficult and challenging parts of the entire college admissions process. If that includes you, this book will ease your mind.

With the coming of every year, a new crop of students prepares for the SAT. In bookstores, online, and in libraries, they face an untold number of SAT preparation books, with each one claiming to offer new, unbeatable strategies or to have somehow solved the SAT. Strategies can be vital test tools but they are not infallible guides. The SAT is not a mystery that needs to be cracked open but rather a known quantity that needs to be mastered.

The fact is, there are no instant answers or pat solutions when it comes to taking the new SAT.

That's where this book comes in. Think of it as your personal Verbal tutor for the SAT. It is intended to aid you significantly in preparing for the Writing and Critical Reading sections of the new SAT. By studying with this book, you will learn how to work through SAT questions by applying simple, systematic rules to enable you to reach the right answers.

The practice questions you will find inside this book have been thoughtfully patterned after the actual SAT. Each answer is fully explained to provide you with a greater understanding of what the SAT expects from you.

You'll find this book to be perfect for self-guided study. Open it up anywhere and any time you are free to answer even just one question—on the bus, waiting in line in the cafeteria, or even between classes. The more you work at it, the more your skills will improve.

Understanding the SAT: Question Types

As you proceed through this book, you will learn and identify types of questions that appear on the two verbal sections of the SAT Reasoning Test. Part I reviews the Writing Section. Part II covers the Critical Reading section.

Each part begins with a review that briefly explains the strategies you should use in attacking the different question types. These reviews are followed by questions and their answers, which illustrate the points made over the course of the review material. All questions that follow the review material are representative of the questions on the actual SAT and will prove to be an excellent source of practice in studying for the exam.

Be sure to spend extra time on the question types that pose the most difficulty to you.

1. Locate the question type you are looking for by referring to the Contents in the front of this book.
2. Refer to the review material pertaining to the question type. You should become acquainted with the material discussed there.
3. Review the questions following the review material, in the order given. As in the actual SAT, the questions are arranged in order of complexity, from the simplest to the more difficult.
4. To learn and understand a question type, it will generally be necessary for students to review a question several times. Repeated review is essential to gain experience in recognizing how to answer the different question types.

To Find a Particular Problem

To locate one or more problems related to a particular question type, refer to the index. In using the index be certain to note that the numbers given there refer to question numbers, not to page numbers. This arrangement of the index is intended to facilitate finding a question more rapidly, since two or more questions may appear on a page.

If a particular question type cannot be found, refer to the Contents in the front pages, and then turn to the part that is applicable to the question being sought. By scanning or glancing at the material that is boxed, it will generally be possible to find questions related to the one being sought, without wasting considerable time. After the questions have been located, the explanations can be reviewed and studied in detail. For locating questions rapidly, acquaint yourself with the organization of the book as found in the Contents.

THE NEW SAT: WHAT'S IT ALL ABOUT?

The introduction of the New SAT in March 2005 stands as one of the most publicized events in college-admission testing. By now you may have seen or heard any number of talking heads on television and radio, or perhaps you read some of the countless articles in newspapers or webzines. A lot of people seem to have a lot to say about the SAT. Millions have taken the SAT and millions more will do so in the future, but right now you care about the SAT only at the point where it intersects with **you**. So let's get down to business.

The New SAT notably differs from its previous version in that ETS has added a third component, the all-new Writing section. Whether you consider yourself a good writer or not, there's no time like the present to learn to do it better. By adding this section, ETS is really doing you a big favor! If you're not getting your message across now, just picture how much worse it will be down the line when you lose a promotion at work to someone who can!

Each of the three test sections is scored using a 200–800 scale, making 2400 the highest score possible. You will also receive subscores on the multiple-choice and Essay portions of the Writing section. The total testing time is 3 hours and 45 minutes.

The Essay section asks you to take a position on an issue and support it with examples from your studies and experience. The question is designed to be open-ended so you can successfully write your Essay in many different ways. You are not required to have any prior specific knowledge about the topic to write your Essay. The Writing section also includes multiple-choice questions that test your ability to identify errors in sentences, improve sentences, and improve paragraphs.

You are allotted 60 minutes to complete the Writing sections.

The Critical Reading (formerly known as Verbal) portions of the revised SAT still focus on vocabulary skills, though perhaps less obviously. Quite simply, a solid vocabulary remains a bedrock requirement for good across-the-board performance on the Critical Reading sections. Other questions test your ability to read at a strong pace while grasping a solid understanding of the material.

Analogies have been eliminated from the New SAT. The time allotted for these sections is 70 minutes.

THE NEW FORMAT

Writing Sections: 60 minutes

In the Writing sections, you will answer multiple-choice questions that test your grammar and reasoning skills as well as write an essay similar to the type required on in-class college essay exams.

- Writing (35 minutes): 49 multiple-choice questions to measure your ability to identify sentence errors, improve sentences, and improve paragraphs.
- Student Essay (25 minutes): Write an essay that effectively communicates your viewpoint as well as defines and supports your position.

Critical Reading Sections: 70 minutes

There are two types of Critical Reading questions on the SAT:

- Reading Comprehension & Sentence Completion: 67 multiple-choice questions. Reading Comprehension questions follow four reading passages that test your reading comprehension and analysis skills. Sentence Completion questions require you to choose the word or words that best fit the meaning of each sentence provided.

The following chart summarizes the format of the Writing and Critical Reading sections of the SAT.

Section	Content	Item Type	Time	Score
Writing (brand-new section!)	Grammar, usage, and word choice	• Student-written essay • Multiple-choice questions	60 min. total: 25 min. for the student-written short essay and 35 min. for multiple-choice questions.	200–800. The essay will be graded on a six-point scale similar to the old SAT II Writing Subject Test grading system.
Critical reading (formerly called Verbal)	Critical Reading and sentence-level reading.	• Sentence completions • Reading Comprehension: includes a new short passages section in addition to the traditional paragraph-length long passages. • No more analogies!	70 min. total (previously 75 min.): two 25-min sections and one 20-min. section.	200–800

ABOUT THE TEST

Who takes the SAT? What is it used for?

Juniors and seniors in high school are the ones most likely to take the SAT. College admissions personnel use your test results as a way to decide if you can be accepted to their school. Because high schools across the nation have a variety of grading systems, the SAT score is designed to put all students on an equal footing. Your SAT score, along with your grades and other school information, helps colleges predict how well you will do at the college level.

If you score poorly on the SAT, it does not mean you should change your plans about going to college. Nor does it mean you will not do well in college. It just means you scored low. Should this happen, remember that you have options:

First, you can register to take the SAT again. Use the time before the next SAT administration to prepare as best you can.

Second, a poor score does not automatically shut the door to all colleges. College admissions officers use several criteria when reviewing applicants including your high school grades, your extracurricular activities, and the levels of your courses in high school.

Who administers the test?

ETS, a client of the College Board, which owns the SAT, develops and scores the test and currently administers it with the assistance of educators across the United States.

When is it best to take the SAT?

You should take the test as a junior or senior in high school. We recommend taking the SAT early in the school year. This allows you more time to retake the test if you are not satisfied with your first set of scores.

When and where do I take the SAT?

The SAT is normally offered seven times a year nationwide. The test can be taken at hundreds of locations throughout the country, including high schools. The standard test day is normally on Saturday, but alternate days are permitted if a conflict—such as a religious obligation—exists.

For information on upcoming SAT testing dates, see your guidance counselor for an SAT Registration Bulletin or request a registration bulletin from ETS as follows:

Educational Testing Service
Rosedale Road
Princeton, NJ 08541
phone: (609) 921–9000 | e-mail: etsinfo@ets.org | www.ets.org

What about the registration fee?

You must pay a fee to register for the SAT. Some students may qualify to have this fee waived.

To find out if you qualify for a fee waiver, contact your guidance counselor.

What is the Student Search Service?

The Student Search Service provides your SAT scores to colleges. Colleges enrolled in this service receive information about you, especially if you express interest in their school. On your SAT answer sheet, you can indicate that you want enrollment in this service.

AFTER THE TEST

Once your test materials have been collected, you will be dismissed. Then your day is free. Go home and relax. Or reward yourself with some shopping. Or play a video game. Or hang with friends. The good news is that the hard part is over. Now you just have to wait for the results.

Part I Writing

UNIT 1: THE SHORT ESSAY

The SAT Essay contains one writing exercise. You will have 25 minutes to plan and write an essay on a given topic. You must write on only that topic. Because you will have only 25 minutes to complete the essay, efficient use of your time is essential.

Writing under pressure can be frustrating, but if you study this review, practice and polish your essay skills, and have a realistic sense of what to expect, you can turn problems into possibilities. The following review will show you how to plan and write a logical, coherent, and interesting essay.

ABOUT THE DIRECTIONS

The directions are straightforward.

DIRECTIONS: You have 25 minutes to plan and write an essay on the following topic. You may write on only the assigned topic.

Make sure to give examples to support your thesis. Proofread your essay carefully and take care to express your ideas clearly and effectively.

PREWRITING/PLANNING

Before you actually begin to write, there are certain preliminary steps you need to take. A few minutes spent planning pays off—your final essay will be more focused, well-developed, and clear. For a 25-minute essay, you should spend about five minutes on the prewriting process.

Understand the Question

Read the essay question very carefully and ask yourself the following questions:

- What is the meaning of the topic statement?

- Is the question asking me to persuade the reader of the validity of a certain opinion?

- Do I agree or disagree with the statement? What will be my thesis (main idea)?

- What kinds of examples can I use to support my thesis? Explore personal experiences, historical evidence, current events, and literary subjects.

Consider Your Audience

Essays would be pointless without an audience. Why write an essay if no one wants or needs to read it? Why add evidence, organize your ideas, or correct bad grammar? The reason to do any of these things is because someone out there needs to understand what you mean or say.

What does the audience need to know to believe you or to come over to your position? Imagine someone you know listening to you declare your position or opinion and then saying, "Oh, yeah? Prove it!" This is your audience—write to them. Ask yourself the following questions so that you will not be confronted with a person who says, "Prove it!"

- What evidence do I need to prove my idea to this audience?

- What would the audience disagree with me about?

- What does the audience share with me as common knowledge? What do I need to tell them?

WRITING YOUR ESSAY

Once you have considered your position on the topic and thought of several examples to support it, you are ready to begin writing.

Organizing Your Essay

Decide how many paragraphs you will write. In a 25-minute exercise, you will probably have time for no more than four or five paragraphs. In such a format, the first paragraph will be the introduction, the next two or three will develop your thesis with specific examples, and the final paragraph should be a strong conclusion.

The Introduction

The focus of your introduction should be the thesis statement. This statement allows your reader to understand the point and direction of your essay. The statement identifies the central idea of your essay and should clearly state your attitude about the subject. It will also dictate the basic content and organization of your essay. If you do not state your thesis clearly, your essay will suffer.

The thesis is the heart of the essay. Without it, readers won't know what your major message or central idea is in the essay.

The thesis must be something that can be argued or needs to be proven, not just an accepted fact. For example, "Animals are used every day in cosmetic and medical testing," is a fact—it needs no proof. But if the writer says, "Using animals for cosmetic and medical testing is cruel and should be stopped," we have a point that must be supported and defended by the writer.

The thesis can be placed in any paragraph of the essay, but in a short essay, especially one written for evaluative exam purposes, the thesis is most effective when placed in the last sentence of the opening paragraph.

Consider the following sample question:

ESSAY TOPIC

"That government is best which governs least."

__ASSIGNMENT__: Do you agree or disagree with this statement? Choose a specific example from current events, personal experience, or your reading to support your position.

After reading the topic statement, decide if you agree or disagree. If you agree with this statement, your thesis statement could be the following:

"Government has the right to protect individuals from interference, but it has no right to extend its powers and activities beyond this function."

This statement clearly states the writer's opinion in a direct manner. It also serves as a blueprint for the essay. The remainder of the introduction should give two or three brief examples that support your thesis.

Supporting Paragraphs

The next two or three paragraphs of your essay will elaborate on the supporting examples you gave in your introduction. Each paragraph should discuss only one idea. Like the introduction, each paragraph should be coherently organized with a topic sentence and supporting details.

The topic sentence is to each paragraph what the thesis statement is to the essay as a whole. It tells the reader what you plan to discuss in that paragraph. It has a specific subject and is neither too broad nor too narrow. It also establishes the author's attitude and gives the reader a sense of the direction in which the writer is going. An effective topic sentence also arouses the reader's interest.

Although it may occur in the middle or at the end of the paragraph, the topic sentence usually appears at the beginning of the paragraph. Placing the topic sentence at the beginning is advantageous because it helps you stay focused on the main idea.

The remainder of each paragraph should support the topic sentence with examples and illustrations. Each sentence should progress logically from the previous one and be centrally connected to your topic sentence. Do not include any extraneous material that does not serve to develop your thesis.

Conclusion

Your conclusion should briefly restate your thesis and explain how you have shown it to be true. Since you want to end your essay on a strong note, your conclusion should be concise and effective.

Do not introduce any new topics that you cannot support. If you were watching a movie that suddenly shifted plot and characters at the end, you would be disappointed or even angry. Similarly, conclusions must not drift away from the major focus and message of the essay. Make sure your conclusion is clearly on the topic and represents your perspective without any confusion about what you really mean and believe. The reader will respect you for staying true to your intentions.

The conclusion is your last chance to grab and impress the reader. You can even use humor, if appropriate, but a dramatic close will remind the reader that you are serious, even passionate, about what you believe.

EFFECTIVE USE OF LANGUAGE

Clear organization, although vitally important, is not the only factor the graders of your essay consider. You must also demonstrate that you can express your ideas clearly, using correct grammar, diction, usage, spelling, and punctuation.

Point of View

Depending on the audience, essays may be written from one of three points of view:

1. Subjective/Personal Point of View:

   "I think . . . "

   "I believe cars are more trouble than they are worth."

   "I feel . . . "

2. Second Person Point of View (We . . . You; I . . . You):

   "If you own a car, you will soon find out that it is more trouble than it is worth."

3. Third Person Point of View (focuses on the idea, not what "I" think of it):

   "Cars are more trouble than they are worth."

It is very important to maintain a consistent point of view throughout your essay. If you begin writing in the first-person ("I"), do not shift to the second- or third-person in the middle of the essay.

Such inconsistency is confusing to your reader and will be penalized by the graders of your essay.

Tone

A writer's tone results from his or her attitude toward the subject and the reader. If the essay question requires you to take a strong stand, the tone of your essay should reflect this.

Your tone should also be appropriate for the subject matter. A serious topic demands a serious tone. For a more light-hearted topic, you may wish to inject some humor into your essay.

Whatever tone you choose, be consistent. Do not make any abrupt shifts in tone in the middle of your essay.

Verb Tense

Make sure to remain in the same verb tense in which you began your essay. If you start in the past, make sure all verbs are past tense. Staying in the same verb tense improves the continuity and flow of ideas. Avoid phrases such as "now was," a confusing blend of present and past. Consistency of time is essential to the reader's understanding.

Transitions

Transitions are like the links of a bracelet, holding the beads, or major points, of your essay together. They help the reader follow the smooth flow of your ideas and show a connection between major and minor ideas. Transitions are used either at the beginning of a paragraph, or to show the connections among ideas within a single paragraph. Without transitions, you will jar the reader and distract him from your true ideas.

Here are some typical transitional words and phrases:

Linking similar ideas

again	for example	likewise
also	for instance	moreover
and	further	nor
another	furthermore	of course
besides	in addition	similarly
equally important	in like manner	too

Linking dissimilar/contradictory ideas

although	however	otherwise
and yet	in spite of	provided that
as if	instead	still
but	nevertheless	yet
conversely	on the contrary	on the other hand

Indicating cause, purpose, or result

as	for	so
as a result	for this reason	then
because	hence	therefore
consequently	since	thus

Indicating time or position

above	before	meanwhile
across	beyond	next
afterwards	eventually	presently
around	finally	second
at once	first	thereafter
at the present time	here	thereupon

Indicating an example or summary

as a result	in any event	in short
as I have said	in brief	on the whole
for example	in conclusion	to sum up
for instance	in fact	in other words

Common Writing Errors

The four writing errors most often made by beginning writers are run-ons (also known as fused sentences), fragments, lack of subject-verb agreement, and incorrect use of object:

1. **Run-ons:** "She swept the floor it was dirty" is a run-on, because the pronoun "it" stands as a noun subject and starts a new sentence. A period or semicolon is needed after "floor."

2. **Fragments:** "Before Jimmy learned how to play baseball" is a fragment, even though it has a subject and verb (Jimmy learned). The word "before" fragmentizes the clause, and the reader needs to know what happened before Jimmy learned how to play baseball.

3. **Problems with subject-verb agreement:** "Either Maria or Robert are going to the game" is incorrect because either Maria is going or Robert is

going, but not both. The sentence should say, "Either Maria or Robert is going to the game."

4. **Incorrect object:** Probably the most common offender in this area is saying "between you and I," which sounds correct, but isn't. "Between" is a preposition that takes the objective case "me." The correct usage is "between you and me."

SAT Essay test graders also cite lack of thought and development, misspellings, and incorrect pronouns or antecedents, and lack of development as frequently occurring problems. Finally, keep in mind that clear, coherent handwriting always works to your advantage. Readers will appreciate an essay they can read with ease.

Five Words Weak Writers Overuse

Weak and beginning writers overuse the vague pronouns "you, we, they, this, and it" often without telling exactly who or what is represented by the pronoun.

1. Beginning writers often shift to second person **"you,"** when the writer means, "a person." This shift confuses readers and weakens the flow of the essay. Although "you" is commonly accepted in creative writing, journalism, and other arenas, in a short, formal essay, it is best to avoid "you" altogether.

2. **"We"** is another pronoun that should be avoided. If by "we" the writer means "Americans," "society," or some other group, then he or she should say so.

3. **"They"** is often misused in essay writing, because it is overused in conversation: "I went to the doctor, and they told me to take some medicine." Tell the reader who "they" are.

4. **"This"** is usually used incorrectly without a referent: "She told me she received a present. This sounded good to me." This what? This idea? This news? This present? Be clear—don't make your readers guess what you mean. The word "this" should be followed by a noun or referent.

5. **"It"** is a common problem among weak writers. To what does "it" refer? Your readers don't appreciate vagueness, so take the time to be clear and complete in your expression of ideas.

Use Your Own Vocabulary

Is it a good idea to use big words that sound good in the dictionary or thesaurus, but that you don't really use or understand? No. So whose vocabulary should you use? Your own. You will be most comfortable with your own level of vocabulary.

This "comfort zone" doesn't give you license to be informal in a formal setting or to violate the rules of standard written English, but if you try to write in a style that is not yours, your writing will be awkward and lack a true voice.

You should certainly improve and build your vocabulary at every opportunity, but remember: you should not attempt to change your vocabulary level at this point.

Avoid the Passive Voice

In writing, the active voice is preferable because it is emphatic and direct. A weak, passive verb leaves the doer unknown or seemingly unimportant. However, the passive voice is essential when the action of the verb is more important than the doer, when the doer is unknown, or when the writer wishes to place the emphasis on the receiver of the action rather than on the doer.

PROOFREADING

Make sure to leave yourself enough time at the end to read over your essay for errors such as misspellings, omitted words, or incorrect punctuation. You will not have enough time to make large-scale revisions, but take this chance to make any small changes that will make your essay stronger. Consider the following when proofreading your work:

- Are all your sentences really sentences? Have you written any fragments or run-on sentences?

- Are you using vocabulary correctly?

- Did you leave out any punctuation? Did you capitalize correctly?

- Are there any misspellings, especially of difficult words?

If you have time, read your essay backwards from end to beginning. By doing so, you may catch errors that you missed reading forward only.

DRILLS

DIRECTIONS: **You have 25 minutes to plan and write an essay on the topic below. You may write on only the assigned topic.**

Make sure to give examples to support your thesis. Proofread your essay carefully and take care to express your ideas clearly and effectively.

■ ESSAY TOPIC I.1.1   TIME: 25 MINUTES

> Educator and writer Richard Rodriguez claims that education entails a "radical transformation" for some students. As opposed to the view that education is merely career training, this group experiences deep and abiding changes in the way they perceive the world, in their values. Quite simply, according to Rodriguez, some students are completely changed by their experiences in school while others remain relatively untouched.
>
> **ASSIGNMENT: Do you agree or disagree with Rodriguez that some students are utterly changed by education, and if you agree, why are some students thus transformed while others are not? Plan and write an essay in which you defend your point of view on this issue. Support your examples with reasoning and examples taken from your reading, studies, experience, and observations.**

ESSAY

Some students travel through their entire education, from Kindergarten through perhaps college and even graduate school, without being much touched by the experience. However, as Richard Rodriguez asserts, others are completely changed, even their values and the way they see the world. Whatever such a student's home life might be, whether rich or poor, Christian or Muslim or atheist, born to loving or dysfunctional parents, he or she cannot help but be changed by the information to which their teachers expose them.

The main difference between these two groups of students, those who are transformed and those who are not, is the degree to which they are actively engaged in the process. The latter group only regurgitates information for a grade, perhaps by doing their best to say exactly what they think any given teacher wants to hear. By contrast, the first group critically analyzes each assignment, carefully connecting it to anything else they have learned and thereby building a more complete picture of the world than they had previously. Maybe historical information about the 19th century makes much more sense after learning about Darwin's theory of evolution, and maybe even something learned in psychology is now more completely understood.

The smartest person I ever knew is one of these actively engaged learners. In fact, my father has never stopped learning and has never stopped being transformed by what he learns. He was the first in his family to go to college, and he took advantage of the opportunity to escape not only poverty but ignorant habits like racism. He is still fascinated by the world around him, by books, and by world events, even though he has not been in school for several years. Many of our conversations begin with him saying things like, "Did you know . . . ," or "I learned today that . . . " This indicates to me that the man will never stop being transformed and that his values will continue to evolve as his perception of the world becomes more complete. He is also one of my teachers because of these conversations and one of the reasons I am constantly being transformed too.

Active learners are the leaders of the world, the ones who move us forward because they are not stuck on one way of seeing the world to the exclusion of any information that does not fit their preconceived notions. This means that many of these people are not only smart but brave. Einstein was one of these people, "thinking outside the box" when it came to the very nature of the universe, but Martin Luther King was also one of these people. He knew that even the laws of the United States could be wrong, and he set out to prove it, paying with his life but making the world a better place in the process.

My father is not one of the heroes changing the world (he is an architect), but his life is fuller for being constantly changed by what he learns. It remains to be seen if I can change the world on some grand scale, but the more of us who are changed by what we learn, the more evolved our species will become. At the very least, my father and I are helping the species move forward in our small way, by achieving the kind of "radical transformation" Rodriguez mentions.

ANALYSIS

This Essay has a score range of 5–6. It is well-organized, presenting a thesis in the introduction, developing that idea throughout the essay, and expanding upon it yet further in the conclusion. The author offers examples to prove the main idea. The writing demonstrates a variety of sentence structure and length, and the grammar and punctuation are correct. The vocabulary is also sophisticated.

ESSAY TOPIC I.1.2

> The Internet makes doing research much easier.
>
> The Internet makes doing research dangerous.
>
> **ASSIGNMENT**: Consider the two contrasting statements above. Select the one that more closely reflects your view. Then write an essay that explains your choice. To support your view, use an example or examples from history, literature, the arts, current events, politics, science and technology, or your experience or observation.

ESSAY

Although research on the Internet can be very easy and give instant access to many sources, it can also be frustrating, difficult, and dangerous. A search may yield far too many sources, some of which may lead the researcher down some really strange paths, and there is no way to discriminate easily between good and bad.

While a search engine brings up responses to a search, it does not discriminate among the items it finds. A very large topic, say Scottish history, may bring up hundreds of thousands of hits. It can be very difficult to go through the items and decide which are going to be helpful and which are not. When calling up an item that appears to be just right, the Web site may be found to be "out of service," and there is no way to learn how to get the people behind that Web site to find out where they are and if they might send information, or if they have published material that can be found in a library.

An individual can put anything he or she likes on the Internet; all it takes is the ability to post and run a website. In contrast, the process of getting a book published by a reputable publisher takes the author through a process that weeds out individuals with half-baked ideas and people who believe they know a lot about a subject even though they haven't done much work in that field.

The Internet is filled with postings by people who have an agenda when it comes to a certain subject, and the unsophisticated researcher might be persuaded by information that is misleading or downright wrong. To take an extreme example, there are individuals who maintain that the Holocaust never happened, and they will give all manner of information that they claim supports their position.

In conclusion, although the Internet is an easy first step in locating material for a research project, the researcher needs to exercise great care in going through what is often an overabundance of information to be able to use those sources that will help.

ANALYSIS

This essay has a score range of 5–6. It is a well-reasoned essay that takes a stand and supports it. The introductory paragraph sets up the thesis. The four body paragraphs supply information that supports the thesis, and the concluding paragraph restates it. The writing demonstrates a variety of sentence structure, some fairly sophisticated vocabulary, and—importantly—it is grammatically correct.

ESSAY TOPIC I.1.3

Polls of American youth suggest they want high-paying jobs, not necessarily satisfying careers. This reflects the current cultural value implied in the popular media that money is the key that opens the golden door to satisfaction, unlike the traditional value of work for its own reward.

ASSIGNMENT: Do you agree or disagree with the statement? Support your opinion with specific examples from history, politics, science and technology, literature, the arts, current events, or your own experience or observation.

ESSAY

American youth are more interested in high-paying jobs rather than a satisfying career because our culture is very materialistic, income is more impressive than a title to a job, and more money implies more power.

Our culture is very materialistic. A pair of faded, worn-out blue jeans costs close to $70.00 and seems to be a necessity for teenagers. It doesn't matter if your job is one that "sounds" good or makes you happy, as long as your income keeps you in step with the Joneses. Status symbols speak out for the high-paying jobs. When people see you riding around in your new shiny Jaguar, they don't know if you're a garbage man or a lawyer, but what they do know is that you're making money, lots of it.

Income is more impressive than a title. If they can make more money running a junk yard than being a lawyer, the youth of today will become a junk dealer in a heartbeat. The question, "What is your average yearly income?" is just as popular now as the ancient question, "What do you do for a living?" Nobody really cares anymore what you do if you're making plenty of money.

The more money you have, the more power you have. You can easily impress your peers and people in lower social standing with your beliefs and ideas because they are all saying to themselves, "Well he must know what he's doing, or else how did he get all this money?" Money and power have always gone hand-in-hand and probably always will.

Income is more important to American youths than a satisfying career because this is a very materialistic culture we live in, income is far more impressive than a title, and more money implies more power. A satisfying career may satisfy you while you are at work, but a good income will satisfy you all of the time. With a high income, what job wouldn't be satisfying?

ANALYSIS

This essay has a score range of 5–6. Even though it has some obvious flaws, its virtues of clear and concise organization, reasonable development with specific examples, and a clear conclusion help outweigh the problems. The quality of thought is clearly a bit superficial. The traditional three-part thesis, which outlines the structure here, serves almost as much as a mechanical formula as it does a guide map for the reader. The essay, however, is unified about its thesis, and good organization in itself counts for a great deal. In general, word choice is not particularly sophisticated, and such phrases as "our culture is very materialistic" are repeated throughout the essay. Nevertheless, given the 25-minute time limit, this essay stands up reasonably well.

UNIT 2: MULTIPLE-CHOICE QUESTIONS

The elimination of Analogy questions and the introduction of Short Passages are significant changes to the SAT. But what really makes the New SAT new is the inclusion of a Writing section that tests just what you might expect: your ability to write and edit prose effectively. The New SAT begins with a 25-minute Essay section. Two multiple-choice sections, one 25 minutes and the other 10 minutes, will consist of questions on Usage, Sentence Correction, and Paragraph Improvement. The 10-minute multiple-choice Writing section will always be the final section of the SAT. The remaining 25-minute section can appear in any order.

ABOUT THE DIRECTIONS

Make sure to study and learn the directions to save yourself time during the actual test. You should simply skim them when beginning the section.

Sentence Correction Questions

For Sentence Correction questions, the directions will read similar to the following:

DIRECTIONS: In each of the following sentences, some portion of the sentence is underlined. Under each sentence are five choices. The first choice has the same wording as the original. The other four choices are reworded. Sometimes the first choice containing the original wording is the best; sometimes one of the other choices is the best. Choose the letter of the best choice. Your choice should produce a sentence that is not ambiguous or awkward and that is correct, clear, and precise.

This is a test of correct and effective English expression. Keep in mind the standards of English usage, punctuation, grammar, word choice, and construction.

EXAMPLE

When you listen to opera, <u>a person may not appreciate it.</u>
- (A)   a person may not appreciate it.
- (B)   it may not be appreciated by a person.
- (C)   you may not appreciate it.
- (D)   which may not be appreciated by you.
- (E)   appreciating it may be a problem for you.

EXAMPLE ANSWER

Ⓐ Ⓑ ● Ⓓ Ⓔ

Usage Questions

For Usage questions, the directions will read as follows:

DIRECTIONS: Each of the following sentences may contain an error in diction, usage, idiom, or grammar. Some sentences are correct. Some sentences contain one error. No sentence contains more than one error.

If there is an error, it will appear in one of the underlined portions labeled A, B, C, or D. If there is no error, choose the portion labeled E. If there is an error, select the letter of the portion that must be changed in order to correct the sentence.

EXAMPLE

He drove <u>slowly</u> and <u>cautiously</u> in order to <u>hopefully</u> avoid having an
       A   B   C

<u>accident</u>. <u>No error</u>.
   D   E

EXAMPLE ANSWER

Ⓐ Ⓑ ● Ⓓ Ⓔ

Paragraph Improvement Questions

For Paragraph Improvement questions, the directions will be presented as follows:

DIRECTIONS: The following passages are considered early draft efforts of a student. Some sentences need to be rewritten to make the ideas clearer and more precise.

Read each passage carefully and answer the questions that follow. Some of the questions are about particular sentences or parts of sentences and ask you to make decisions about sentence structure, diction, and usage. Some of the questions refer to the entire essay or parts of the essay and ask you to make decisions about organization, development, appropriateness of language, audience, and logic. Choose the answer that most effectively makes the intended meaning clear and follows the requirements of standard written English. After you have chosen your answer, fill in the corresponding oval on your answer sheet.

EXAMPLE

(1) On the one hand, I think television is bad, But it also does some good things for all of us. (2) For instance, my little sister thought she wanted to be a policeman until she saw police shows on television.

Which of the following is the best revision of the underlined portion of sentence (1) below?

One the one hand, I think television <u>is bad, But it also</u> does some good things for all of us.

(A)   is bad; But it also
(B)   is bad. but it also
(C)   is bad, but it also
(D)   is bad, and it also
(E)   is bad because it also

EXAMPLE ANSWER

(A)　(B)　●　(D)　(E)

MASTERING USAGE QUESTIONS

In all likelihood, you'll find that the Usage questions cover familiar territory. They'll test your ability to identify typical writing errors, the kind that your English teachers have been warning you about for years.

The Usage questions, for the most part, focus on the relatively small number of error types that many writers—even proficient ones—are prone to committing. In this unit, we will cover the most common types of errors you'll encounter in the Writing section.

Steps for Mastering Usage Questions

STEP 1   Listen for an error. Even if you lack confidence in your knowledge of grammar, you probably know enough to "hear" most errors as you encounter them.

STEP 2 Having identified the part of the sentence that seems incorrect, try to determine what makes that part wrong, and then replace the underlined error with the correct word or phrase. Doing so will help you to test your intuition.

STEP 3 If you do not "hear" anything wrong with the sentence, it may be error-free. Nevertheless, mentally review the kinds of errors you are told to expect and apply them to the underlined parts of the sentence. If you see evidence of a given type of error, apply STEP 2 to that part of the sentence.

USAGE QUESTION FORMAT

Each usage question will consist of a sentence that may or may not contain an error. Choose the underlined part that contains the error or select "No error."

Be sure to read the sentence exactly as it is written:

<u>Some people</u> fail <u>to realize</u> that regular dental cleaning, accompanied by
   A   B

a thorough exam, <u>are</u> essential to avoid <u>more</u> serious complications later.
              C   D

<u>No error.</u>
  E

STEP 1 As you read the preceding sample questions, you may have "heard" something wrong with "are" (choice C). When a verb such as "are" doesn't sound right, the cause is almost always noun-verb disagreement. In other words, the verb doesn't agree with the subject in number.

STEP 2 The reason "are" sounds wrong is that the subject of the sentence, "dental cleaning," is singular, not plural. To agree with this singular subject, the form of the verb "to be" must be present singular, "is."

STEP 3 If you didn't hear the error in the sample question, it's probably because you didn't "hear" that the subject of the sentence is singular. After all, the phrase "accompanied by a thorough exam" follows the subject, creating the impression that both "dental cleaning and exam are the subject—in other words, a compound (and therefore plural) subject. But the phrase mentioning "exam" only modifies the subject; it is not a part of it.

KINDS OF USAGE ERRORS

The following mini-review is not exhaustive, but it does cover the major kinds of errors likely to appear on the Writing exam.

Disagreement Errors—Noun-Verb

Each of the following sentences illustrates a classic way in which noun-verb disagreement manages to slip past our "grammar radar."

1.   Attendance at <u>poetry festivals</u> over the past few years <u>have</u> increased
                    A   B
      dramatically as a <u>result of</u> poetry clubs and <u>writers'</u> workshops.
                        C   D

(B)   The subject of the sentence is "attendance," which is singular. The main verb should be "has," not "have." Because the plural nouns "festivals" and "years" come between the subject and the verb, the writer failed to hear the disagreement.

2.   There <u>is</u>, when you consider the issue, several reasons <u>for supporting</u> the
            A   B
      current legislation now <u>before</u> the <u>Appropriations Committee</u>.
                              C   D

(A)   The subject of a clause beginning with "There is" or "There are" comes after the verb. The subject of sentence 2 is "reasons," a plural noun, so the main verb should be "are," not "is."

3.   In the <u>depths</u> of the <u>woods</u> live a species of bird that <u>hasn't</u> been thor-
              A   B   C
      oughly studied <u>by</u> wild-life experts.
                     D

(B)   A typical word order can occur in contexts other than the one mentioned above. The subject of sentence 3 is " species," a singular noun. Therefore the verb should be "lives," not "live." Plural "woods" and "depths," which occur in prepositional phrases, probably encouraged the writer to use the plural verb form.

Disagreement Errors—Noun-Pronoun

Disagreement can also occur between nouns and pronouns:

4.   Both the geography book I used <u>as</u> a high school student and <u>the one</u> I
                                      A   B
       used as a college student <u>have</u> the same vivid photograph of Mount
                                  C
       Everest on <u>its cover</u>.
                  D

(D)   The subject of sentence 4 is a compound noun—in other words, it's
plural. Consequently, the same photograph appears on two separate "covers."
Choice D should be "their covers."

5.   In <u>today's</u> competitive world, even a student <u>who</u> earns high grades and
          A   B
       top test scores may <u>have</u> a tough time getting into the college of <u>their</u>
                            C   D
       choice.

(D)   "Student" in sentence 5 is, of course, singular. But because the gender
of student is not specified, the writer mistakenly uses the gender-free plural possessive pronoun "their."

Shift Errors

There are two kinds of shift errors: tense shift and pronoun shift.

6.   When I saw her again after <u>almost</u> twenty years, I <u>can't</u> help but ap-
                                  A   B
       proach her and <u>say</u> "How's life <u>been</u> treating you?"
                       C   D

(B)   The action of the sentence is taking place in the past—"I saw her"
"Can't" is a present tense modal. The modal helping to describe the nature and
conditions of the encounter needs to be in the past tense: "I couldn't help but
approach her"

7.   Experience <u>teaches</u> us that we have <u>to work</u> hard and play hard if <u>you</u>
                  A   B   C
       want to have a <u>genuinely</u> fulfilling life.
                       D

(C)   In conversation, speakers often use the pronoun "you" to refer to people
in general. Sometimes writers lapse into this conversational tendency in their
writing, even when it violates pronoun consistency. The writer of sentence 7

errs by going from "we" and "us"—both first person plural pronouns—to second person "you."

Comparison Errors

Two types of comparison errors may occur in the Writing section: comparative/superlative errors and unequal comparison errors.

8.   Olympus Mons, a volcanic mountain <u>on</u> Mars, is the <u>taller</u> of all the
                                         A   B

other <u>known</u> <u>mountains</u> in the Solar System.
       C   D

(B)   The writer discusses Olympus Mons in superlative terms: no mountain is taller than it. Hence, it is the "tallest" of all the other mountains, not simply "taller." Also, the comparative "taller" should appear with the conjunction "than," which does not appear in the sentence.

9.   From a <u>distance</u>, Betty seems <u>rather</u> short to me, but, when I stand next
            A   B

to her, <u>she's</u> clearly the <u>tallest</u>.
        C   D

(D)   The writer compares his or her height to that of one other person. If two things or people are being compared, the adjective needs to be in the comparative form, not the superlative.

10.   My high school's track team <u>is</u> much <u>better</u> at long distance running <u>than</u>
                                   A   B   C

the <u>high school</u> that won the state championship last year.
    D

(D)   The writer clearly intended to compare two track teams; grammatically, the writer is comparing a track team to a high school. Although it's acceptable to substitute the whole for the part—for example, high school = track team—this substitution should be applied consistently, a rule the writer fails to apply in this case.

Word Choice Errors

In a sense, all grammatical errors are the result of choosing the wrong word or phrase. But in the grammatical mistakes we've considered so far, the errors in word choice have been logical errors. Treating a plural noun as though it's singular, or grammatically comparing unequal things, is simply illogical. The category "Word Choice Errors" concerns violations of accepted idioms and definitions. Nonnative speakers of English have particular difficulty identifying these kinds of errors.

Try to "hear" improperly used words and expressions in the following:

11.   After three hours <u>of</u> negotiations, the Trade Union insisted that mana-
                            A
      gement agree <u>on</u> <u>its</u> demands for a reduced work week and improved
                      B   C
      <u>working</u> conditions.
         D

(B)   Like many verbs, "agree" combines with several prepositions to form
new concepts. To "agree with" someone is to share his or her opinion; to "agree
to" something is to concede to a demand or request. A trade union usually
doesn't care if management agrees with its philosophy, so long as it agrees to
(concedes to) the union's demands.

12.   <u>Despite of</u> the bad weather, <u>Mark</u> and Heather's garage sale went <u>well</u>,
           A   B   C
      earning the couple a <u>tidy</u> sum.
                              D

(A)   "In spite of" and "despite" have virtually the same meaning and sound
alike. Consequently, characteristics of each are sometimes erroneously blended,
as in sentence 12.

13.   <u>Even</u> at an early age, Picasso displayed signs <u>of</u> <u>imaginary</u> genius that
         A   B   C
      would fuel <u>ground-breaking</u> artwork.
                     D

(C)   Imaginary and imaginative are adjectives derived from the same root
word. Nevertheless, they have very different meanings. "Imaginative" means
"gifted with imagination"—which Picasso was; "imaginary" means "illusory."

Faulty Parallelism

Consider the following sentence:

   Jim likes hiking, skiing, and to snowboard.

   Clearly, the third element in the series of things Jim likes should be "snowboard-
ing," not "to snowboard." Whenever possible, elements catalogued or linked with
conjunctions should be grammatically equal. This rule of "parallelism"—think
"equal"—is more typically violated when the sentence is more complex than the
preceding one. See if you can identify the faulty parallelisms below.

14.   A <u>low-calorie</u> diet, most nutritionists <u>agree</u>, is the best <u>way</u> to reduce
        A   B   C
       cholesterol and <u>the achievement</u> of weight loss.
                              D

(D)   In naming the two things that a low-calorie diet helps the dieter to achieve, the writer begins with an infinitival phrase: "to reduce" Disobeying the rule of parallelism, the writer describes the second benefit of dieting as "the achievement of weight loss"—a noun phrase. Clearly, following the first infinitival phrase with another to create "to lower cholesterol and to achieve weight loss" sounds better and improves clarity.

15.   When <u>one</u> takes a high-stakes test, <u>it's</u> perfectly natural to <u>be a</u> little ner-
             A   B   C
       vous, irritable, <u>sweaty palms</u>.
                              D

(D)   "Nervous" and "irritable" are adjectives. "Sweaty" is also an adjective, but, because it is followed by "palms," the third element in this catalogue is a noun phrase modified by an adjective. Parallelism could be achieved simply by removing "palms."

Additional Error Types

The preceding review is a representative sample of the kinds of errors you will encounter; it doesn't cover all error types. Below is a "mixed bag" of other error types.

Double Negative:
I can't hardly *see the bridge from here due to the fog.*

Explanation: The writer's view of the bridge is obscured. He or she either *can't* see the bridge or *can hardly* see it. Joined together, "can't " and "hardly" cancel each other out.

Who/Which/That Substitution:
The students that *protested the tuition increase actually had lots of disposable income.*

Explanation: "Who" is an animate relative pronoun (i.e., it refers to people and sometimes to pets/animals). "Which" and "that" are inanimate relative pronouns (i.e., they refer to things).

Correlative Conjunctions (Misused):
The new movie was seen both by my friend Mary as well *as her brother.*

Explanation: Correlative conjunctions function as pairs. If you see one half of a correlative conjunction pair in a sentence, the second half should soon follow. "And," not "as well as," should appear soon after "both." Here are some other common corrective conjunctions:

either . . . or   neither . . . nor   not only . . . but also

MASTERING SENTENCE CORRECTION QUESTIONS

These questions test your ability to make appropriate revisions in accordance with the rules of standard written English. In the following sentences some part of the sentence, or all of the sentence, is underlined. Below each you will find five ways of phrasing the underlined part. Choose the answer that most effectively expresses the meaning of the original sentence. If you think the original sentence needs no revision, choose (A), which is always the same as the underlined part.

Although familiarity with the error types described in the Usage Questions review may help you to answer some Sentence Correction questions, be advised that this section focuses particularly on the following error types:

1. Ambiguous (unclear) sentences

2. Awkward sentences

3. Fragments (incomplete sentences)

4. Run-on sentences

Read the sentence carefully:

Intelligence is determined contrary to public opinion not by the size of the brain but by the number and complexity of the dendrites in the brain.

(A) Intelligence is determined contrary to public opinion not by

(B) Intelligence is contrary to public opinion and determined not by

(C) Contrary is public opinion, intelligence is determined not by

(D) Not by public opinion is intelligence determined but by

(E) Contrary to public opinion, intelligence determines not by

If you determine that the sentence contains an error, proceed as follows:

STEP 1   Eliminate choice (A) because it restates exactly what is underlined in the sentence.

STEP 2
Eliminate the obviously incorrect choices.
(B) ELIMINATE—changes the meaning of the sentence
(C) Maybe
(D) Maybe
(E) ELIMINATE—awkward and unclear

STEP 3
Choose between the most likely answers
(C) is clearer than (D). (C) directly links the phrase "Intelligence is determined not by" with the part of the sentence that logically follows this statement.

Note that the preceding sample question falls under the "awkward sentences" category; it is best revised by placing part of the underlined portion at the beginning of the sentence.

Answer the following questions and try to identify the kind of error contained in each.

1.   When I arrived at the stadium, which was jam-packed with spectators, <u>the halftime show under way</u>.

(A)   the halftime show under way.

(B)   the halftime show being under way.

(C)   under way, the half-time show was nearly over.

(D)   the halftime show was under way.

(E)   was under way.

(D)   The underlined portion is the main clause of the sentence, yet it lacks a verb. Choice (D) provides the appropriate verb (i.e., "was"). The remaining choices still result in a sentence fragment, either by not supplying an appropriate verb (choices (B) and (C)), or by eliminating the main clause's subject (choice (E)).

2.   Leaving behind a middle-class existence in <u>France, Paul Gaugin's sojourn in Tahiti brought the artist much-needed inspiration</u>.

(A)   France, Paul Gaugin's sojourn in Tahiti brought the artist much-needed inspiration.

(B)   France, Paul Gaugin sojourned in Tahiti and gained much-needed inspiration.

(C)   A sojourn in Tahiti brought Paul Gaugin much-needed inspiration.

(D)   Paul Gaugin was inspired to sojourn in Tahiti.

(E)   Much-needed inspiration was sought by Gaugin in Tahiti.

(B)   The original sentence is both confusing and ungrammatical. Paul Gaugin, not his "sojourn," is "leaving behind a middle-class existence in France." Choices

(C) and (E) similarly confuse the reader by failing to mention Gaugin directly after the participial phrase. Choice (D) doesn't commit this grammatical error—known as a dangling modifier—but it does not reproduce the original sentence's intended meaning. Choice (B) reproduces the original sentence's intended meaning and eliminates the dangling modifier. The correct answer is (B).

3.   Today's poetry lovers don't really read much <u>poetry, they prefer books about poetry and poets</u>.

   (A)   poetry, they prefer books about poetry and poets.

   (B)   poetry; they prefer books about poetry and poets.

   (C)   poetry because of books about poetry and poets themselves.

   (D)   poetry; books about poetry are largely read by poets themselves.

   (E)   poetry, poetry itself being less preferable to books about poetry.

(B)   The sentence in question 3 contains two clauses. Separate clauses should either be joined with conjunctions or separated by a period or semicolon. If the sentences are short and structurally similar, a semicolon is preferable to a period. The correct answer is (B). The remaining choices either alter the original meaning or result in a grammatical error.

4.   <u>America's literacy rates have increased far from being in decline</u>, as book sales suggest.

   (A)   America's literacy rates have increased far from being in decline,

   (B)   Far from being in decline, America's literacy rates have increased

   (C)   Far from the literacy rates of Americans being in decline, they have actually increased

   (D)   Unlike the decline of literacy rates among most Americans, there is an increase

   (E)   American's literacy rates far from being in decline have actually increased

(B)   The underlined portion of sentence 4 is awkward; its elements need to be rearranged. Choice (B) moves a participial phrase to the beginning of the sentence and separates it from the main clause with a comma. Now it is clear that what is "far from being in decline" is, in fact, "America's literacy rates." Choice (C) is ambiguous because it's unclear whether "they" refers to literacy rates or to Americans. In choice (D), it's not clear what "the decline in literacy rates" is being contrasted with. Choice (E) would be acceptable if the phrase "far from being in decline" was offset by commas. Also, "American's literacy rates" means the literacy rates of just one American, a nonsensical notion.

MASTERING PARAGRAPH IMPROVEMENT QUESTIONS

As its name implies, Paragraph Improvement questions are more about strengthening paragraph cohesion and essay unity than about correcting out-and-out errors. A paragraph's elements may be grammatically correct but stylistically and rhetorically inadequate.

Problem Types

Below is a chart listing some of the stylistic deficiencies typically encountered in the Improving Paragraphs questions:

Problem	Solution
wordy, redundant	eliminate unnecessary words
choppy sentences	combine sentences
unclear relationships between sentences	clarify relationships (usually with conjunctions)
vague language	replace with specific words
awkward passive voice	use active voice
off-topic sentence	find and eliminate sentence
lacking in support/details	select appropriate details

Steps for Mastering Paragraph Improvement Questions

The following is an introduction excerpted from a student's essay. The essay was written in response to a writing prompt asking the student to explain how his or her use of language differs from proper English when speaking with a friend.

(1) The language I use in talking to a friend would certainly differ from Standard English. (2) In talking with a friend I would be prone to phrases drawn from popular culture that we are both aware of. (3) I would know that by employing certain phrases that my friends and I were members of a peer group, and thus friends.

Which of the following revisions most clearly states the meaning of sentence 3?

(A) No change

(B) I would know, by employing certain phrases, that my friends and I shared certain interests.

(C) My friends and I would be peers by employing certain phrases that show we are friends.

(D) I would know that my friends and I had things in common by our similar uses of language.

(E) I would know, that by employing certain phrases and words, that my friends and I shared common interests and were, because of this knowledge, peers.

If you feel that the sentence is not in need of revision, choose answer choice (A). If you determine that the sentence would benefit from revision, proceed as follows:

 STEP 1   Eliminate choice (A) because it makes no revision.

STEP 2   Eliminate the obviously incorrect choices. Choice (D) says something completely different from the idea implied by the original sentence, while (E) is a verbose and repetitive run-on sentence.

STEP 3   Choose between the most likely answers. Choice (B) is clearer than (C), and (B) better expresses the thought that sentence 3 attempts to convey.

Now read the extended passage below and apply the steps to the questions that follow. Also, keep in mind the typical error types and their solutions as you both read the passage and answer the questions.

(1) Some high schools are making community service a requirement for graduating from high school. (2) School officials assert that students benefit from this policy. (3) Officials believe community service has both educational value as well as making students civic-minded. (4) They learn good work habits and assistance is provided where they are needed.

(5) Almost everyone has positive feelings about the new graduating requirement. (6) Some students feel the community service requirement, which involves volunteering one's time and assistance for forty hours or more, is too demanding. (7) Many students already have very full schedules. (8) They participate in sports. (9) They work part-time jobs. (10) Some even belong to clubs.

(11) Many of which already provide valuable services to the community. (12) Also, teenagers just need those relatively care-free years to enjoy themselves, which won't last forever.

(13) More students would be in favor of the community service requirement if changes were made. (14) The number of community service hours required to graduate should be reduced.

(15) Participation in community-centered clubs should be counted toward a student's community service requirement.

1.   Which is the best way to revise the underlined portion of sentence 3 (reproduced below)?

     Officials believe community service <u>has both educational value as well as making students civic-minded</u>.

     (A)   has both educational value as well as making students civic-minded.

     (B)   teaches students valuable lessons and makes students civic-minded.

     (C)   has both educational and civic value.

     (D)   both educates and civilizes students.

     (E)   is educationally as well as civically valuable.

(B)   The underlined portion is wrong for two reasons. First, it uses the correlative conjunction "both" but not its partner, "and." Second, the elements linked by the phrase "as well as" are not grammatically equal. Choice (B) correctly joins two verb phrases with the conjunction "and." Choice (B) is the right answer. Choice (C) properly uses the correlative conjunctions "both" and "and"; it also links two grammatically equal phrases. But it does not reproduce the meaning of the original. Similarly, (D) and (E) are grammatically correct but alter what the writer is saying.

2.   In context, which of the following best replaces the word "They" in sentence 4?

     (A)   They

     (B)   Students

     (C)   Educators

     (D)   Officials

     (E)   Aid recipients

(B)   The "they" is ambiguous, if only grammatically. The context strongly suggests that "they" refers to the students, making choice (B) correct. But because two plural nouns are mentioned in the previous sentence, the reader may initially be unclear about who "they" are. Choice (C) is clearly wrong because "educators" are previously mentioned. Choice (E) is wrong for the same reason.

3.   In context, which is the best way to revise the underlined portion of sentence 4 (reproduced below)?

They learn good work habits <u>and assistance is provided where they are needed</u>.

(A)   and assistance is provided where they are needed.

(B)   and provide assistance where it is needed.

(C)   and assist the needy and provide other kinds of assistance.

(D)   and, where needed, assist in providing for others.

(E)   and assistance skills provided where they are needed.

(B)   The underlined portion contains two passive voice constructions. Although the passive voice is acceptable, it should be used sparingly. Using the passive voice can also unnecessarily increase your chances of writing an awkward and grammatically ambiguous sentence. Does the "they" in "they are needed" refer to "habits" or "students"? The correct answer, choice (B), puts the first passive construction into the active voice and replaces the ambiguous "they" with "it," which unambiguously refers to "assistance." Choice (C), with its overuse of "and," lacks concision. Similarly, choice (D) needlessly complicates and expands the sentence. Choice (E) tries, but fails, to eliminate correctly one of the passive voice constructions.

4.   In context, which is the best way to revise the underlined portion of sentence 5 (reproduced below)?

<u>Almost everyone</u> has positive feelings about the new graduating requirement.

(A)   Almost everyone

(B)   Although hardly anyone

(C)   Not everyone

(D)   Because everyone

(E)   No one

(C)   The relationship between sentences 5 and 6 needs to be clarified. The underlined part of sentence 5—"almost everyone"—downplays the existence of the minority that has negative feelings. But it soon becomes clear that the writer wants to focus on, not dismiss, the minority. Choice (C) properly signals the discussion of a dissatisfied minority. Choices (B) and (D) both contain subordinating conjunctions and would turn sentence 5 into a dependent clause fragment. Choice (E) would create a contradiction in the paragraph, which discusses students' negative feelings.

5.   Which of the following is the best way to revise the underlined portion
      of sentence 6 (reproduced below)?

      Some students feel the community service requirement, <u>which involves
      volunteering one's time and assistance for forty hours or more,</u> is too de-
      manding.

      (A)   which involves volunteering one's time and assistance for forty
            hours or more

      (B)   which involves volunteering forty or more hours of one's time

      (C)   which involves volunteering forty or more hours

      (D)   which involves volunteering one's time and assistance

      (E)   a forty-hour or more volunteer commitment

(C)   The underlined portion in question 5 is too wordy and redundant. In
the context of the essay, "volunteering" means devoting one's "time and assistance." Choice (C) eliminates this redundant phrase. In choice (B), "of one's
time" is redundant because "hours" clearly establishes that time is being volun-
teered. (D) eliminates valuable information while retaining the original redundancy. Choice (E) introduces a new redundancy. "Volunteer" needlessly modifies "commitment," which we already know is of a volunteer nature.

6.   In context, which is the best way to revise and combine the underlined
      portions of sentences 8, 9, and 10 (reproduced below)?

      <u>They participate in sports. They work part-time jobs. Some even belong
      to clubs.</u>

      (A)   They participate in sports. They work part-time jobs. Some even
            belong to clubs.

      (B)   They participate in sports, work part-time jobs, and belong to
            clubs.

      (C)   They already devote time to sports, to working part-time, and to
            belong to clubs.

      (D)   Their participation in sports, part-time work, and clubs is a kind of
            community service.

      (E)   Sports, working part-time jobs, and clubs take up lots of a student's
            time.

(B)   Choppy sentences should be combined. Be sure to choose the option that
combines the sentences grammatically without changing the original meaning
or creating an awkward sentence. Choice (B) combines the sentences by forming a parallel structure that consists of verb phrases. The sentence is clear and
grammatical. (B) is the correct answer. Choice (C) is a faulty parallelism con-

sisting of two noun phases and one infinitival phrase. Both choices (D) and (E) alter the original meaning of the sentences. They are also awkward—notice how late the main verb occurs in each sentence.

7.   Which of the following would be the most appropriate sentence to insert after sentence 15?

    (A)   A community service requirement should recognize the reality of students' lives.

    (B)   Community service should be a volunteer program for busy students.

    (C)   The benefits of a community service program should be weighed against its potential liabilities.

    (D)   Community service isn't the only way students contribute their time and effort.

    (E)   As long as students' concerns are addressed, community service programs will remain counterproductive.

(A)   The final question of a given Paragraph Improvement set may ask you to choose an appropriate final sentence for the passage. This sentence should be a good concluding sentence for the passage as a whole. The passage focuses on why many students are unhappy with the community service requirement, which doesn't really seem to take into account just how busy most students are. The best answer is (A). Choice (B) is incorrect because the writer never suggests totally eliminating the requirement for one group of students. Choice (C) looks like an attractive choice; the writer does begin by mentioning the supposed benefits of community service. But the writer never really specifies how the community service requirement has impacted students (e.g., the jobs they've had to forego, the activities they've given up). Choice (D) does follow from sentence 15, but it does not account for the passage's overall meaning or purpose. (E) contradicts the passage, which implies that students' concerns have yet to (and very much need to) be taken into account.

DRILLS

SENTENCE CORRECTION QUESTIONS

DIRECTIONS: In each of the following sentences, some portion of the sentence is underlined. Under each sentence are five choices. The first choice has the same wording as the original. The other four choices are reworded. Sometimes the first choice containing the original wording is the best; sometimes one of the other choices is the best. Choose the

letter of the best choice. Your choice should produce a sentence which is not ambiguous or awkward and which is correct, clear, and precise.

This is a test of correct and effective English expression. Keep in mind the standards of English usage, punctuation, grammar, word choice, and construction.

EXAMPLE:

When you listen to opera, <u>a person may not appreciate it.</u>

(A) a person may not appreciate it.

(B) it may not be appreciated by a person.

(C) which may not be appreciated by one.

(D) you may not appreciate it.

(E) appreciating it may be a problem for you.

EXAMPLE ANSWER

Ⓐ Ⓑ Ⓒ ⬤ Ⓔ

■ QUESTION I.2.1

<u>Slavery or dulosis is practiced to</u> varying degrees by a wide array of ant species.

(A) Slavery or dulosis is practiced by

(B) Slavery, or dulosis, is practiced to

(C) Slavery, or dulosis, is practice for

(D) Slavery, or dulosis, is practiced by

(E) Slavery, or dulosis, is practiced for

ANSWER

(B) "Dulosis" is another word for "slavery" and thus must be set off by commas. The correct preposition is "to."

■ QUESTION I.2.2

When pursued by dogs the steenbok will take refuge in an underground burrow or den.

(A) When pursued by dogs, the steenbok will take refuge

(B) The steenbok will take refuge when pursued by dogs

(C) Pursued by dogs, the steenbok will take refuge

(D) The steenbok, when pursued by dogs will take refuge

(E) The steenbok pursued by dogs will take refuge

ANSWER

(A)   "When . . . " is an introductory clause and therefore requires a comma.

■ QUESTION I.2.3

Obstruction or infection of the appendix causes inflammation and serious cases it may rupture, spreading infection to the abdominal lining, and organs.

(A) rupture, spreading infection to the abdominal lining and nearby organs

(B) inflammation and in serious cases it may rupture spreading infection to the abdominal lining and nearby organs

(C) inflammation, and in serious cases it may rupture in order to spread infection to the abdominal lining and nearby organs

(D) serious cases that spread infection to the abdominal lining and nearby organs

(E) inflammation, and in serious cases it can rupture, spreading infection to the abdominal lining and organs

ANSWER

(E)   There are other ways to fix this construction, but none of the choices listed is correct except (E). The use of "and" will require a comma if the remainder of the sentence is fixed as follows: inserting "in" to make the first clause introductory, which then makes the remainder of the construction an independent clause. The final comma in the sentence that needs repair is misplaced (this "and" does not signal an independent clause or the last entry in a sequence).

■ QUESTION I.2.4

The archeologist develops his or her understanding of the past from the traces of things that ancient man made tools, weapons, utensils, and other objects of daily use.

(A) which ancient man made: tools, weapons, utensils, and other objects of daily use

(B) that ancient manmade: tools, weapons, utensils, and other objects of daily use

(C) that ancient man made; tools, weapons, utensils, and other objects of daily use

(D) things. Ancient man made: tools, weapons, utensils, and other objects of daily use

(E) that ancient man made: tools, weapons, utensils, and other objects of daily use

ANSWER

(E)   The insertion of a colon is correct because what follows is a list of what "ancient man made."

■ QUESTION I.2.5

The introduction of coinage into <u>Gaul and later during the second quarter of the first century B.C. into Britain,</u> was another sign both of a growing economic complexity and increasing political integration in the final stages of prehistory.

(A) Gaul and later during the second quarter of the first century B.C. into Britain

(B) Gaul and, later, during the second quarter of the first century B.C., into Britain,

(C) Gaul and later during the second quarter of the first century B.C., into Britain

(D) Gaul and Britain later, during the second quarter of the first century B.C.,

(E) Gaul and later into Britain during the second quarter of the first century B.C.,

ANSWER

(B)   Without setting off all qualifying clauses with commas, either the resulting construct is wrong grammatically or the sentence will be misread. For example, option (C) would make this sentence read as if both countries adopted coinage in the second quarter of the first century, which is not apparent from the sentence in need of repair. The correction now rightly informs the reader that only Britain adopted coinage during this timeframe and Gaul's adoption occurred earlier.

◼ QUESTION I.2.6

The progressive extension of the Roman Empire finally brought <u>the whole Celtic world under control, with the notable exception of Ireland and parts of Scotland</u>.

(A) the whole Celtic world under control, with the notable exceptions of Ireland and parts of Scotland

(B) the whole Celtic world, under control, with the notable exceptions of Ireland and parts of Scotland

(C) the whole Celtic world under control, with exceptions of Ireland and parts of Scotland

(D) with the notable exceptions of Ireland and parts of Scotland, the whole Celtic world under control

(E) under control the whole Celtic world, with the notable exceptions of Ireland and parts of Scotland

ANSWER

(A)   This choice is grammatically correct, and the usage is cleaner than other options. The word "exceptions" must also be plural.

■ QUESTION I.2.7

Because of its relatively low cost main uses of argon is in incandescent light bulbs.

(A) Because the main use of argon is in incandescent light bulbs, it has a relatively low cost.

(B) Because of its relatively low cost the main use of argon is in incandescent light bulbs.

(C) Because of its relatively low cost, the main use of argon is in incandescent light bulbs.

(D) Relatively low cost incandescent light bulbs are mainly used for argon.

(E) Relatively low cost, the main use of argon is in incandescent light bulbs.

ANSWER

(C)   This choice is grammatically correct, and the usage is discernibly cleaner than the other options.

■ QUESTION I.2.8

> Mythical animals, simple heraldic groups, <u>and an occasional myth-</u>
> <u>ological scene are apparent in the architecture at Carchemish in the</u>
> <u>early orthostates, which were made of alternating light and dark</u>
> <u>stones.</u>
>
> (A) and an occasional mythological scene in the architecture at
> Carchemish in the early orthostates were made of alternating light
> and dark stones.
>
> (B) and an occasional mythological scene in the early orthostates
> are apparent in the architecture at Carchemish, which were made of
> alternating light and dark stones.
>
> (C) and an occasional mythological scene apparent in the archi-
> tecture at Carchemish in the early orthostates, which were made of
> alternating light and dark stones.
>
> (D) and an occasional mythological scene are apparent in the ar-
> chitecture at Carchemish in the early orthostates, which were made
> of alternating light and dark stones.
>
> (E) and an occasional mythological scene at Carchemish in the
> early orthostates are apparent in the architecture, which were made
> of alternating light and dark stones.

ANSWER

(D)   This choice is grammatically correct, and the clauses are correct relative
to the nouns they modify. Some choices may appear grammatically correct (i.e.,
[C]), but the incorrect noun is modified.

■ QUESTION I.2.9

Thomas Amory, an English author was born in Ireland in 1691 but resided for most of his life in Westminster.

(A) An English author was born in Ireland in 1691 but resided for most of his life in Westminster, Thomas Amory.

(B) Thomas Amory an English author was born in Ireland in 1691 but resided for most of his life in Westminster.

(C) Thomas Amory, an English author, born in Ireland in 1691 but residing for most of his life in Westminster.

(D) Thomas Amory, an English author, was born in Ireland in 1691 but resided for most of his life in Westminster.

(E) An English author, Thomas Amory, was born in Ireland in 1691 but residing for most of his life in Westminster.

ANSWER

(D)   The author's name requires commas to set it apart from the introductory clause, and the correct version of the verb is "resided." One other choice is grammatically correct (A), but this version is not common usage or good writing.

■ QUESTION I.2.10

Calvin Fairbanks' <u>efforts, on behalf of Kentucky slaves, were interrupted in 1849 when he was seized by agents from Kentucky in Indiana to which he had fled.</u>

(A) efforts on behalf of Kentucky slaves were interrupted in 1849, when he was seized by agents from Kentucky in Indiana, to which he had fled

(B) efforts on behalf of Kentucky slaves were interrupted in 1849 when he was seized by agents from Kentucky in Indiana to which he had fled

(C) efforts were interrupted in 1849 on behalf of Kentucky slaves, when he was seized by agents from Kentucky in Indiana, to which he had fled

(D) 1849 efforts on behalf of Kentucky slaves were interrupted when he was seized by agents from Kentucky in Indiana, to which he had fled

(E) efforts on behalf of Kentucky slaves were interrupted in 1849 when seized by agents from Kentucky in Indiana, to which he had fled

ANSWER

(A) The adverbial clause "when . . . Indiana" must be set off by commas.

QUESTION I.2.11

Bedouins are frequently involved in intertribal feuds, which involve not only property such as water-use rights, but also honor.

(A) Bedouins frequently involved in intertribal feuds, which include not only property, such as water-use rights, but also honor.

(B) Bedouins are frequently involved in intertribal feuds which include not only property, such as water-use rights, but also honor.

(C) Bedouins frequently involved in intertribal feuds include not only property, such as water-use rights, but also honor.

(D) Bedouins, frequently involved in intertribal feuds, including not only property, such as water-use rights, but also honor.

(E) Bedouins are frequently involved in intertribal feuds, which include not only property, such as water-use rights, but also honor

ANSWER

(E)   The nonrestrictive clause (signaled by "which") requires a comma.

QUESTION I.2.12

The thieves compared notes, and they agreed that it would be imprudent to try to rob the bank they had researched because of its security arrangements.

(A) notes, and they agreed that it would be imprudent

(B) notes and they agreed that it would be imprudent

(C) notes, and they agreed to be imprudent

(D) notes, and agreed that it would be imprudent

(E) notes, and agreed that to be imprudent

ANSWER

(A)   There is no error as written.

QUESTION I.2.13

There are winners and losers, but no one could whine about the outcome of this contest, which was as fair as it could possibly be given the circumstances.

(A) There are winners and losers,

(B) Winners and losers

(C) There were winners and losers,

(D) There can be winners and losers

(E) The winners and losers were berated,

ANSWER

(C)   The remainder of the sentence is past tense, and thus the first verb must be changed from "are" to "were."

QUESTION I.2.14

In 1973, Richard Nixon gave his famous I am not a crook speech.

(A) Richard Nixon gave his famous I am not a crook speech

(B) Richard Nixon gave his famous "crook" speech

(C) Richard Nixon, a famous crook, gave his speech

(D) Richard Nixon gave his famous "I am not a crook" speech

(E) Richard Nixon gave his famous speech: I am not a crook

ANSWER

(D)   The name of the speech needs to be set off with quotation marks.

■ QUESTION I.2.15

Rabies, or hydrophobia, is an acute viral infection of the central nervous system in <u>dogs, foxes, raccoons, skunks, bats, and other animals, which can also occur in humans</u>.

(A) dogs, foxes, raccoons, skunks, bats, and other animals, which can also occur in humans

(B) dogs foxes raccoons skunks bats and other animals, which can also occur in humans

(C) dogs, foxes, raccoons, skunks, bats, and other animals which can also occur in humans

(D) dogs, foxes, raccoons, skunks, bats, and other animals, and which can also occur in humans

(E) dogs, foxes, raccoons, skunks, and bats, and other animals, and which can also occur in humans

ANSWER

(A)   No error as written. The commas are used correctly to divide a series and to designate the nonrestrictive clause ("which").

QUESTION I.2.16

Condensed from an even longer work, Tabari's annals <u>are not a continuous narrative but contain vociferous versions of the same story</u> and are thus a prime collection of Arabic sources.

(A) are not a continuous narrative but contain vociferous versions of the same story

(B) are not a continuous narrative but contain differing versions of the same story

(C) are not a continuous narrative but contain petulant versions of the same story

(D) are not a continuous narrative but contain stipulated versions of the same story

(E) are not a continuous narrative but contain exaggerated versions of the same story

ANSWER

(B)   The word "differing" is the best choice of those offered. The use of the word "collection" later in the sentence is a clue.

■ QUESTION I.2.17

A taste bud consists of about 20 long, slender cells; a tiny hair proj-ects from each cell to the surface of the tongue through a tiny pore. The taste cells contain the endings of nerve filaments that convey impulses to the taste center in the brain.

(A) A taste bud consists of about 20 long, slender cells; a tiny hair projects from each cell

(B) A taste bud consists of about 20 long, slender cells, a tiny hair projects from each cell

(C) A taste bud consists of about 20 long, slender cells; a tiny hair would project from each cell

(D) A taste bud consists of about 20 long, slender cells a tiny hair projects from each cell

(E) A taste bud consists of about 20 long, slender cells; a tiny hair projections from each cell

ANSWER

(A)   No error as written. The semicolon is used correctly, and the "projects" portion of the sentence is both grammatically correct and clear.

■ QUESTION I.2.18

An unrhymed Japanese poem recording the essence of a moment keenly perceived and in which nature is linked to human nature, a haiku usually consists of 17 *jion* (Japanese symbol-sounds).

(A) An unrhymed Japanese poem recording the essence of a moment keenly perceived and in which nature is linked to human nature, a haiku usually consists of 17 *jion* (Japanese symbol-sounds).

(B) An unrhymed Japanese poem recording the essence of a moment keenly perceived in which nature is linked to human nature usually consists of 17 *jion* (Japanese symbol-sounds).

(C) An unrhymed Japanese poem recording the essence of a moment keenly perceived, which nature is linked to human nature, a haiku usually consists of 17 *jion* (Japanese symbol-sounds).

(D) An unrhymed Japanese poem recording the essence of a moment keenly perceived linked to human nature, a haiku usually consists of 17 *jion* (Japanese symbol-sounds).

(E) A haiku, an unrhymed Japanese poem recording the essence of a moment keenly perceived and in which nature is linked to human nature, usually consists of 17 *jion* (Japanese symbol-sounds).

ANSWER

(E)   Although the underlined sentence is not grammatically incorrect, it is a passive construction and therefore (E) is the better choice. The other options are either not grammatically correct or alter the meaning of the original.

■ QUESTION I.2.19

She mistook the small garter snake for a poisonous <u>variety, and killed it with her hoe, afterwards</u> she was very remorseful.

(A) variety, and killed it with her hoe, afterwards

(B) variety and killed it with her hoe, afterwards

(C) variety and killed it with her hoe afterwards

(D) variety and killed it with her hoe. Afterwards,

(E) variety, and killed it with her hoe. Afterwards

ANSWER

(D)   The comma is not required before the "and" in the absence of a subject in the clause that follows. A new sentence follows, and consequently, the period is required after the word "hoe."

■ QUESTION I.2.20

<u>Reportedly, the horse jumped three fences and broke through another before it was hit by a car going south on the highway.</u>

(A) Reportedly, the horse jumped three fences and broke through another before it was hit by a car going south on the highway.

(B) Reportedly the horse jumped three fences, and broke through another before it was hit by a car going south on the highway.

(C) Reportedly, the horse jumped three fences, broke through another, before it was hit by a car going south on the highway.

(D) Reportedly, the horse jumped three fences and broke through another before it hit a car going south on the highway.

(E) Reportedly, the horse jumped three fences and broke through another before going south on the highway.

ANSWER

(A)   No error as written. The other choices are either comma faults or change the meaning of the sentence, as in (E).

■ QUESTION I.2.21

If you <u>understand</u> the math, the physics of planetary movement would have been no problem at all; however, not many among us can decipher those equations.

(A) understand

(B) understood

(C) would understand

(D) did understand

(E) did comprehend

ANSWER

(B)   The verb's tense in the underlined section does not match that in the rest of the sentence.

■ QUESTION I.2.22

<u>An altar boy as a child,</u> but as a young man, he took a wrong turn on life's pathway and wound up behind bars.

(A) An altar boy as a child,

(B) He was an altar boy as a child,

(C) An altar boy child,

(D) The altar boy as a child,

(E) When a child, an altar boy,

ANSWER

(B)   Some of these choices are simply very awkward, and therefore (B) is the better choice. The use of the word "but" precludes choice (A).

■ QUESTION I.2.23

The 14th Dalai Lama, Tenzin Gyatso (1935-), was installed in 1940. In 1959, following a Tibetan revolt against Chinese rule, <u>he fled into exile and traveling</u> widely, pleading the Tibetan cause.

(A) he fled into exile traveling

(B) he was exiled. He has traveled

(C) he fled into exile traveling

(D) he has traveled into exile

(E) he fled to exile and has traveled

ANSWER

(B)   This choice corrects the tense and also makes the passage more readable.

■ QUESTION I.2.24

<u>He had been wounded in battle, and consequently, he was allowed to return home, where he is still convalescing.</u>

(A) He had been wounded in battle, and consequently, he was allowed to return home, where he is still convalescing.

(B) He had been wounded in battle and consequently he was allowed to return home, where he is still convalescing.

(C) He had been wounded in battle and consequently, he was allowed to return home, where he is still convalescing.

(D) He had been wounded in battle, and consequently he was allowed to return home where he is still convalescing.

(E) He had been wounded in battle, and, consequently, he was allowed to return home where he is still convalescing.

ANSWER

(A)   No error as written. Whereas all other choices are wrong because of comma placement, choice (E) is technically correct; however, one comma can be deleted and still be correct, as in choice (A), which is preferable in order to enhance readability.

■ QUESTION I.2.25

In Roman religion, a Bacchanalia is a festival in honor of Bacchus, god of wine. Originally a religious ceremony, it gradually became an occasion for drunken, licentious excesses and was finally <u>instituted</u> by law in 186 B.C.

(A) instituted

(B) forbidden

(C) incorporated

(D) attributed

(E) convened

ANSWER

(B)   This word is the only logical choice among those offered.

■ QUESTION I.2.26

Upon leaving the nursery, Mr. Greene, together with his wife, <u>put the plants in the trunk of the car they had just bought.</u>

(A) put the plants in the trunk of the car they had just bought.

(B) put in the plants to the trunk of the car they had just bought.

(C) put into the trunk of the car they had just bought the plants.

(D) put the plants they had just bought in the trunk of the car.

(E) put the plants into the trunk of the car.

ANSWER

(D)   It is obvious that the Greenes have just purchased plants: "Upon leaving the nursery." The location of the modifying phrase, "they had just bought," should be carefully placed in the sentence so it clearly modifies "plants" and not "car." Choice (D) has the modifying phrase immediately following "plants," and the meaning is clear. The wording of choices (A), (B), and (C) makes the reader think the car has just been purchased. Choice (E) omits the concept "they had just bought."

■ QUESTION I.2.27

The way tensions are increasing in the Middle East, some experts <u>are afraid we may end up with a nuclear war.</u>

(A) are afraid we may end up with a nuclear war.

(B) being afraid we may end up with a nuclear war.

(C) afraid that a nuclear war may end up over there.

(D) are afraid a nuclear war may end there.

(E) are afraid a nuclear war may occur.

ANSWER

(E)   Choice (E) retains the central idea while eliminating the wording problems of the other choices. There is no antecedent for "we" in choices (A) and (B). Also, the phrase "end up" is redundant; "up" should be eliminated; therefore, choice (C) is incorrect. Choice (D) introduces a new concept of "war may end over there," an idea clearly not intended by the original.

QUESTION I.2.28

Whether Leif Erickson was the first to discover America or not is still a debatable issue, but there is general agreement that there probably were a number of "discoveries" through the years.

(A) Whether Leif Erickson was the first to discover America or not

(B) That Leif Erickson was the first to discover America

(C) That Leif Erickson may have been the first to have discovered America

(D) Whether Leif Erickson is the first to discover America or he is not

(E) Whether or not Leif Erickson was or was not the first discoverer of America

ANSWER

(B)   Choice (B) clearly and precisely states the issue of debate. Choice (C) is eliminated because it is too wordy and not the precise issue under debate. The correlative conjunctions, "whether . . . or," should be followed by parallel structures. Choice (A) follows "Whether" with a subject-verb combination not seen after "not." Choice (D) is parallel but in the wrong tense. Choice (E) has "Whether or not" run together and uses poor wording in the rest of the sentence.

QUESTION I.2.29

People who charge too much are likely to develop a bad credit rating.

(A) People who charge too much are likely to develop

(B) People's charging too much are likely to develop

(C) When people charge too much, likely to develop

(D) That people charge too much is likely to develop

(E) Charging too much is likely to develop for people

ANSWER

(A)   Choice (A) has both correct agreement and clear reference. Choice (B) has a subject-verb agreement problem, "charging . . . are." Choice (C) produces a fragment. It is unclear in choice (D) who will have the bad credit rating, and the wording of choice (E) has the obvious subject, "people," in a prepositional phrase.

■ QUESTION I.2.30

The museum of natural science has a special exhibit of gems and minerals, <u>and the fifth graders went to see it on a field trip.</u>

(A)   and the fifth graders went to see it on a field trip.

(B)   and seeing it were the fifth graders on a field trip.

(C)   when the fifth graders took a field trip to see it.

(D)   which the fifth graders took a field trip to see.

(E)   where the fifth graders took their field trip to see it.

ANSWER

(D)   Choice (D) correctly presents the fifth grade field trip in a subordinate clause modifying "exhibit." Choices (A) and (B) have the coordinating conjunction "and," but the first part of the sentence is not equal in meaning or importance to the second part of the sentence. Choice (C) introduces "when" with no antecedent. Choice (E) uses "where" as the subordinating conjunction, but it is too far from its antecedent and is not the important idea of the sentence.

■ QUESTION I.2.31

<u>When the case is decided, he plans appealing</u> if the verdict is unfavorable.

(A)   When the case is decided, he plans appealing

(B)   When deciding the case, he plans appealing

(C)   After the case is decided, he is appealing

(D)   After deciding the case, he is planning to appeal

(E)   When the case is decided, he plans to appeal

ANSWER

(E) In choice (E) the present infinitive is correctly used to express an action following another action: "plans to appeal." Choices (A) and (B) use the wrong form, "appealing." Choice (C) uses the wrong tense, "is appealing." Choice (D) sounds as if the same person is deciding the case and appealing the case.

◼ QUESTION I.2.32

> We decided there was hardly any reason for his allowing us to stay up later on weeknights.
>
> (A) We decided there was hardly any reason for his allowing us
>
> (B) We, deciding there was hardly any reason for his allowing us,
>
> (C) Deciding there was hardly any reason, we allowed
>
> (D) We decided there were none of the reasons for him to allow us
>
> (E) For him to allow us there was hardly any reason we decided

ANSWER

(A) Choice (A) has clear wording. Choice (B) is a fragment because it puts the verb in the nonessential phrase. Choices (C), (D), and (E) produce twisted wording. Choice (C) has no object for the verb "allowed" and sounds as if the speakers were allowed to stay up later. Choice (E) needs commas and sounds as if the speakers decided to stay up later.

◼ QUESTION I.2.33

> At this time it is difficult for me agreeing with your plan of having everyone in the club working on the same project.
>
> (A) it is difficult for me agreeing with your plan of having everyone
>
> (B) I find it difficult to agree to your plan of having everyone
>
> (C) for my agreement with your plan is difficult for everyone
>
> (D) an agreement to your plan seems difficult for everyone
>
> (E) finding it difficult for me to agree to your plan of having everyone

ANSWER

(B)   Choice (B) plainly states the subject and the verb, "I find." Choices (A) and (E) have the subject in a prepositional phrase, "for me." Choice (E) produces a fragment. Choice (C), a fragment, has no subject because both potential subjects are in prepositional phrases: "agreement" and "plan." Choices (C) and (D) imply "everyone" as the main subject.

▪ QUESTION I.2.34

When the Whites hired a contractor to do remodeling on their home, he <u>promised to completely finish the work inside of three months.</u>

(A) promised to completely finish the work inside of three months.

(B) promised to complete the work within three months.

(C) completely promised to finish the work inside of three months' line span.

(D) promising to completely finish the work in three months.

(E) completely finished the work within three months.

ANSWER

(B)   Choice (B) avoids the split infinitive and the incorrect expression, "inside of." Choices (A) and (D) split the infinitive "to finish" with the adverb "completely." Choice (C) uses "inside of," an expression that is incorrect to use because it is redundant ("of" should be deleted) and because it should not be used with measuring time. Choice (E) erroneously changes the idea and would employ two verbs in simple past tense: "hired" and "finished."

■ QUESTION I.2.35

> Women live longer and have fewer illnesses than men, <u>which proves that women are the strongest sex.</u>
>
> (A) which proves that women are the strongest sex.
>
> (B) which proves that women are the stronger sex.
>
> (C) facts which prove that women are the stronger sex.
>
> (D) proving that women are the strongest sex.
>
> (E) a proof that women are the stronger sex.

ANSWER

(C)   General reference should be avoided. The pronoun "which" does not have a clear reference in choices (A) or (B). In choice (C) "which" clearly refers to "facts." The reference "proving" in choice (D) is too general. In choice (E) "a proof" is an incorrect number to refer to the two strengths of women.

■ QUESTION I.2.36

> Wealthy citizens often protest <u>about the building of</u> low-cost housing in the affluent communities where they reside.
>
> (A) about the building of
>
> (B) whether they should build
>
> (C) if builders should build
>
> (D) the building of
>
> (E) whether or not they should build

ANSWER

(D)   Because the verb "protest" can be transitive and have a direct object, choice (D) avoids awkward wordiness and use of the unnecessary preposition "about." Choices (B) and (E) include unnecessary words and use the pronoun "they" that has no clear antecedent; choice (C) is also unnecessarily wordy and contains the repetitious words "builders should build."

■ QUESTION I.2.37

Siblings growing up in a family do not necessarily have equal op-portunities to achieve, <u>the difference being their placement in the family, their innate abilities, and their personalities.</u>

(A) the difference being their placement in the family, their innate abilities, and their personalities.

(B) because of their placement in the family, their innate abilities, and their personalities.

(C) and the difference is their placement in the family, their innate abilities, and their personalities.

(D) they have different placements in the family, different innate abilities, and different personalities.

(E) their placement in the family, their innate abilities, and their personalities being different.

ANSWER

(B)   Choice (B) best shows the causal relationship between sibling opportunities and their placement in the family, their abilities, and their personalities and retains the subordination of the original sentence. Choices (A) and (E) provide dangling phrases. Choice (C) with its use of the coordinating conjunction "and" treats the lack of opportunity and its cause as if they are equal ideas and does not show the causal relationship between them, and choice (D) results in a run-on sentence.

QUESTION I.2.38

Two major provisions of the United States Bill of Rights <u>is freedom of speech and that citizens are guaranteed a trial by jury.</u>

(A) is freedom of speech and that citizens are guaranteed a trial by jury.

(B) is that citizens have freedom of speech and a guaranteed trial by jury.

(C) is freedom of speech and the guarantee of a trial by jury.

(D) are freedom of speech and that citizens are guaranteed a trial by jury.

(E) are freedom of speech and the guarantee of a trial by jury.

ANSWER

(E)   Only choice (E) corrects the two major problems in the sentence, the lack of subject-verb agreement and the lack of parallelism. In choices (A), (B), and (C), the verb "is" does not agree with its plural subject, "provisions." Choices (A) and (D) have unlike constructions serving as predicate nominatives, the noun "freedom" and the clause "that citizens are guaranteed a trial by jury." Choice (E) correctly uses the plural verb "are" to agree with the plural subject, and the predicate nominative is composed of two parallel nouns, "freedom" and "guarantee."

QUESTION I.2.39

<u>Eating chips of dried paint,</u> children who live in old houses are at risk for lead poisoning.

(A) Eating chips of dried paint

(B) Having eaten chips of dried paint

(C) Because of eating chips of dried paint

(D) Chips of dry paint being eaten

(E) Because they may eat chips of dried paint

ANSWER

(E) This sentence starts with a dangling participial phrase that must be followed by the noun or pronoun that it modifies or be eliminated from the sentence all together. Choice (E) correctly replaces the phrase with a subordinate clause that shows the causal relationship between the eating of paint chips and lead poisoning. Choices (B), (C), and (D) are also dangling phrases and create the same basic problem as the phrase in the original sentence.

■ QUESTION I.2.40

French architect Pierre Charles L'Enfant was hired to plan the United States capital <u>although he and President Washington had a disagreement</u>, L'Enfant's plan was used in the design of Washington, D.C.

(A) although he and President Washington had a disagreement,

(B) and, although he and President Washington had a disagreement,

(C) who had a disagreement with President Washington, but,

(D) although having had a disagreement with President Washington,

(E) he and President Washington had a disagreement.

ANSWER

(B) Only choice (B) corrects the run-on sentence in this exercise in an acceptable fashion by adding the conjunction "and" to join the two sentences. Choice (C) corrects the run-on but poses the problem of the relative pronoun "who" that does not follow its antecedent; choice (D) retains the run-on and adds an awkward participial phrase; and choice (E) results in two run-on errors.

■ QUESTION I.2.41

While trying to reduce cholesterol, <u>you should eat lentils in casseroles, salads, and soups, the reason being that lentils</u> provide an excellent source of protein.

(A) you should eat lentils in casseroles, salads, and soups, the reason being that lentils

(B) lentils should be eaten in casseroles, salads, and soups, the reason being that lentils

(C) you should eat lentils in casseroles, salads, and soups because lentils

(D) eating lentils in casseroles, salads, and soups will

(E) you should eat lentils in casseroles, salads, and soups, which

ANSWER

(C) Choice (C) retains the pronoun "you" after the participial phrase that modifies it but eliminates the wordy dangling phrase, "the reason being that"; the revision expresses clearly the causal relationship. Choices (B) and (D) leave the introductory phrase dangling; and choice (E) results in an unclear antecedent for the pronoun "which" and fails to show the causal relationship.

■ QUESTION I.2.42

Being that the first Library of Congress had been destroyed in the War of 1812, Congress purchased the personal library of Thomas Jefferson to replace it.

(A) Being that the first Library of Congress had been destroyed in the War of 1812,

(B) Although the first Library of Congress was destroyed in the War of 1812,

(C) The first Library of Congress was destroyed in 1812, was restored because

(D) The first Library of Congress was destroyed in the War of 1812, so

(E) Having destroyed the first Library of Congress in the War of 1812,

ANSWER

(D)   Only choice (D) corrects the opening independent clause while retaining the original meaning of the sentence. Choice (A) is incorrect because "Being" is both an unattached participle and an improper conjugation of "to be," which must always be used as the main verb. Choices (B) and (E) are idiomatically incorrect and change the meaning. Choice (E) also contains an unattached participle. Choice (C) is excessively wordy.

■ QUESTION I.2.43

The fewer people you tell your secret to, there are fewer people to divulge it to others.

(A) there are fewer people to divulge it to others.

(B) there will be fewer people to divulge it to others.

(C) there being fewer people to divulge it to others.

(D) the fewer people there are to divulge it to others.

(E) the fewer people can divulge it to others.

ANSWER

(E) The problem here is one of parallel construction; choice (E) completes the comparison in parallel fashion and avoids the wordiness of choice (D). Choice (B) unnecessarily changes the tense but does not eliminate the problem; choice (C) replaces the second clause with a dangling phrase.

■ QUESTION I.2.44

Lisbon, Portugal, is a large city <u>whose history goes back</u> to ancient Greek and Roman times.

(A) whose history goes back

(B) which history goes back

(C) the history of which goes back

(D) its history goes back

(E) who's history goes back

ANSWER

(A) This sentence is correct in standard written English because "whose," a possessive relative pronoun, is appropriate to refer to a city. Choice (B) eliminates the required possessive pronoun and is not idiomatically correct; choice (C) is wordy and awkward; choice (D) results in a run-on sentence; and choice (E) replaces the possessive pronoun with the contraction that means "who is."

◼ QUESTION I.2.45

The young entertainer gets unusual opportunities <u>due to the fact that he is a man whose</u> father is famous.

(A) due to the fact the he is a man whose

(B) due to the fact that he is a man who's

(C) due to the fact that his

(D) because he is a man whose

(E) because his

ANSWER

(E)   The problem is one of wordiness, and choice **(E)** correctly shows the relationship and eliminates words that add nothing to the meaning of the sentence. Each of the other choices retains unnecessary words.

USAGE QUESTIONS

<u>DIRECTIONS</u>: **Each of the following sentences may contain an error in diction, usage, idiom, or grammar. Some sentences are correct. Some sentences contain one error. No sentence contains more than one error.**

If there is an error, it will appear in one of the underlined portions labeled A, B, C, or D. If there is no error, choose the portion labeled E. If there is an error, select the letter of the portion that must be changed in order to correct the sentence.

EXAMPLE:

He drove <u>slowly</u> and <u>cautiously</u> in order to <u>hopefully</u> avoid having an
        A   B   C
<u>accident</u>. <u>No error</u>
    D   E

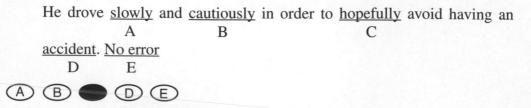

■ QUESTION I.2.46

In establishing chronologies for cultures that existed before <u>written</u>
                                                                                    A
<u>history</u> <u>the archeologist</u> is primarily dependent upon the fabric of
                        B
knowledge he or she <u>has been able to reconstruct through the prin-</u>
                                                    C
<u>ciples of</u> typological seriation and stratigraphy. <u>No error</u>.
          D   E

ANSWER

(A)   The introductory prepositional phrase ("In . . . history") requires a
comma.

■ QUESTION I.2.47

<u>Pericles building campaign</u> centered on <u>the Acropolis, a natural</u>
                    A   B
<u>outcropping</u> of rock that had originally served as <u>the citadel, it had</u>
                                                                      C
<u>served</u> that same purpose <u>even during the Persian wars</u>. <u>No error</u>.
                                                    D   E

ANSWER

(C)   A comma in this section should be replaced by a period, and "it" should
be capitalized because a complete sentence follows.

■ QUESTION I.2.48

Thomas Jefferson's model for the State Capitol in Richmond was
     A   B

the Mason Carrée in Nîmes, which he deemed "the model of cubi-
                   C   D

cal architecture." No error.
             E

ANSWER

(E)   There is no error in this construction.

■ QUESTION I.2.49

An arabesque is a complex decorative motive painted or in low relief
     A   B

composed of interlacing bands geometric devices, and sprays of
                              C

foliage, among other layered designs. No error.
             D   E

ANSWER

(C)   The comma should not be used in this section because it does not set off a modifying clause nor divide a series.

QUESTION I.2.50

Almost two thirds of <u>Argentine industrial production takes</u> place in
A

or around <u>Buenos Aires. The main industries being</u> meat-packing, oil
B

refining, metal <u>working, and the production of textiles,</u> <u>electrical-</u>
C

<u>machinery, appliances, and transportation equipment.</u> <u>No error.</u>
D   E

ANSWER

(B)   The section beginning "The main industries" is not a sentence. Either a comma needs to follow "Buenos Aires" or the verb "being" needs to be changed to "are" to make this construct correct.

QUESTION I.2.51

<u>Heparin, a substance inhibiting blood clotting,</u> and fibrinogen,
A

<u>a protein that</u> <u>forms the network of a clot,</u> <u>are both in the liver.</u>
B   C   D

<u>No error.</u>
E

ANSWER

(E)   No error.

■ QUESTION I.2.52

> Among the <u>protozoans the radiolarians</u> have <u>elaborate, geometrically</u>
>   A   B
> designed siliceous (silicon) <u>skeletons; and</u> the foraminiferans have
>   C
> calcareous (calcium) shells <u>in elaborate</u> designs. <u>No error</u>.
>   D   E

ANSWER

(A)   The introductory clause "Among . . . protozoans" requires a comma.

■ QUESTION I.2.53

> <u>Feathers, which</u> evolved from reptilian <u>scales,</u> <u>are the most outstan-</u>
>   A   B   C
> ding characteristic of <u>birds skin</u>. <u>No error</u>.
>   D   E

ANSWER

(D)   The possessive is required: "birds' skin."

■ QUESTION I.2.54

> <u>In the eighth century B.C.</u>, the Phrygians made <u>some of their sculpture</u>
>   A   B
> <u>in tentative imitation of</u> the oriental <u>designs but</u> the overall style
>   C   D
> remained indigenous. <u>No error</u>.
>   E

ANSWER

(D)   A comma is required before "but," which serves as a coordinating conjunction here.

■ QUESTION I.2.55

Economically, then, the American Revolution created <u>not only new</u>
        A   B
<u>wealth but</u> new sources of <u>wealth, particularly</u> <u>in the form of the</u>
                                C   D
<u>war debt of</u> the states and the central government. <u>No error.</u>
                                                                        E

ANSWER

(E)   No error.

■ QUESTION I.2.56

<u>The impressive mound site</u> of Cempoala <u>25 miles inland</u> <u>was</u> the
                A   B   C
capitol of the Totonac tribe <u>in late Post-classic times</u>. <u>No error.</u>
                                                 D   E

ANSWER

(B)   There is not an error, but commas used to set off "25 miles inland" enhance the readability of the sentence.

■ QUESTION I.2.57

The Cathedral of Siena <u>was</u> a rare but triumphant example of the
                        A
Italian Gothic, has <u>a richly</u> ornamental façade <u>that was conceived</u>
                        B   C
<u>by Giovanni Pisano (c. 1245-c. 1320)</u>. <u>No error</u>.
                        D   E

ANSWER

(A)   The verb "was" must be deleted to make the construction grammatically correct. Other options would work, but no other section that is underlined would be one of those options.

■ QUESTION I.2.58

The <u>warrior</u> of ancient Greece wore <u>a helmet</u>, <u>breastplate and back-</u>
        A   B   C
<u>plate</u>, <u>and greaves</u> (leg armor). <u>No error</u>.
        D   E

ANSWER

(E)   No error.

■ QUESTION I.2.59

<u>During the last 30 years of his life</u>, <u>Matthew Arnold's</u> literary <u>ener-</u>
                A   B
<u>gies was devoted</u> to prose, <u>of which</u> he published more than 15 vol-
        C   D
umes. <u>No error</u>.
        E

ANSWER

(C)   "Energies" is plural, and therefore, the verb must be "were."

■ QUESTION I.2.60

> Another Renaissance device <u>for using space</u> to represent time <u>were</u>
>   A   B
> the sequencing of small <u>panels, typically</u> below the central subject,
>   C
> each containing a key episode <u>from the story</u>. <u>No error</u>.
>   D   E

ANSWER

(B)   The noun "device" is singular, and therefore, the verb must be "was."

■ QUESTION I.2.61

> The Etruscans <u>migrated</u> to central <u>Italy during</u> the eighth century B.C.,
>   A   B
> probably <u>from Asia Minor, their</u> ascendancy <u>was</u> secured by the sixth
>   C   D
> century B.C., when they occupied the region from the Po to the Tiber.
>
> <u>No error</u>.
>   E

ANSWER

(C)   A period must follow "Asia Minor," creating another sentence out of what follows.

QUESTION I.2.62

The pseudo-historical tradition established <u>by Geoffrey however</u>
                                                        A

includes no mention of <u>Tristan, Lancelot, or the Grail legends</u> <u>that</u>
                                        B   C

became famous <u>in the Middle Ages</u> through the French romances.
                        D

<u>No error</u>.
    E

ANSWER

(A)   The word "however" serves as a conjunction and must be set off by commas.

QUESTION I.2.63

Prostheses <u>are fitted</u> to individuals of all <u>ages. This</u> includes ampu-
                A   B

tees <u>who</u> are children <u>to adults 70 years old and older</u>. <u>No error</u>.
        C   D   E

ANSWER

(E)   No error.

QUESTION I.2.64

Charles Draper developed the <u>theory of</u> and invented the <u>technology for</u>
                                        A   B

inertial navigation, a guidance system <u>which</u> does not <u>rely on</u> external
                                                C   D

sources. <u>No error</u>.
            E

ANSWER

(E) The sentence is correct as written. Choices (A) and (B) are a compound structure and are in proper parallel form. Choice (C) has a clear reference to "system." Choice (D) is a correct idiom.

◼ QUESTION I.2.65

Inertial navigation is a system of navigation <u>employed</u> in submarines
A

when <u>they are</u> underwater, missiles used <u>for</u> defense purposes, air-
BC

craft, and <u>to get</u> man to the moon in the Apollo exploration series.
D

<u>No error</u>.
E

ANSWER

(D) The preposition "in" has three objects: "submarines," "missiles," and choice (D), which must be made parallel to the previous two nouns. Choice (A) is a participle modifying "navigation." Choice (B) is a part of a subordinate clause modifying "submarines." Choice (C) is a correct preposition.

◼ QUESTION I.2.66

Much <u>to</u> <u>everyone's</u> surprise, the company president, <u>known for</u> his
ABC

intelligence and good business judgment, <u>and enjoying</u> a hobby of
D

sky diving. <u>No error</u>.
E

ANSWER

(D)   This sentence is a fragment made by the conjunction "and" linking "enjoying" with "known," the participial adjective of choice (B); "and" should be eliminated and "enjoying" changed to "enjoys" to be the subject of "president." Choice (A) is an idiom. Choice (B) is the correct possessive form to complete the idiom.

■ QUESTION I.2.67

> They are very grateful the city has set up a special fund that helps pay
> ‎A   B   C   D
> for electric bills of the elderly and the handicapped. No error.
>   E

ANSWER

(A)   There is no antecedent for this pronoun, although it is implied that the elderly and the handicapped are the logical ones to be grateful. Choices (B) and (D) are elliptical constructions, "grateful [that] the city" and "helps [to] pay." Choice (C) is a verb.

■ QUESTION I.2.68

> In order to stay cool during the summer months, Americans not only
>   A   B
> are using ceiling fans, but they are also using devices to add humidity
>   C
> to the air in particularly arid climates such as Arizona. No error.
>   D   E

ANSWER

(B)   This sentence is not parallel. Two actions are mentioned, connected by "not only" and "but also." The sentence should read, "not only are Americans . . . but also they are." Choices (A) and (C) contain properly used infinitives. Choice (D), "particularly," is the adverb form modifying the adjective, "arid."

■ QUESTION I.2.69

> After seeing the technique demonstrated on television, Janie baked
>   A
> homemade bread for the first time yesterday, and her brother
>   B
> thought it tasted good, an opinion everyone agreed with. No error.
>   C   D   E

ANSWER

(D)　Sentences should not end with a preposition; the sentence should read, "an opinion with which everyone agreed." Choice (A) is a gerund as the object of a preposition. Choice (B) is an appropriate conjunction; and choice (C), "good," is the positive form of the adjective to follow the linking verb "tasted."

■ QUESTION I.2.70

> Although not so prevalent as they once were, hood ornaments still
>   A   B
> exist, some of which are quite distinctive, such as the symbol for
>   C   D
> Mercedes-Benz and Jaguar. No error.
>   E

ANSWER

(A)　The expression should read, "as prevalent as" for the proper comparison. Choice (B) is a noun used as an adjective. Choice (C), "some of which," has clear reference to "ornaments." Choice (D), "such as," is correct to mean, "for example."

■ QUESTION I.2.71

> If I <u>were</u> that tourist, I would not <u>argue with</u> those two members of
>   A   B
> the Guardia Civil because, although they are <u>speaking politely</u>, it is
>   C
>
> obvious they are <u>becoming angry</u>. <u>No error</u>.
>   D   E

ANSWER

(E)   Choice (A) is subjunctive mood to indicate a condition contrary to fact. Choice (B) is a correct idiom. Choice (C) uses the adverb "politely" to modify "speaking," and choice (D) uses the adjective "angry" to follow the linking verb "becoming."

■ QUESTION I.2.72

> Mr. Burns is fully <u>aware of</u> statistics proving the <u>harmful</u> conse-
>   A   B
> quences of smoking; <u>irregardless</u>, he <u>persists</u> in his habit. <u>No error</u>.
>   C   D   E

ANSWER

(C)   "Irregardless," an incorrect expression, is a combination of "irrespective" and "regardless." (Taking into account the prefix and the suffix of "irregardless," the combination would mean, "not, not regarding," and so would be redundant.) Usually, "regardless" is used, although "irrespective" is also correct. The idioms in choices (A) and (D) are correct. Choice (B) is an adjective.

■ QUESTION I.2.73

David was not capable <u>to win</u> the singles tennis match because he
                         A

<u>had been</u> injured <u>in</u> a game last week and the doctor prohibited him
    B   C

<u>from</u> playing for two weeks. <u>No error</u>.
  D   E

ANSWER

(A)   The idiom should be "capable of winning." The verb in choice (B) indicates the prior action of two past actions; the prepositions in choices (C) and
(D) are correct.

■ QUESTION I.2.74

<u>In spite of</u> the doctor's orders, David is playing tennis today because
    A

he is <u>one of those</u> athletes who <u>are</u> determined to play, no matter what
          B   C

the <u>coach and she</u> say. <u>No error</u>.
        D   E

ANSWER

(E)   Choice (A) is a correct expression. Choice (B) uses an indefinite pronoun as the predicate nominative, and "those" as the object of a preposition.
The verb in (C), "are," is plural because a plural verb must be used in a subordinate clause following the phrase "one of those." Choice (D) uses the nominative
form of the pronoun as the subject of "say."

■ QUESTION I.2.75

> Although <u>unequal in</u> ability compared to other team members, Wilt
>   A
> <u>practices</u> his free throws every <u>afternoon</u> so he would become a
>   B   C
> <u>member of</u> the varsity squad. <u>No error</u>.
>   D   E

ANSWER

(B) The verb should be in the past tense, "practiced," as signaled by "would become." Choice (A) is a correct idiom. Choice (C) is one word as used in this sentence. Choice (D) contains a correct preposition.

■ QUESTION I.2.76

> If you <u>would have</u> listened to me <u>carefully</u>, you would have heard
>   A   B
> me <u>advise against</u> your <u>subscribing to</u> the magazine of that ultra-
>   C   D
> conservative political group. <u>No error</u>.
>   E

ANSWER

(A) In the prior of two past actions, the verb should be past perfect: "had listened" comes before "would have heard." Choice (B), "carefully," is an adverb modifying "would have heard." Choices (C) and (D) are correct idioms.

■ QUESTION I.2.77

A graduating high school senior who <u>wants to attend</u> a university
                                                    A
must <u>attend to</u> many details, such as taking the SAT or ACT, sending
         B
an official transcript to the university, <u>arranging for</u> a dormitory
                                              C
room, <u>and etc</u>. <u>No error</u>.
        D   E

ANSWER

(D)   The expression "and etc." is redundant; it would mean "and, and." In this case, "etc." or "and so on" would be acceptable. Choice (A) is an infinitive; choice (B) and choice (C) are correct idioms.

■ QUESTION I.2.78

<u>Running</u> errands for upperclassmen, pushing pennies, and being
   A
<u>thrown in</u> mud holes are all <u>factors of</u> being hazed <u>as</u> a freshman.
     B   C   D
<u>No error</u>.
   E

ANSWER

(C)   A "factor" is something that contributes toward a result. This phrase could be reworded to read, "are part of being hazed as a freshman" or "are part of freshman hazing." Choice (A) is a gerund parallel to the others: "pushing" and "being." Choices (B) and (D) are correct.

■ QUESTION I.2.79

> She worked hard to <u>prepare for</u> the final <u>exam, reading</u> every assigned
>   A   B
> passage <u>as reviewing</u> every worksheet the instructor <u>had given</u> to the
>   C   D
> class. <u>No error</u>.
>   E

ANSWER

(C)   The word "and," instead of "as," should connect two parallel verb forms ("reading" and "reviewing") to form a compound predicate. Choice (A) correctly uses the preposition "for" after "prepare." Choice (B) correctly uses a comma to separate the modifier from the main clause. Choice (D) correctly uses a past perfect verb ("had given") for an action that had occurred prior to the action in the main clause.

■ QUESTION I.2.80

> What the <u>politicians say</u> in their campaign speeches <u>are</u> not necessarily
>   A   B
> what they <u>actually do</u>, once they are <u>in office</u>. <u>No error</u>.
>   C   D   E

ANSWER

(B)   The subject of the sentence is the singular pronoun "what," which requires the singular verb "is," instead of "are." Choice (A) correctly uses the plural verb "say" to agree with the plural subject "politicians." Choice (C) correctly uses the adverb "actually" to modify the verb "do." Also, the plural verb "do" agrees with the plural subject "they." And Choice (D) correctly uses the prepositional phrase "in office."

■ QUESTION I.2.81

> Las Vegas, Nevada, has been called the "entertainment capital
>   A   B
> of the world" because it offering countless drinking and eating
>   C
> establishments, casinos, music shows, and other forms of enter-
>   D
> tainment. No error.
>   E

ANSWER

(C) Choice (C) correctly uses "offers" as the verb of "it." The participle "offering" cannot stand alone as the verb. Choice (A) correctly uses a comma after the city and another one after the state. Choice (B) correctly uses the present perfect verb "has been called." Choice (D) uses a comma to separate items in a series. The items—both nouns ("establishments" and "casinos")—are parallel.

■ QUESTION I.2.82

> Over the past year, the little boy has learned to walk, to say
>   A
> several words, and is feeding himself with a spoon. No error.
>   B   C   D   E

ANSWER

(C) Items in a series must be parallel; the present progressive verb "is feeding" is not parallel with the infinitives "to walk" and "to say." So "is feeding" must be changed to "to feed," an infinitive that is parallel with the other infinitives ("to walk" and "to say"). Choice (A) correctly uses to present-perfect verb "has learned" to show action that began in the past but extends into the present. Choice (B) correctly uses the plural adjective "several" with the plural noun "words." Choice (D) uses an appropriate prepositional phrase "with a spoon" to modify "to feed."

■ QUESTION I.2.83

The strict rules about <u>students'</u> attire <u>is causing</u> several people to
                              A   B

protest <u>that</u> their civil rights <u>are being</u> violated. <u>No error.</u>
      C   D   E

ANSWER

(B)   This choice contains a subject-verb agreement error; the plural subject "rules" requires the plural verb "are causing," instead of the singular verb "is causing." Choice (A) correctly uses the plural possessive "students,'" with the apostrophe after the "s." Choice (C) uses the subordinating conjunction "that" to introduce a noun clause ("their . . . violated"). Choice (D) appropriately uses the plural present progressive verb "are being violated" to agree with the plural subject "rights" and to show action that is occurring.

■ QUESTION I.2.84

<u>Being</u> the only <u>mammal</u> that <u>flies,</u> the bat <u>intrigues zoologists</u>.
 A   B   C   D
<u>No error.</u>
  E

ANSWER

(E)   This sentence has no errors. In Choice (A), the participle "being" correctly serves to introduce an adjective phrase. The singular noun in Choice (B) agrees with the singular noun ("bat") in the main clause. Choice (C) correctly uses a singular verb ("flies") to agree with its singular subject ("mammal"). In Choice (D), a singular verb ("intrigues") agrees with its singular subject ("bat"), and the direct object "zoologists" is correct.

■ QUESTION I.2.85

> An <u>effective presenter</u> not only <u>appeals to</u> his audience's <u>interests</u>
>   A   B   C
> and emotions <u>and also</u> uses appropriate humor. <u>No error</u>.
>   D   E

ANSWER

(D) The phrase "not only" requires "but also" to create an appropriate correlative construction. Choice (A) correctly uses the adjective "effective" to modify the noun "presenter." Choice (B) uses the singular verb "appeals" to agree with the singular subject "presenter"; it also uses the preposition "to" to create an appropriate idiom. In Choice (C), the plural noun "interests" contains no error.

■ QUESTION I.2.86

> Some portions of the test <u>are</u> timed; <u>therefore</u>, you must work as
>   A   B
> <u>quick</u> <u>as</u> possible. <u>No error</u>.
> C D   E

ANSWER

(C) Choice (C) is the correct answer; "quick" must be changed to "quickly," since it serves as an adverb modifying the verb "work." Choice (A) correctly uses a plural verb ("are") to agree with a plural subject ("portions"). With the use of "therefore," Choice (B) appropriately shows the relationship between the two clauses. Choice (D) correctly completes the phrase "as . . . as."

PARAGRAPH IMPROVEMENT QUESTIONS

<u>DIRECTIONS</u>: **The following passages are considered early draft efforts of a student. Some sentences need to be rewritten to make the ideas clearer and more precise.**

Read each passage carefully and answer the questions that follow. Some of the questions are about particular sentences or parts of sentences and ask you to make decisions about sentence structure, diction, and usage. Some of the questions refer to the entire essay or parts of the essay and ask you to make decisions about organization, development, appropriateness of language, audience, and logic. Choose the answer that most effectively makes the intended meaning clear and follows the requirements of standard written English. After you have chosen our answer, fill in the corresponding oval on your answer sheet.

EXAMPLE

(1) On the one hand, I think television is bad, But it also does some good things for all of us. (2) For instance, my little sister thought she wanted to be a policeman until she saw police shows on television.

Which of the following is the best revision of the underlined portion of sentence 1 below?

On the one hand, I think television <u>is bad, But it also</u> does some good things for all of us.

(A)   is bad; But it also

(B)   is bad. but is also

(C)   is bad, and it also

(D)   is bad, but it also

(E)   is bad because it also

EXAMPLE ANSWER

Ⓐ   Ⓑ   Ⓒ   ⬤   Ⓔ

Questions I.2.87–I.2.92 are based on the following passage.

(1) Actually, the term "Native Americans" is incorrect. (2) Indians migrated to this continent from other areas, just earlier then Europeans did. (3) The ancestors of the Anasazi—Indians of the four-state area of Colorado, New Mexico, Utah, and Arizona—probably crossed from Asia into Alaska. (4) About 25,000

years ago while the continental land bridge still existed. (5) This land bridge arched across the Bering Strait in the last Ice Age. (6) About A.D. 500 the ancestors of the Anasazi moved onto the Mesa Verde a high plateau in the desert country of Colorado. (7) The Wetherills, five brothers who ranched the area, is generally given credit for the first exploration of the ruins in the 1870s and 1880s. (8) There were some 50,000 Anasazi thriving in the four-corners area by the 1200s. (9) At their zenith A.D. 700 to 1300, the Anasazi had established widespread communities and built thousands of sophisticated structures—cliff dwellings, pueblos, and kivas. (10) They even engaged in trade with Indians in surrounding regions by exporting pottery and other goods.

■ QUESTION I.2.87

Which of the following best corrects the grammatical error in sentence 7?

(A) The Wetherills, a group of five brothers who ranched in the area, is generally given credit for the first exploration of the ruins in the 1870s and 1880s.

(B) The Wetherills, five brothers who ranched in the area, are generally given credit for the first exploration of the ruins in the 1870s and 1880s.

(C) The Wetherills are generally given credit for the first exploration of the ruins in the 1870s and 1880s, five brothers who ranched in the area.

(D) The Wetherills, generally given credit for the first exploration of the area, is five brothers who ranched in the area.

(E) Best as it is.

ANSWER

(B)   "The Wetherills" is plural, and the verb must agree. Choice (B) correctly changes "is" to "are"; the rest of the sentence is fine. (A) adds the singular "a group" which may make the verb "is" seem right, though it still modifies "The Wetherills" and must agree accordingly. (C) corrects the verb problem, but misplaces the clause "five brothers who ranched in the area" at the end of the sentence where it is unclear. (D) fails to correct the verb disagreement and places the clause at the end of the sentence, which alters the sense.

■ QUESTION I.2.88

Which of the following sentences would best fit between sentences 9 and 10 of the passage?

(A) Artifacts recovered from the area suggest that the Anasazi were artistic, religious, agricultural, classless, and peaceful.

(B) By 12,000 to 10,000 B.C., some Indians had established their unique cultures in the southwest.

(C) The Navaho called their ancestors the Anasazi, the Ancient Ones.

(D) I think it is unfortunate that such a unique and innovative culture should have disappeared from the country.

(E) Before Columbus reached the New World, the Anasazi had virtually disappeared.

ANSWER

(A)   Choice (A) best continues the topic of sentence 9, which concerns the cultural achievements of the Anasazi, and provides a nice transition toward the final sentence. (B) concerns an entirely different historical epoch, and is clearly irrelevant. (C) may fit somewhere in this essay, but not between sentences 9 and 10, where this new fact would seem obtrusive. (D) introduces the personal voice of the author which is contrary to the expository tone in the passage thus far, and which would not fit between the factual content of sentences 9 and 10. (E) would be a good topic sentence for a new paragraph, but would not be good here.

■ QUESTION I.2.89

Which of the following is an incomplete sentence?

(A) 4   (D) 7

(B) 5   (E) 10

(C) 6

ANSWER

(A) Sentence 4 is a dependent prepositional clause and would be best added onto sentence 3.

■ QUESTION I.2.90

Which of the following best corrects the underlined portion of sentence 9?

At their zenith A.D. 700 to 1300, the Anasazi has established widespread communities and built thousands of sophisticated structures—cliff dwellings, pueblos, and kivas.

(A) At their zenith which was from A.D. 700 to 1300

(B) At their zenith B.C. 700 to 1300

(C) At their zenith, from A.D. 700 to 1300,

(D) At their zenith, being A.D. 700 to 1300,

(E) At their zenith, of A.D. 700 to 1300,

ANSWER

(C)   The years of the Anasazi's zenith are best set off by commas and turned into a prepositional phrase, and of the two choices which do this, (C) uses "from," which is more appropriate than (D) "being." Without the punctuation, choice (A) is awkward; if the phrase were set off by commas, it would be acceptable, though (C) is more concise. (B) is just wrong; from the context of the passage it is clear that the Anasazi thrived in the years A.D. and not B.C.

■ QUESTION I.2.91

Which of the following would be the best way to punctuate sentence 6?

(A) About A.D. 500, the ancestors of the Anasazi moved onto the Mesa Verde a high plateau, in the desert country of Colorado.

(B) About A.D. 500 the ancestors of the Anasazi moved, onto the Mesa Verde: a high plateau in the desert country of Colorado

(C) About A.D. 500 the ancestors of the Anasazi moved onto the Mesa Verde: a high plateau, in the desert country of Colorado.

(D) About A.D. 500, the ancestors of the Anasazi moved onto the Mesa Verde, a high plateau in the desert country of Colorado.

(E) Best as it is.

ANSWER

(D) Choice (D) best utilizes commas which clarify the sense of the sentence. Choice (A) places the second comma incorrectly. (B) and (C) both utilize a colon, and each has an unnecessary comma. Choice (E) is correct as written.

■ QUESTION I.2.92

Which of the following sentences contains a spelling/grammatical error?

(A) 1   (D) 10

(B) 2   (E) 5

(C) 3

ANSWER

(B) Sentence 2 uses "then," a temporal reference, instead of "than," which should be used for the comparison in this sentence.

Question I.2.93 through I.2.96 are based on the following passage:

(1) Stock-car racing is a major spectator sport in this country, but an estimated thirty percent of Americans claiming to be fans of the 53-year-old sport. (2) However, racing has not always been so popular. (3) As a matter of fact, it had a rather shaky start, with a negative reputation and problems with the law.

(4) During the 1920s, with the Prohibition came moonshining; and with moonshining came bootleggers who were moonshine runners that illegally ran whiskey from the illegal stills to the markets. (5) These drivers ran races with the law; the losers were subject to jail time and steep fines. (6) Soon racing among the bootleggers became a weekend sport; they used their "whiskey run" cars to prove who was the fastest. (7) And of course the area denizens came out to watch. (8) These races became popular. (9) They continued even after the end of the Prohibition.

(10) In 1938 Bill France organized the first Daytona Beach race. (11) Winners received such prizes as rum, cigars, and motor oil. (12) After a hiatus during World War II, in the late 1940s France held a meeting of promoters.

▪ QUESTION I.2.93

> What is the best way to deal with sentence 1 (reproduced below)?
> Stock-car racing is a major spectator sport in this country, but an estimated thirty percent of Americans claiming to be fans of the 53-year-old sport.
>
> (A) Leave it as it is.
>
> (B) Change "but" to "with."
>
> (C) Change "claiming" to "claim."
>
> (D) Change "is" to "was."
>
> (E) Remove the comma and insert a semicolon.

ANSWER

(B)   The use of "with" reinforces the idea presented in the first clause. In Choice (A), the use of "but" incorrectly implies that the idea in the second half of the sentence contrasts with that of the main clause. Also, the use of "but" makes the second part of the sentence a fragment, since a participle ("claiming") cannot serve as the verb of a clause. Choice (C) incorrectly implies that the idea in the second half of the sentence contrasts with that of the main clause. In Choice (D) the switch to past tense is incorrect because the information is current information. Choice (E) is incorrect, since a comma is the correct punctuation to separate two independent clauses, if the second clause begins with a coordinating conjunction ("but").

■ QUESTION I.2.94

Which of the following best describes the relationship between sentences 2 and 3?

(A) Sentence 3 contradicts the idea presented in Sentence 2.

(B) Sentence 3 provides examples to illustrate the idea presented in Sentence 2.

(C) Sentence 3 offers a new idea that is unrelated to Sentence 2.

(D) Sentence 3 defines a term that Sentence 2 presents.

(E) Sentence 2 leads to Sentence 3 with an explanation of a situation presented in Sentence 3.

ANSWER

(B)   Sentence 3 gives two examples to show that racing has not always been so popular—its negative reputation and its problems with the law. Choice (A) is incorrect, since the sentences are not contradictory. Choice (C) is wrong, since Sentences 2 and 3 are related, and Sentence 3 does not offer a new idea. Choice (D) is incorrect since Sentence 3 does not define a term. And Choice (E) is incorrect because Sentence 3 does not present a situation that Sentence 3 explains.

▪ QUESTION I.2.95

Which of the following is the best revision of the underlined portion of Sentence 4 (reproduced below)?

During the 1920s, with the Prohibition came moonshining; and with moonshining came <u>bootleggers who were moonshine runners that illegally ran whiskey</u> from the illegal stills to the markets.

(A) bootleggers, who were also called moonshine runners, because they illegally ran whiskey

(B) bootleggers, or moonshine runners, who ran whiskey

(C) the illegal running of whiskey by bootleggers, or moonshine runners,

(D) bootlegging, or moonshine running whiskey

(E) bootleggers who are moonshine runners who ran whiskey

ANSWER

(B) It uses no unnecessary words and contains no redundancy. It correctly uses an apostrophe to set apart the appositive "or moonshine runners." Choice (A) is redundant with the words "illegally" and "illegal." It contains the unnecessary words "who were also called . . . because." This sentence is confusing because it is difficult to determine what the clause "because . . . markets" modifies. Choice (C) is awkwardly worded and creates a confusing sentence. Choice (D) is illogical with the phrase "moonshine running whiskey." Choice (E) shifts from past tense to present tense, and the repetition of the word "who" is awkward although grammatically correct.

■ QUESTION I.2.96

What is the best way to revise the underlined wording in order to combine sentences 8 and 9?

These races became popular. They continued even after the end of the Prohibition.

(A) Although these races became popular, they continued even after the end of the Prohibition.

(B) These races became popular, but they continued even after the end of the Prohibition.

(C) These races became popular even after they continued at the end of the Prohibition.

(D) These races became popular, since they continued even after the end of the Prohibition.

(E) These races became so popular that they continued even after the end of the Prohibition.

ANSWER

(E)   The use of "so popular that" correctly reflects the reason for the races' continuing. Choices (A) and (B) are incorrect because the conjunctions "although" and "but" incorrectly implies that the two clauses are contradictory. Choice (C) is illogical, incorrectly implying that the races did not become popular until after the end of Prohibition. In Choice (D), the use of the conjunction "since" creates an illogical relationship between the two clauses, implying that the races became popular as a result of their continuation after the end of Prohibition.

■ QUESTION I.2.97

In relation to the passage as a whole, which of the following best describes the writer's intention in paragraph 2?

(A) To provide an example

(B) To provide a summary

(C) To detail a chain of events

(D) To describe a location

(E) To propose a solution

ANSWER

(C)   Paragraph 2 focuses on the progress of racing from illegal whiskey runs to popular entertainment. It does not (A) provide an example, (B) provide a summary, (D) describe a location, or (E) propose a solution.

■ QUESTION I.2.98

Which of the following sentences would be the best sentence to add immediately after Sentence 12?

(A) This three-day meeting resulted in the establishment of the rules, specifications, and official name of the organization—the National Association of Stock Car Auto Racing (NASCAR).

(B) These promoters were interested in racing.

(C) Stock-car racing continues to be popular today, with many fans who attend in person or who watch the races on television.

(D) Although bootlegging is almost non-existent today, much racing still goes on both on and off the track.

(E) Not many people know who Bill France was, but he definitely played an important role in the history of racing.

ANSWER

(A)   It provides information that is relevant to the specific issue at hand in this paragraph—the meeting that Bill France held with promoters at Daytona Beach in the late 1940s. Although all the other choices are related to the topic of racing, none develop the specific topic that the first part of the paragraph has introduced.

Questions I.2.99–I.2.100 are based on the following passage.

(1) In the poem "The Raven" by Edgar Allan Poe, a man has nodded off in his study after reading "many a quaint and curious volume of forgotten lore." (2) His mood is melancholy. (3) He is full of sorrow. (4) He is grieving for "the lost Lenore."

(5) When he hears the tapping at his window, he lets in a raven. (6) The raven perches on the bust of Pallas Athena, a goddess often depicted with a bird on her head by the Greeks who believed that birds were heralds from the dead. (7) At first, the man thinks the bird might be a friend but one who would leave soon, but the raven says, "Nevermore," an affirmation which makes the man smile. (8) However, the bird's repetition of "Nevermore" leads the speaker to the realization that Lenore will never return, the bird becomes an omen of doom and is called "evil" by the mournful speaker. (9) He becomes frantic, imploring the raven to let him know if there is comfort for him or if he will ever again hold close the sainted Lenore. (10) To both questions, the bird replies, "Nevermore." (11) Shrieking with anguish, the bird is ordered to leave, but it replies, "Nevermore." (12) At the end of the poem, the man's soul is trapped in the Raven's shadow "that lies floating on the floor" and "shall be lifted—nevermore."

(13) Thus, the bird evolves into an ominous bird of ill omen. (14) Some argue that the bird deliberately drives the speaker insane. (15) While others feel the bird is innocent of any premeditated wrong doing, and I think the bird doesn't do anything but repeat one word. (16) One thing is certain, however. (17) The poem's haunting refrain is familiar, one that students of American literature will memorize and forget "nevermore."

QUESTION I.2.99

Which of the following is the best way to combine sentences 2, 3, and 4?

(A) He is melancholy and sorrowful and grieving for "the lost Lenore."

(B) He is grieving for "the lost Lenore," full of melancholy and sorrow.

(C) Melancholy and sorrowful, he is grieving for "the lost Lenore."

(D) Melancholy and full of sorrow, he is grieving for "the lost Lenore."

(E) Full of melancholy mood and sorrow, he is grieving for "the lost Lenore."

ANSWER

(C)   Choice (C) correctly and smoothly combines the two adjectives while providing sentence variety. Choice (A) is not parallel; "grieving" is not parallel with the other two adjectives. In choice (B), the adjectives appear to modify the dead Lenore. In choices (D) and (E), the ideas of melancholy and grief are not stated in concise parallel structure.

■ QUESTION I.2.100

> Which of the following is the best revision of the underlined portion of sentence 8 below?
>
> However, the bird's repetition of "Nevermore" leads the speaker to <u>the realization that Lenore will never return, the bird becomes an omen of doom and is called "evil" by the mournful speaker</u>.
>
> (A) realize the following—Lenore will never return, the bird is evil and an omen of doom.
>
> (B) the realization of Lenore's failure to return, the evil and the omen of doom of the bird.
>
> (C) realize that Lenore will never return, so the bird, called "evil" by the mournful speaker, becomes an omen of doom.
>
> (D) the realization that Lenore will never return, the bird becomes an omen of doom and is called "evil" by the mournful speaker.
>
> (E) that Lenore will never return, that the bird is an omen of doom, and that the bird should be called "evil."

ANSWER

(C) Choice (C) is the most concise expression of the major ideas. Choice (A) is too abrupt and states that the bird "is evil" instead of being "called evil." Choice (B) contains awkward wording; "the realization of" and "the evil omen of doom of the bird." The wording of choice (D) creates a run-on sentence. Choice (E) incorrectly twists the idea of evil.

Part II

Reading

UNIT 1: SENTENCE COMPLETIONS

Regardless of the Critical Reading or Writing SAT section in which one is working, all problem solving techniques should be divided into two main categories: skills and strategies. This unit will present skills and strategies that are effective in helping the test-taker successfully answer Sentence Completions. These techniques include the recognition of a context clue, a knowledge of the levels of difficulty in a Sentence Completion section, the application of deductive reasoning, and familiarity with the logical structure of sentence completions. You will encounter Sentence Completion questions in two different sections.

ABOUT THE DIRECTIONS

The directions for Sentence Completion questions are relatively straightforward.

DIRECTIONS: Each sentence below has one or two blanks, each blank indicating that something has been omitted. Beneath the sentence are five lettered words or sets of words. Choose the word or set of words that BEST fits the meaning of the sentence as a whole.

EXAMPLE:

Although the critics found the book _____, many of the readers found it rather _____.

(A) obnoxious . . .perfect   (D) comical . . . persuasive

(B) spectacular . . . interesting   (E) popular . . . rare

(C) boring . . . intriguing

EXAMPLE ANSWER

(A) (B) ● (D) (E)

ABOUT THE QUESTIONS

You will encounter two main types of questions in the Sentence Completion section of the SAT. In addition, the questions will appear in varying difficulties, which we will call Level I (easy), Level II (average), and Level III (difficult). The following explains the structure of the questions.

Question Type 1: One-Word Completions

One-Word Completions will require you to fill in one blank. The one-word completion can appear as a Level I, II, or III question depending on the difficulty of the vocabulary included.

Question Type 2: Two-Word Completions

Two-Word Completions will require you to fill in two blanks. As with the one-word completion, this type may be a Level I, II, or III question. This will depend not only on the difficulty of the vocabulary, but also on the relationship between the words and between the words and the sentence.

The remainder of this review will provide explicit details on what you will encounter when dealing with Sentence Completion questions, in addition to strategies for correctly completing these sentences.

ANSWERING SENTENCE COMPLETION QUESTIONS

Follow these steps as you attempt to answer each question.

STEP 1   Identifying context clues is one of the most successful ways for students to locate correct answers in Sentence Completions. Practicing constantly in this area will help you strengthen one of your main strategies in this type of word problem.

Example: Level I Question

The Sentence Completion below is an example of a Level I question.

Pamela played her championship chess game _____, avoiding all traps and making no mistakes.

(A) hurriedly   (D) imaginatively

(B) flawlessly   (E) aggressively

(C) prodigally

The phase "avoiding all traps and making no mistakes" is your context clue. Notice that the phrase both follows and modifies the word in question. Since you know that Sentence Completions are exercises seeking to test your vocabulary knowledge, attack these problems accordingly. For example, ask yourself what word means "avoiding all traps and making no mistakes." In so doing, you discover the answer flawlessly (B), which means perfectly or without mistakes. If Pamela played hurriedly (A), she might well make mistakes.

Difficult words are seldom the answer in easier questions; therefore, prodigally (C) stands out as a suspicious word. This could be a magnet word. However, before you eliminate it, ask yourself whether you know its meaning. If so, does it surpass flawlessly (B) in defining the context clue, "making no mistakes"? It does not.

Imaginatively (D) is a tempting answer, since one might associate a perfect game of chess as one played imaginatively; however, there is no connection between the imagination and the absence of mistakes. Aggressively (E) playing a game may, in fact, cause you to make mistakes.

Example: Level II Question

Here is an example of a Level II Sentence Completion. Try to determine the context clue.

> Although most people believe the boomerang is the product of a _____ design, that belief is deceptive; in fact, the boomerang is a _____ example of the laws of aerodynamics.
>
> (A) foreign . . . modern   (D) primitive . . . sophisticated
>
> (B) symbolic . . . complex   (E) faulty . . . invalid
>
> (C) practical . . . scientific

The most important context clue in this sentence is the opening word "although," which indicates that some kind of antonym relationship is present in the sentence. It tells us there is a reversal in meaning; therefore, be on the lookout for words that will form an opposite relationship. The phrase "that belief is deceptive" makes certain the idea that there will be an opposite meaning between the missing words.

Primitive . . . sophisticated (D) is the best answer, since the two are exact opposites. "Primitive" means crude and elementary, whereas "sophisticated" means refined and advanced.

Foreign . . . modern (A) and symbolic . . . complex (B) have no real opposite relationship. Also, "complex" is a magnet word that sounds right in the context of scientific laws, but "symbolic" is not its counterpart.

Practical . . . scientific (C) and faulty . . . invalid (E) are rejectable because they are generally synonymous pairs of relationships.

Example: Level III Question

The following is an example of a Level III question:

> The weekly program on public radio is the most _____ means of educating the public about pollution.
>
> (A) proficient   (D) capable
>
> (B) effusive   (E) competent
>
> (C) effectual

The context clue in this sentence is "means of educating the public about pollution." Effectual (C) is the correct answer. Effectual means having the power to produce the exact effect or result. Proficient (A) is not correct as it implies competency above the average—radio programs are not described in this manner. Effusive (B) does not fit the sense of the sentence. Both capable (D) and competent (E) are incorrect because they refer to people, not things.

STEP 2   Because the Critical Reading SAT sections are fundamentally a vocabulary test, they must resort to principles and techniques necessary for testing your vocabulary. Therefore, certain dynamics like antonyms (word opposites) and synonyms (word similarities) become very useful in setting up a question or word problem. This idea can be taken one step further.

Another type of technique that utilizes the tension of opposites and the concurrence of similarities is *word values*. Word values begin with the recognition that most pivotal words in an SAT word problem can be assigned a positive or negative value. Marking a "+" or "−" next to choices may help you eliminate inappropriate choices. In turn, you will be able to more quickly identify possible correct answers.

Dealing with Positive Value Words

Positive value words are usually easy to recognize. They usually convey a meaning that can be equated with gain, advantage, liveliness, intelligence, virtue, and positive emotions, conditions, or actions:

The ability to recognize positive and negative word values, however, will not bring you very far if you do not understand how to apply it to your advantage in Sentence Completions. Below you will find examples of how to do this, first with a study of positive value Sentence Completions, then with a study of negative value Sentence Completions. The following is an example of a Level I question:

An expert skateboarder, Tom is truly _____ ; he smoothly blends timing with balance.

(A) coordinated

(B) erudite

(C) a novice

(D) supportive

(E) casual

As you know, the context clue is the clause after the word in question, which acts as a modifier. Naturally, anyone who "smoothly blends" is creating a *positive* situation. Look for the positive answer.

An expert skateboarder, Tom is truly __+__; *he smoothly blends timing with balance.*

+(A) coordinated

+(B) erudite

−(C) a novice

+(D) supportive

−(E) casual

Coordinated (A), a positive value word that means ordering two or more things, fits the sentence perfectly.

Erudite (B) is positive, but it is too difficult to be a Level I answer.

A novice (C) in this context is negative.

Supportive (D) and casual (E) don't fulfill the definition of the context clue, and casual is negative, implying a lack of attention. Notice that eliminating negatives *immediately reduces the number of options from which you have to choose.*

This raises the odds of selecting the correct answer. (One of the analytic skills you should develop for the SAT is being able to see the hidden vocabulary question in any exercise.)

A Level II question may appear as follows:

Despite their supposedly primitive lifestyle, Australian aborigines developed the boomerang, a _____ and _____ hunting tool that maximizes gain with minimum effort.

(A) ponderous . . . expensive   (D) sophisticated . . . efficient
(B) clean . . . dynamic   (E) useful . . . attractive
(C) dangerous . . . formidable

In this case, the context clues begin and end the sentence (in italics below).

Despite their supposedly primitive lifestyle, Australian aborigines developed the boomerang, a __+__ and __+__ hunting tool that maximizes gain with minimum effort.

–(A) ponderous . . . expensive   +(D) sophisticated . . . efficient
+(B) clean . . . dynamic   +(E) useful . . . attractive
–(C) dangerous . . . formidable

The first context clue (*despite*) helps you determine that this exercise entails an antonym relationship with the word primitive, which means simple or crude. The second context clue offers a definition of the missing words. Since the meaning of primitive in this context is a negative word value, you can be fairly confident that the answer will be a pair of positive word values.

Sophisticated . . . efficient (D) is positive *and* it satisfies the definition of the latter context clue. This is the best answer.

Ponderous . . . expensive (A) is not correct.

Clean . . . dynamic (B) is positive, but does not meet the definition of the latter context clue.

Dangerous . . . formidable (C) is negative.

Useful . . . attractive (E) is positive, but it does not work with the latter context clue.

Here is a Level III example:

When physicians describe illnesses to colleagues, they must speak an _____ language, *using professional terms and concepts understood mostly by members of the profession.*

(A) extrinsic
(D) esoteric

(B) inordinate
(E) abbreviated

(C) ambulatory

Looking at this question, we can see an important context clue. This appears in italics below.

When physicians describe illnesses to colleagues, they must speak an __+__ language, *using professional terms and concepts understood mostly by members of the profession.*

+(A) extrinsic
+(D) esoteric

−(B) inordinate
−(E) abbreviated

+(C) ambulatory

This clue gives us a definition of the missing word. Begin by eliminating the two obvious negatives, inordinate (B) and abbreviated (E). This leaves us with three positives. Because this is a Level III exercise, at first you may be intimidated by the level of vocabulary. In the section on etymology you will be given insights into how to handle difficult word problems.

For now, note that esoteric (D) is the best answer, since it is an adjective that means *inside* or *part of a group.*

Ambulatory (C) is positive, but it is a trap. It seems like an easy association with the world of medicine. In Level III there are *no* easy word associations.

Extrinsic (A) is positive, but it means *outside of*, which would not satisfy the logic of the sentence.

Dealing with Negative Value Words

Here are examples of how to work with negative value Sentence Completion problems. The first example is Level I.

Although Steve loves to socialize, his fellow students find him _____ and strive to _____ his company.

(A)   generous . . . enjoy   (D)   sinister . . . delay

(B)   boring . . . evade   (E)   weak . . . limit

(C)   altruistic . . . accept

The context clue (in italics) tells us that a reversal is being set up between what Steve thinks and what his fellow students think.

> *Although Steve loves to socialize*, his fellow students find him __–__ and strive to __–__ his company.

+(A) generous . . . enjoy   –(D) sinister . . . delay

–(B) boring . . . evade   –(E) weak . . . limit

+(C) altruistic . . . accept

Boring . . . evade (B) is the best answer. The words appearing in Level 1 questions are not overly difficult, and they satisfy the logic of the sentence. Generous . . . enjoy (A) is positive. Altruistic . . . accept (C) is not only positive but contains a very difficult word (altruistic), and it would be unlikely that this would be a Level I answer. The same is true of sinister . . . delay (D), even though it is negative. Weak . . . limit (E) does not make sense in the context of the sentence.

This next example is Level II.

> Because they reject _____ , conscientious objectors are given jobs in community work as a substitute for participation in the armed services.

(A)   labor   (D)   dictatorships

(B)   belligerence   (E)   poverty

(C)   peace

Essentially, this example is a synonym exercise. The description of conscientious objectors (in italics) acts as a strong context clue. Conscientious objectors avoid ("reject") militancy.

> Because they reject __–__ , conscientious objectors *are given jobs in community work as a substitute for participation in the armed services.*

+(A) labor   –(D) dictatorships

–(B) belligerence   –(E) poverty

+(C) peace

Because we are looking for a negative word value (something to do with militancy), labor (A) is incorrect since it is positive. Belligerence (B) fits perfectly, as this is a negative value word having to do with war. Not only is peace (C) a positive value word, it is hardly something to be rejected by conscientious objectors. Dictatorships (D), although a negative word value, has no logical place in the context of this sentence. The same is true of poverty (E).

Here is a Level III example:

Dictators understand well how to centralize power, and that is why they combine a(n) _____ political process with military _____.

(A) foreign . . . victory   (D) domestic . . . decreases

(B) electoral . . . escalation   (E) totalitarian . . . coercion

(C) agrarian . . . strategies

Totalitarian . . . coercion (E) is the best answer. These are difficult words, and both have to do with techniques useful in the centralizing of power by a dictator. *Totalitarian* means centralized, and *coercion* means force.

> *Dictators* understand well how to *centralize power*, and that is why they combine a(n) __–__ political process with military __–__.
>
> +(A) foreign . . . victory   +(D) domestic . . . decreases
>
> +(B) electoral . . . escalation   –(E) totalitarian . . . coercion
>
> +(C) agrarian . . . strategies

Foreign . . . victory (A) are not only easy words, they do not appear to be strictly negative. Remember that easy word answers should be suspect in Level III. Agrarian . . . strategies (C) is positive. Domestic . . . decreases (D) is a positive combination. Since you are searching for two negatives, this answer is incorrect. There will be more about this in the next section.

Dealing with Mixed Value Words

In examples with two-word answers so far, you have searched for answers composed with identical word values, such as negative/negative and positive/positive. Every SAT Sentence Completion section, however, will have exercises in which two-word answers are found in combinations. Below you will find examples of how to work with these. Here is a Level I example:

> Despite a healthy and growing environmental _____ in America, there are many people who prefer to remain _____ .
>
> (A) awareness . . . ignorant   (D) crisis . . . unencumbered
>
> (B) movement . . . enlightened   (E) industry . . . satisfied
>
> (C) bankruptcy . . . wealthy

The context clue *despite* sets up the predictable antonym warning. In this case, the sentence seems to call for a positive and then a negative value word answer.

Despite a healthy and growing environmental __+__ in America, there are many people who prefer to remain __–__ .

+/–(A)   awareness . . . ignorant

+/+(B)   movement . . . enlightened

–/+(C)   bankruptcy . . . wealthy

–/+(D)   crisis . . . unencumbered

+/+(E)   industry . . . satisfied

Awareness . . . ignorant (A) is the best answer. These are logical antonyms, and they fit the meaning of the sentence. Notice that the order of the missing words is positive, *then* negative. This should help you eliminate (C) and (D) immediately, as they are a reversal of the correct order. Furthermore, industry . . . satisfied (E) and movement . . . enlightened (B) are both identical values, and so are eliminated. Practice these techniques until you confidently can recognize word values and the order in which they appear in a sentence.

Here is a Level II example:

Prone to creating characters of _____ quality, novelist Ed Abbey cannot be accused of writing _____ stories.

(A)   measly . . . drab   (D)   sinister . . . complete

(B)   romantic . . . imaginative   (E)   two-dimensional . . . flat

(C)   mythic . . . mundane

The best answer is mythic . . . mundane (C). Measly . . . drab (A) does not make sense when you consider the context clue cannot, which suggests the possibility of antonyms. The same is true for sinister . . . complete (D), romantic . . . imaginative (B), and two-dimensional . . . flat (E).

Prone to creating characters of __+__ quality, novelist Ed Abbey *cannot* be accused of writing __–__ stories.

–/–(A)   measly . . . drab

+/+(B)   romantic . . . imaginative

+/–(C)   mythic . . . mundane

–/+(D)   sinister . . . complete

–/–(E)   two-dimensional . . . flat

Notice that the value combinations help you determine where to search for the correct answer.

Here is a Level III example:

> Reminding his students that planning ahead would protect them from __
> ___ , Mr. McKenna proved to be a principal who understood the virtues
> of _____ .
>
> (A) exigency . . . foresight
>
> (B) grades . . . examinations
>
> (C) poverty . . . promotion
>
> (D) deprivation . . . abstinence
>
> (E) turbulence . . . amelioration

The best answer is exigency . . . foresight (A). The first context clue tells us
that we are looking for a negative value word. The second context clue tells us
the missing word is most likely positive. Furthermore, exigency . . . foresight is
a well-suited antonym combination. Exigencies are emergencies, and foresight
helps to lessen their severity, if not their occurrence.

> Reminding his students that planning ahead would *protect them* from
> __–__ , Mr. McKenna proved to be a principal who understood the *vir-*
> *tues* of __+__ .
>
> –/+(A)   exigency . . . foresight
>
> 0/0(B)   grades . . . examinations
>
> –/+(C)   poverty . . . promotion
>
> –/–(D)   deprivation . . . abstinence
>
> –/+(E)   turbulence . . . amelioration

Grades . . . examinations (B) are a trap, since they imply school matters.
Furthermore, they are neutrals. There will be more on this below. Poverty . . .
promotion (C) is an easy word answer and should be immediately suspect, especially if there are no difficult words in the sentence completion itself. Also,
this answer does not satisfy the logic of the sentence. Turbulence . . . amelioration (E) is a negative/positive combination, but it does not make sense in this
sentence. Even if you are forced to guess between this answer and exigency . . .
foresight (A), you have narrowed the field to two. These are excellent odds for
success.

Dealing with Neutral Value Words

There is another category of word values that will help you determine the correct answer in a Sentence Completion problem. These are neutral word values.
Neutral words are words that convey neither loss nor gain, advantage nor disad-
vantage. Consider the example above, once again:

Reminding his students that planning ahead would *protect them* from
_____−_____ , Mr. McKenna proved to be a principal who understood the *virtues* of __+__ .

−/+(A)   exigency . . . foresight

0/0(B)   grades . . . examinations

−/+(C)   poverty . . . promotion

−/−(D)   deprivation . . . abstinence

−/+(E)   turbulence . . . amelioration

Notice that grades . . . examinations (B) is rated as neutral. In fact, in this case, both words are considered of neutral value. This is because neither word conveys a usable value. Grades in and of themselves are not valued until a number is assigned. Examinations are not significant until a passing or failing value is implied or applied.

Neutral word values are significant because they are *never* the correct answer; therefore, when you identify a neutral word or combination of words, you may eliminate that choice from your selection. You may eliminate a double-word answer even if only one of the words is obviously neutral.

Neutral words are rare, and you should be careful to measure their value before you make a choice. Here is another example from an exercise seen previously (Note: The answer choices have been altered.):

Dictators understand well how to *centralize power*, and that is why they combine a(n) _____−_____ political process with military _____−_____ .

0/+(A)   foreign . . . victory

0/+(B)   electoral . . . escalation

0/+(C)   agrarian . . . strategies

0/0(D)   current . . . jobs

−/−(E)   totalitarian . . . coercion

Here, current . . . jobs (D) is an obvious neutral word combination, conveying no positive or negative values. You may eliminate this choice immediately. There is no fixed list of words that may be considered neutral. Rather, you should determine *from the context* of a word problem whether you believe a word or word combination is of a neutral value. This ability will come with practice and a larger vocabulary. As before, the correct answer remains totalitarian . . . coercion (E).

STEP 3   Another way to determine the correct answer is by using etymology. Etymology is the study of the anatomy of words.

The most important components of etymology on the SAT
are prefixes and roots. SAT vocabulary is derived almost
exclusively from the etymology of Greek and Latin word
origins, and that is where you should concentrate your study.
In this section, you will learn how to apply your knowledge of
prefixes and roots to Sentence Completion problems.

Etymological skills will work well in conjunction with other techniques you
have learned, including positive/negative word values. Furthermore, the technique of "scrolling" will help you understand how to expand your knowledge
of etymology.

Scrolling is a process whereby you "scroll" through a list of known related
words, roots, or prefixes to help you discover the meaning of a word. As an example, consider the common SAT word *apathy*. The prefix of apathy is *a*. This
means *without*. To scroll this prefix, think of any other words that may begin
with this prefix, such as *a*moral, *a*typical, *a*symmetrical. In each case, the meaning of the word is preceded by the meaning *without*.

At this point, you know that *apathy* means without something. Now try to
scroll the root, *path*, which comes from the Greek word *pathos*. Words like
pathetic, sympathy, antipathy, and empathy may come to mind. These words all
have to do with feeling or sensing. In fact, that is what *pathos* means: feeling.
So apathy means without feeling.

With this process you can often determine the fundamental meaning of a
word or part of a word, and this may give you enough evidence with which to
choose a correct answer. Consider the following familiar Level I example:

An expert skateboarder, Tom is truly __+__ ; he smoothly blends timing
with balance.

+(A) coordinated   +(D) supportive

+(B) erudite   −(E) casual

−(C) a novice

As you should remember, the correct answer is coordinated (A). The prefix
of this word is *co*, meaning together, and the root is *order*. Something that
is "ordered together" fits the context clue perfectly. Combining that with the
knowledge that you are looking for a positive value word certifies coordinated
(A) as the correct answer.

Here is a Level II example:

Because they reject __−__ , conscientious objectors *are given jobs in
community work as a substitute for participation in the armed services.*

+(A) labor   –(D) dictatorships

–(B) belligerence   –(E) poverty

+(C) peace

From working with this example previously, you know that the correct answer is belligerence (B). The root of this word is *bellum,* Latin for war. Belligerence is an inclination toward war. Other words that may be scrolled from this are bellicose, belligerent, and antebellum, all of which have to do with war. Study your roots and prefixes well. A casual knowledge is not good enough. Another root, *bellis*, might be confused with *bellum. Bellis* means beauty. Is it logical that a conscientious objector would reject beauty? Know when to use which root and prefix. This ability will come with study and practice.

Here is a Level III example:

When physicians describe illnesses to colleagues, they must speak an __+__ language, *using professional terms and concepts understood mostly by members of the profession.*

+(A) extrinsic   +(D) esoteric

–(B) inordinate   –(E) abbreviated

+(C) ambulatory

Recalling this example, you will remember that the context clue defines the missing word as one meaning language that involves a special group of people—that is, "inside information." The correct answer is esoteric (D). *Eso* is a prefix that means *inside*. The prefix of extrinsic (A) is *ex*, which means *out*, the opposite of the meaning you seek. Inordinate (B) means *not ordered*. In this case, the prefix *in* means *not*. This is Level III, so beware of easy assumptions! The root of ambulatory (C) is *ambulare*, which means to walk. Abbreviated (E) breaks down to *ab*, meaning *to*, and *brevis*, Latin for brief or short.

In many Level III words you may not be able to scroll or break down a word completely. However, often, as in the example above, a partial knowledge of the etymology may be enough to find the correct answer.

Now, take what you have learned and apply it to the following questions.

DRILLS

DIRECTIONS: Each sentence below has one or two blanks, each blank indicating that something has been omitted. Beneath the sentence are five lettered words or sets of words. Choose the word or set of words that BEST fits the meaning of the sentence as a whole.

■ QUESTION II.1.1

_____ swept the crowd when the natural _____ suddenly occurred.

(A) Infirmary . . . dispensation

(B) Pandemonium . . . catastrophe

(C) Vehemence . . . iodides

(D) Rectification . . . cravenness

(E) Turbulence . . . atmosphere

ANSWER

(B) The way that the word "when" is used in this sentence produces a cause-and-effect relationship. We must choose the two nouns that are related in such a way that the occurrence of one will directly cause the other to happen. Choice (B) is the best answer because "pandemonium" (a wild uproar) will sweep a crowd when a natural "catastrophe" (great disaster) occurs.

Choice (A) is incorrect because the noun "infirmary" (a clinic for sick people) does not make sense followed by the active verb "swept."

Choice (C) is incorrect because although "vehemence" (great force) can sweep a crowd, "iodides" (a chemical term) not only does not relate to the meaning of the entire sentence, but is also awkward followed by the active verb "occurred."

Choice (D) is incorrect because "rectification" (to make or set right) is semantically meaningless in a cause-and-effect relationship with the noun "cravenness" (cowardliness).

For the same reason, choice (E) is wrong, because although "turbulence" (violence or disturbance) may sweep a crowd, it would not be caused by "atmosphere."

■ QUESTION II.1.2

The family left their country to _____ to Utopia and escape _____ because of their beliefs.

(A) immigrate . . . prosecution   (D) wander . . . arraignment

(B) peregrinate . . . extortion   (E) roam . . . censure

(C) emigrate . . . persecution

ANSWER

(C)   In this cause-and-effect sentence, we are looking for a verb whose action is caused by a noun with a negative connotation. (C) is the correct answer because to "emigrate" (leave a place to settle elsewhere) is synonymous with the action described earlier in the sentence, "left their country," and people often experience "persecution" (constant affliction for reasons of religion, race, etc.) because of their beliefs.

Choice (A) is wrong because "immigrate" (come into a foreign country) does not work as well with the word "left," and it would be unlikely for a family to be "prosecuted" (served with a law suit) because of beliefs rather than actions.

Choice (B) is wrong because although "peregrinate" (to travel) fits into the sentence, "extortion" (drawing something from someone by force) does not, as it is commonly used to describe a means of gathering money or material possessions and would be unrelated to a family's beliefs.

Choices (D) and (E) are incorrect because both "wander" and "roam" imply movement with no fixed destination, and we know that the family went specifically to Utopia.

■ QUESTION II.1.3

The _____ was _____ .

(A) desert . . . pudding   (D) condiment . . . stew

(B) dessert . . . parfait   (E) compliment . . . pastry

(C) hors d'oeuvre . . . ice cream

ANSWER

(B) The sentence calls for two nouns which are related as a category and a member of that category. Choice (B) is correct because "dessert" is a category of food and "parfait" (a frozen dessert of rich cream and eggs) is a type of dessert, and therefore fits into that category.

Choice (A) is incorrect because to describe a "desert" (an area of dry, arid land) as "pudding," makes no sense. This option was probably included in order to call attention to the similar spellings of "dessert" and "desert."

Choice (C) is incorrect because it is unlikely that "ice cream" would be served as an "hors d'oeuvre" (an appetizer before the main course).

Choice (D) is wrong because "stew" is not used as a "condiment" (a seasoning or relish, as pepper, mustard, etc.).

Choice (E) does not make sense because a "compliment" (something said in praise) is verbal, and "pastry" (pies, tarts, etc.) is a material object.

■ QUESTION II.1.4

The _____ associated with drug abuse and alcoholism are often _____ .

(A) outgrowth . . . impromptu

(B) consequences . . . grave

(C) compensation . . . inconsequential

(D) fruit . . . malnutrition

(E) benefit . . . illumination

ANSWER

(B) To complete this sentence it is necessary to choose a plural noun and an adjective to describe it. The correct answer is (B) because "grave" (serious) is an appropriate description of the "consequences" (results) associated with drug abuse and alcoholism.

Choice (A) is incorrect because "outgrowth" (product), being singular, does not agree with the plural verb "are" and because "impromptu" (spur of the moment) does not make sense in the sentence.

In choice (C), "Compensation" (reward) is inappropriate to speak of in relation to drug and alcohol abuse, and, being singular, it does not agree with the plural verb.

The same applies to "fruit" (D), and "malnutrition" does not work because it is a noun and not an adjective. The same reasoning applies once again to option (E); not only is it inappropriate to speak of "benefit" (improvement, advantage) in relation to drug and alcohol abuse, but it is a singular noun, and "illumination" is a noun where an adjective is needed.

■ QUESTION II.1.5

> The _____ of the situation warranted _____ measures.
>
> (A) gravity . . . extreme   (D) levity . . . crass
>
> (B) importance . . . pompous   (E) uniqueness . . . wonted
>
> (C) significance . . . piquant

ANSWER

(A)   In this sentence, the correct answer must contain a noun and an adjective which describes the action taken as a result of the noun. Choice (A) is correct because a situation with "gravity" (seriousness, weight) would be important enough to require "extreme" (very great, drastic) measures in response.

The word "pompous" (B) (unnecessarily showy) has negative connotations of excess, and it is unlikely that any situation would "warrant" (authorize, as by law) something negative, especially if that situation was "important."

This is also true of option (C), in which "significance" fits the sentence, but "piquant" (power to whet the appetite or interest through tartness) is inappropriate to describe warranted measures.

Option (D) is a bad choice because "levity" (frivolity) does not fit with a word as weighty as "warranted," and it does not necessarily result in "crass" (grossness of mind precluding delicacy) actions.

(E) is wrong because "uniqueness" (having the quality of being without like or equal) would require the opposite adjective of "wonted" (customary or accustomed).

■ QUESTION II.1.6

The phenomenon called the "self-fulfilling prophecy" occurs when one holds and acts on a belief that is not true; for example, parents who believe a child is destined to turn out "no good" and treat the child as if he were no good, often have their worst fears realized: false _____ becomes _____ .

(A) belief . . . reality   (D) presumption . . . certain

(B) fear . . . truth   (E) dread . . . proven

(C) anxiety . . . fact

ANSWER

(A)   The statement after the colon in this sentence paraphrases what was set forth in the example and relates it back to the idea set forth in the beginning of the sentence. Option (A) is correct because "belief" connects to "a belief" and "parents who believe," while "reality" connects to "fears realized." The rest of the options may work semantically, but only option (A) exactly mirrors the words of the beginning of the sentence.

■ QUESTION II.1.7

The _____ speaker moved the audience to _____ .

(A) apprehensive . . . solitude

(B) enthusiastic . . . action

(C) vulnerable . . . adversity

(D) authentic . . . tranquility

(E) scrupulous . . . complacency

ANSWER

(B)   Option (B) is the correct answer because it is the choice in which the noun is most clearly caused by the specific adjective in the beginning of the sentence. It is extremely likely that an "enthusiastic" (intensely eager) speaker could move an audience to "action." (B) also makes the most sense because the verb "move" implies activity or "action." In the rest of the options, although they could make sense in unusual contexts, the noun does not follow as inevitably after the adjective.

Choices (A) "solitude," (D) "tranquility," and (E) "complacency" (contentment) are all quiet, passive words that do not make sense with the verb "moved." It would be as illogical as to say that someone was moved to stillness. "Moved" also implies self-motivated, and (C) "adversity" (misfortune) usually comes from outside forces.

■ QUESTION II.1.8

The student's request for early graduation was _____ until all the grades were processed.

(A) denied   (D) ratified

(B) prohibited   (E) obscured

(C) deferred

ANSWER

(C)   The word "until" suggests that the first part of this sentence is conditional upon the second part, and that a passage of time is necessary before the conditions are met. For this reason, (C) is the best choice. "Deferred" (to postpone or delay) also implies that a certain amount of time must pass before a decision is reached.

(A) "Denied," (B) "prohibited," (D) "ratified" (confirmed), and (E) "obscured" (not easily understood) are all very fixed states which are unlikely to change over time or in the very light of new evidence.

■ QUESTION II.1.9

Winston Churchill was such a(n) _____ and _____ speaker that listeners from around the world would postpone whatever they were doing to hear his speeches on the radio.

(A) gullible . . . deliberate   (D) provocative . . . prosaic

(B) impartial . . . obscure   (E) eloquent . . . mesmerizing

(C) incoherent . . . pious

ANSWER

(E)   In this sentence we are looking for two adjectives that positively describe the noun "speaker." We know that the adjectives imply that the speaker was good and captivating because the second half of the sentence tells us that people would interrupt their actions to listen to him speak.

Choice (E) is the only one in which both adjectives are complimentary, and therefore the correct answer.

Many of the other choices, (A) "deliberate," (B) "obscure," or (D) "prosaic," although they may describe an appropriate form of speaking for a teacher or lecturer, suggest a tedious and even boring style, and could not describe a man who commanded attention all over the world. Someone who speaks in an (C) "incoherent" (not logically connected) style is not pleasant to listen to at all.

■ QUESTION II.1.10

After he lost 20 pounds with healthy food choices and exercise, he found that his body responded with more _____ than before.

(A) frivolity   (D) vitality

(B) lethargy   (E) tranquility

(C) diligence

ANSWER

(D)   This sentence tells us that a person lost weight by eating healthy food and by exercising. We know that this person is healthy and that his body will "respond" in a positive way. So we are looking for a noun that is related to the adjective "healthy." (D) "vitality" (having energy) is the best choice.

(A) is incorrect because although "frivolity" (fun) is a positive word, it does not relate semantically to a healthy body.

(B) is wrong because "lethargy" (lazy, passive) is not related to a healthful way of life.

(C) "diligence" (hard work) is related to having a healthy body, because it takes hard work to do so, but it does not tell us how the body responds.

(E) "tranquility" is incorrect because a healthy body is not usually described as responding in a "peaceful, still, or harmonious" manner.

■ QUESTION II.1.11

The sales associate tried to _____ trade by distributing business cards.

(A) elicit   (D) elliptic

(B) solicit   (E) conciliate

(C) illicit

ANSWER

(B)   To complete this sentence we must find a verb related to money and business. (B) is the best answer because "solicit" (to pursue business or legal affairs) connects to "sales" and "business cards."

(A) "elicit" (to draw forth) although it may seem to make sense, is not as good an answer because it does not carry the association with money and business.

(C) "illicit" and (D) "elliptic" are incorrect because, not only do they not make sense semantically, they are also both adjectives where a verb is required.

(E) "conciliate" (to win over or smooth) does not make sense because it usually is used in relation to people or animals and not to an impersonal noun such as "trade."

■ QUESTION II.1.12

To express his reservations without offending anyone, the professor _____ his statements.

(A) lengthened   (D) warranted

(B) formed   (E) qualified

(C) constructed

ANSWER

(E) Judging from the context of this sentence, it is obvious that the professor is aware that his statements are potentially offensive. Since he wishes to express them anyway, the word chosen must imply a balance that will make his statements less likely to anger anyone. (E) "qualified" (to moderate, soften) expresses this balance.

Choice (A) "lengthened" is incorrect because if his statements were likely to be upsetting, the longer they were, the more upsetting they would be.

"Formed" (B) and "constructed" (C) do not work because they are both too neutral to reflect the negative connotations associated with the professor's reservations.

(D) "warranted" (guaranteed or authorized) would make more sense if the professor were sure his audience would agree with his statements and wanted to solidify them.

■ QUESTION II.1.13

A storm of _____ swept over the country when _____ at the highest levels of government became common knowledge.

(A) indignation . . . corruption   (D) uncertainty . . . graft

(B) protest . . . cooperation   (E) indifference . . . actions

(C) praise . . . dedication

ANSWER

(A)   This sentence involves a cause-and-effect relationship in which some action of the government caused a reaction among the people. The words "storm" and "swept" imply that the people reacted to a negative action. For this reason (A) is the best answer. "Corruption" (evilness, depravity, dishonesty) in the government would be certain to raise "indignation" (righteous anger) in the citizens of a country.

Both (B) and (C) contain words, "cooperation," "praise," "dedication," with positive meanings that don't fit into the negative atmosphere of the sentence. Likewise, the words, "uncertainty," "indifference," "actions," from (D) and (E), are too neutral and impassive to carry the meaning of the sentence.

■ QUESTION II.1.14

He knew that all available evidence indicated the invalidity of the theory in question; nevertheless, he personally _____ it.

(A) researched   (D) explored

(B) repudiated   (E) investigated

(C) supported

ANSWER

(C)   The semicolon and the word "nevertheless" in the middle of this sentence indicate that the second half of the sentence contains information that is contrary to that presented in the first half. Therefore, since the beginning of the sentence suggests a negative attitude towards the "evidence," the rest of the sentence must be more positive. The most positive of the options is choice (C) "supported" (to advocate).

Choices (A) "researched," (D) "explored," and (E) "investigated" are too neutral to contradict the thought presented in the first part of the sentence.

Choice (B) "repudiated" (to disavow) is incorrect because it mirrors the negative attitude towards the evidence expressed in the first half of the sentence instead of contradicting it.

■ QUESTION II.1.15

Perhaps one reason for the lesser number of female writers is that women traditionally have lacked the _____ independence and the _____ necessary to permit them to concentrate their efforts on writing.

(A) literary . . . talent   (D) emotional . . . intelligence

(B) intellectual . . . ability   (E) financial . . . leisure

(C) social . . . reputation

ANSWER

(E)   For this sentence, rather than look for grammatical clues, it is necessary to find the words that cause the sentence to make the most sense in the whole sentence. All of the pairs fit in the first part of the sentence, but only one takes into account the key phrase, " . . . to concentrate their efforts on writing," which finishes the sentence.

■ QUESTION II.1.16

The mayor stated that it was _____ knowledge that a campaign should _____ the election.

(A) ordinary . . . supersede   (D) common . . . precede

(B) familiar . . . persecute   (E) vulgar . . . proceed

(C) popular . . . prosecute

ANSWER

(D)   This question relies on your knowledge of campaigns and elections. The easiest way to answer it is to look at the second choice. The best answer is (D). A campaign should "precede" (come before) the election. Choice (A) is incorrect because a campaign doesn't "supersede" or take the place of an election.

Choices (B), (C), and (E) are wrong because they are semantically impossible. A campaign cannot "persecute" (afflict constantly), "prosecute" (serve with a lawsuit), or "proceed" (carry on). Only people or groups of people can do these things.

■ QUESTION II.1.17

I admire his ability; it's just his manner that I find _____ .

(A) appealing   (D) lacking

(B) interesting   (E) compelling

(C) hard

ANSWER

(D)   The semicolon in this sentence divides two opposing thoughts. The word "just" means there are reservations attached to this person's "manner." Thus, we are looking for a word that would describe his "manner" in a negative way, in contrast to "admire . . . ability." The best choice is "lacking" (D).

Choice (A) "appealing," choice (B) "interesting," and choice (E) "compelling" all have positive connotations and are therefore incorrect. Choice (C) is wrong because it would be unusual to use the word "hard" to describe someone's "manner."

QUESTION II.1.18

She was _____ into the prestigious club despite her _____ .

(A) excepted . . . qualifications

(B) accepted . . . reputation

(C) enjoined . . . popularity

(D) inaugurated . . . fame

(E) rejected . . . notoriety

ANSWER

(B) The meaning of this sentence hinges on the word "despite." Something will happen that is contradictory to what is expected. (B) is the best answer because although "reputation" has a neutral denotation, it often has a negative connotation, and it is therefore contradictory to "accept" someone because of their reputation.

Choice (A) is incorrect because "excepted" (taken out) does not work with the word "into," which implies that something was put in. The word is semantically meaningless in the sentence.

Choice (C) "enjoined" and "popularity" do not make any sense because it would mean she was commanded into the club despite her popularity; these words are not contradictory.

Choice (D) is wrong because "inaugurate" means to "put into office with ceremony" and this would not happen "despite" fame, but rather because of it.

Choice (E) is wrong because she would be "rejected" because of "notoriety," which means ill-fame, and not "despite" it; once again, the result is not the opposite of what one would expect.

■ QUESTION II.1.19

After reading the letter, she unhappily _____ that the manager was attempting to _____ a contract with her.

(A) implied . . . abrogate   (D) concluded . . . nullify

(B) inferred . . . negotiate   (E) surmised . . . research

(C) imposed . . . analyze

ANSWER

(D)   To complete this sentence, we must assume the subject wanted a contract with the manager, and choose a verb that suggests she was made unhappy because the manager did not want a contract with her. The words that best convey this meaning to the sentence are in option (D). She unhappily "concluded" (decided) that the manager was trying to "nullify" (cancel out) the contract.

Although "abrogate" (annul, revoke) fits into the sentence, (A) is not as fitting an answer because "unhappily" does not work as well as an adjective for "implied" as it does for "concluded."

(B), (C), and (E) do not work because if the woman wanted a contract, she would not be unhappy if the manager wished to "negotiate" (confer to arrive at a settlement), "analyze" (examine), or "research" (investigate) a contract with her.

■ QUESTION II.1.20

Teenagers in part-time jobs today are relatively well paid: _____, workers in the fast-food segment of the work force can earn up to $5.00 per hour.

(A) additionally   (D) because

(B) however   (E) for example

(C) therefore

ANSWER

(E) "For example" is correct. The second part of this sentence gives supporting information in the form of an example for the assertion made in the first part of the sentence.

(A) "additionally" is wrong because the second part of the sentence does not add new information or another assertion.

(B) "however" is wrong because this word would be followed by information that contradicts or in some way contrasts with the assertion made in the first part of the sentence.

Choices (C) "therefore" and (D) "because" are wrong because they are both used to signal cause-and-effect relationships, and the second part of the sentence is neither a cause nor an effect of the first part of the sentence.

▄ QUESTION II.1.21

> The grant was _____ because the budget was _____ .
>
> (A) denied . . . obvious   (D) reassessed . . . diffident
>
> (B) approved . . . infinite   (E) allocated . . . finite
>
> (C) rejected . . . truculent

ANSWER

(E) The way that the word "because" is used in this sentence gives it a cause-and-effect relationship. The first blank calls for a predicate adjective, which is caused by the quality of the budget described by the adjective used in the second blank. The correct answer is (E) because a grant will be "allocated" (assigned) if the budget is "finite" (has a definite ending), or has a specific number value.

Although all verb forms in the choices are possible answers, the predicate adjectives pose some problems.

Choice (A) is incorrect because it is not logical that a grant would be "denied" because of an "obvious" (evident) budget.

Choice (B) is also incorrect because a grant would not be "approved" if the budget was "infinite" (never ending). Most grants ask for a complete, detailed budget.

Choices (C) and (D) are wrong because both "truculent" (fierce or threatening) and "diffident" (shy or lacking in self-confidence) are adjectives used to
describe people or animals, and are ridiculous when applied to an inanimate
object such as a budget.

■ QUESTION II.1.22

The prisoner finally _____ that he drank to _____ on the night he
committed the murder.

(A) acceded . . . access   (D) eluded . . . escape

(B) conceded . . . excess   (E) alluded . . . abundance

(C) exceeded . . . extreme

ANSWER

(B)   There are few clues to help the reader decide which pair of words is
most appropriate in the sentence. It is necessary to simply decide by a process
of elimination, which two words complete the sentence in such a way that it
makes the most sense.

Saying that the prisoner finally "conceded" (yielded) that he drank to "excess" (too much) on the night of the murder is a perfectly logical sentence; (B)
is the best answer. Saying that a prisoner "acceded" (agreed with) the fact that
he drank to "access" (availability) on a murder night is not logical; therefore,
(A) is not the best selection.

A prisoner who "exceeded" (surpassed) is not a clear thought; therefore, (C)
is not the best answer.

Choice (D) is incorrect because one would not say that the prisoner finally
"eluded" (escaped from) that he drank to "escape" on the night of the murder.

The word "alluded" (E), which means "made a reference to," might fit the
first part of the sentence well, but not when coupled with "abundance."

◼ QUESTION II.1.23

Living out the _____ consequences of choices made, he realized the meager nature of his existence; his life was not to be so _____ as he had once assumed it would be.

(A) surprising . . . intricate   (D) boring . . . predictable

(B) unexpected . . . exciting   (E) happy . . . unusual

(C) inevitable . . . full

ANSWER

(C)   Because the nature of man's existence is "meager" (poor, inadequate) which is a negative term, we can assume that the man's life will be described with another negative term. The "not" after the semicolon, however, when applied to the second blank, turns it to its opposite, so that a positive term is needed there. The only pair of words that fit this pattern is (C).

In the context, "inevitable" (unavoidable) has negative connotations, while a "full" life is desirable. In the remainder of the choices, the two words are too similar in their connotations, and would only work if the word "not" was removed from the sentence.

◼ QUESTION II.1.24

Although the legislative body is sometimes described as lethargic, it can sometimes act in a _____ manner, especially in an emergency.

(A) vigorous   (D) elusive

(B) prudent   (E) virulent

(C) indolent

ANSWER

(A)   The word "although" suggests that the word that would be most appropriate for this sentence is the opposite of "lethargic"; that word would be "vigorous" (A).

"Prudent" (B) (wise, careful) might be considered as a possibility, especially in light of the phrase "in an emergency," but not within the context of the sentence where we are looking for a word opposite in meaning to "lethargic."

Choice (C) is incorrect because "indolent" is synonymous with "lethargic."

Choice (D) doesn't apply because "elusive" is not an antonym of "lethargic," nor would the legislature act in an elusive manner in an emergency.

Choice (E) "virulent" is not appropriate because a legislature hopefully wouldn't act in a malicious manner, under any circumstances, and certainly not in an emergency.

■ QUESTION II.1.25

Faced with a limited budget and many attractive choices, Michael had to _____ the merits of each possibility so that he didn't encounter any debt.

(A) concede   (D) waive

(B) denounce   (E) assess

(C) refute

ANSWER

(E)   Because the phrase "limited budget" is semantically juxtaposed with "many attractive choices," we must choose a term which suggests a balance between these things. (E) "assess" (judge the worth) is just such a word because judging implies weighing or balancing.

The rest of the options, (A) "concede" (acknowledge), (B) "denounce" (condemn), (C) "refute" (disprove), and (D) "waive" (give up possession) are all too definite and fixed and do not carry this sense of making a decision.

■ QUESTION II.1.26

Although the topic embarrassed him, he spoke _____ about his bankruptcy and financial situation.

(A) vainly   (D) bitterly

(B) rapidly   (E) candidly

(C) cryptically

ANSWER

(E)   The key word here is "although," which tells us to interpret the sentence as follows: even though the topic was embarrassing to the speaker, he spoke in a way that didn't show his embarrassment. The best choice for this sentence is (E) "candidly" (truthfully, sincerely).

Choice (A) is wrong because "vainly" (futilely, unsuccessfully) does not suggest the opposite of embarrassment.

Choice (B) "rapidly" is a possibility, but doesn't convey the essence of the meaning of the sentence as well as (E).

Choice (C) "cryptically" (meant to be puzzling) is not meaningful in the sentence.

■ QUESTION II.1.27

In spite of the fact that the professor was _____ , his lecture was so _____ that few students understood him.

(A) articulate . . . abstract   (D) illuminating . . . deliberate

(B) arrogant . . . austere   (E) affable . . . derogatory

(C) taciturn . . . superficial

ANSWER

(A)   The clue here is "in spite of the fact," which means that regardless of the quality that described the professor, the quality of the lecture would have to be contradictory to it. The fact that "few students understood" the lecture is negative, and therefore the adjective to describe the professor must be positive. We can conclude that few students would understand a lecture that is "abstract" (vague, having no clear definition), even though the professor is "articulate" (well-spoken); therefore, (A) is the best choice.

In choice (B), although "arrogant" (haughty) is a possible way to describe the professor, "austere" (harsh, strict, severe) is also a negative term and does not contradict the quality described in the first part of the sentence.

Choice (C) is incorrect because "taciturn" (reserved, quiet) and "superficial" (cursory, shallow) are also both negative.

Choice (D) is incorrect because although the professor might be "illuminating" (make understandable), students would understand a "deliberate" (carefully considered) lecture. This does not go with "in spite of the fact."

Choice (E) "affable" (friendly, amiable, good natured) is a positive way of describing the professor, and "derogatory" (belittling, uncomplimentary) is negative, which is the contradictory relationship we are looking for. This is not the best answer, however, because "derogatory" describes the content of the lecture and not whether or not it was understandable.

■ QUESTION II.1.28

> Tile manufacturers need high-quality clay; this is why brickyards are invariably located in places where high-quality clay is _____ and can be readily _____ .
>
> (A) present . . . verified   (D) abundant . . . accessed
>
> (B) evident . . . procured   (E) visible . . . utilized
>
> (C) nearby . . . obtained

ANSWER

(D)   The first part of this sentence establishes a need, and the second part shows how those needs are met. Therefore, we must find two words that describe a condition of "high-quality clay," which would help tile manufacturers fill their need for it. The best answer is (D); the need can best be met if the clay is "abundant" (plentiful) and can be readily "accessed" (easily obtained).

All of the remaining choices, (A) "present . . . verified" (proven true), (B) "evident . . . procured" (obtained), (C) "nearby . . . obtained," and (E) "visible . . . utilized," make sense within the context of the sentence, but they are not the best answers. Although they maintain that the clay is present and obtainable, choice (D) adds the important connotations that the clay is plentifully present and easily obtainable.

■ QUESTION II.1.29

People who drive when they are drunk put themselves and others on the road in _____ .

(A) guile   (D) distress

(B) discord   (E) dissonance

(C) jeopardy

ANSWER

(C)   It should be common knowledge that many drunk driving accidents result in the death of many of the people involved; therefore, we should look for a word that suggests a threat to life. (C) "jeopardy" (great danger or risk) is just such a word. The implication of this sentence is that drunk drivers are a menace on the road; therefore, if they drive while they are under the influence of alcohol, they put people's lives in "jeopardy" (danger).

(A) "guile" (slyness, deceit), (B) "discord" (disagreement, lack of harmony), and (E) "dissonance" (harsh contradiction) are incorrect answers because they do not fit into the semantic context of the sentence.

Choice (D) "distress" (pain, anguish) is a possibility, but is not the best answer, because it is not as strongly negative a word. It describes pain or suffering, but not possible death.

QUESTION II.1.30

Although the explorers often felt _____ , they managed to _____ the desert.

(A) defeated . . . achieve   (D) relentless . . . finish

(B) elated . . . survive   (E) withdrawn . . . subject

(C) exhausted . . . conquer

ANSWER

(C)   The key word in this sentence is "although," which indicates that the second half of the sentence must contradict the expectations established in the first half. (C) is the correct answer because "exhausted" explorers couldn't normally "conquer" the desert.

Although in choice (A), "defeated" and "achieved" are contradictory, you could never say that someone "achieved" the desert. This is not semantically correct.

Choice (B) is incorrect because "elated" and "survive" do not relate back to "although." They are not contradictory ideas.

"Relentless" explorers (D) would manage to "finish" the desert, but again, this does not make sense with the conditional word "although" in the sentence.

It is possible that the explorers might have felt "withdrawn" (E), but the word "subject" has no meaning in the sentence.

QUESTION II.1.31

A great _____ remained after the tornado completely _____ the population of the small town.

(A) devastation . . . overwhelmed (D) windfall . . . invaded

(B) fallout . . . covered   (E) vacancy . . . augmented

(C) detachment . . . broke

ANSWER

(A)   The meaning of this sentence hinges on your knowledge of the consequences of a tornado. Knowing that a tornado is destructive, the only possible choice is (A) "devastation." A tornado has no relation to (B) "fallout," (C) "detachment," (D) "windfall," or (E) "vacancy."

■ QUESTION II.1.32

Young people who have never experienced serious illness or harm often have an exaggerated sense of _____ that leads them to believe that the really bad things in life only happen to other people.

(A) judgment   (D) well-being

(B) happiness   (E) concern

(C) life

ANSWER

(D)   The correct answer is (D) "well-being," because people who have never been sick or experienced harm do not really believe that illness or bad things could ever happen to them.

Choice (A) "judgment" is incorrect because it has no bearing on the topic of the sentence.

Choice (B) "happiness" is wrong because people who believe that bad things happen only to other people don't have an exaggerated sense of happiness.

Choice (C) is wrong because "life" has no meaning in the sentence. The same applies to choice (E), "concern."

■ QUESTION II.1.33

The crushing _____ suffered by the soccer team left the fans feeling _____ with the bragging goalie.

(A) blow . . . overwhelmed   (D) defeat . . . disenchanted

(B) failure . . . indecisive   (E) loss . . . placid

(C) defense . . . angry

ANSWER

(D)   The word "crushing" in the first sentence should indicate that something bad has happened, and that the fans would be feeling very negative towards the "bragging goalie" who has nothing to brag about.

Choice (D) "defeat" and "disenchanted" (disillusioned) are the best words to meet these conditions.

Choice (A) is only partially correct. Although "blow" (unexpected calamity) would fit into the first part of the sentence, "overwhelmed" would not.

Choice (B) "failure" is appropriate for the first part of the sentence, but "indecisive" is incorrect for the second part as it has neutral rather than negative connotations.

Choice (C) "defense" is inappropriate for the first part of the sentence, so although "angry" fits into the second part, choice (C) is the incorrect answer.

Choice (E) is only partially correct. "Loss" fits in semantically but "placid" is, once again, too neutral a term to convey the negative reactions of the crowd.

■ QUESTION II.1.34

Since the calendar year originally contained only 355 days, an extra month was occasionally _____ .

(A) contingent   (D) superadded

(B) introduced   (E) intercalated

(C) incident

ANSWER

(E) The word "since" creates a cause-and-effect relationship. The second half of the sentence must be caused directly by the information provided in the first half. The word "occasionally" further informs us that the action must be capable of repetition. The correct choice is (E) because "intercalated" (inserted among existing elements) relates to the original information and can be frequently repeated.

Choice (A) "contingent" and choice (C) "incident" imply chance.

Choice (B) "introduced" (to bring forth for the first time) and choice (D) "superadded" (to add to something already complete) are both too finite to happen "occasionally."

■ QUESTION II.1.35

The acquisition of exact knowledge is apt to be _____ , in that it is time-consuming to check for accuracy; but it is essential to every kind of excellence.

(A) wearisome

(D) amorphous

(B) equable

(E) eccentric

(C) erratic

ANSWER

(A) The phrase "in that it is" is an important clue that the correct word will be synonymous or closely related to whatever immediately follows it. In this case the idea is "time-consuming," and the option closest in meaning is (A) "wearisome."

The remainder of the words, (B) "equable" (fair), (C) "erratic" (unpredictable), (D) "amorphous" (having no shape), and (E) "eccentric" (odd, peculiar), have little or no connection to "time-consuming" and make no sense in the sentence.

■ QUESTION II.1.36

There was something _____ about the old house. In many ways one was made to feel that ghosts and demons existed there.

(A) ominous

(B) tutelary

(C) attractive

(D) celestial

(E) mythical

ANSWER

(A) The best answer is (A) "ominous" (foretelling evil, threatening). The context of the sentence tells us that ghosts and demons existed there, and as a result, the adjective that would best describe the "old house" should reflect the feeling of something scary.

(B) "tutelary" (acting as a guardian) has no relationship to the context of the sentence as it does not imply anything frightening.

(C) "attractive" is the opposite of what the sentence context implies and is the wrong answer.

(D) "celestial" (heavenly, divine) is an antonym of the contextual implications in this sentence. This sentence requires a word that describes a house with "demons and ghosts."

(E) "mythical" (legendary narrative that is related to the beliefs of a people or explains a practice or natural phenomena) is not appropriate in the context of the sentence.

■ QUESTION II.1.37

The _____ policy of the Defense Secretary was regarded by the army as a national humiliation.

(A) pliant

(B) impartial

(C) pacific

(D) malleable

(E) histrionic

ANSWER

(C)   A country establishes an army because of a real or implied threat by foreign or domestic agents; therefore, anybody who joins an army would be willing to fight to eliminate this threat. The most humiliating quality for a Defense Secretary would be the opposite of "wanting to fight." (C), therefore, is the best answer because a "pacific" (peaceful) policy would be inappropriate for a military official.

(A) "pliant" (flexible), (B) "impartial" (fair), and (D) "malleable" (adaptable) would be possible answers; however, none of these words implies the opposite of the desirable quality for the Defense Secretary as well as "pacific" and therefore are not the best choices. (E) "histrionic" (relating to the theater) does not relate to the subject of the sentence.

■ QUESTION II.1.38

Her constant stealing of lunch money from others in the class _____ her teacher.

(A) annoys   (D) delectates

(B) irritates   (E) inconveniences

(C) exasperates

ANSWER

(C)   Choice (C) is the best answer because we are looking for a very strong word that illustrates or describes the negative feelings associated with stealing lunch money.

Choice (C) is the extreme feeling of vexation and irritation.

Choice (A) "annoys" is a mild feeling compared to "exasperates."

Although choice (B) "irritates" is a stronger emotion than "annoys," it is a lesser one than "exasperates."

"Delectates" (D) (delight), is not correct, because the teacher would not be delighted about "her stealing lunch money."

Choice (E) "inconveniences" (causes a lack of comfort) is a possibility, but is incorrect because it is not an emotionally strong word.

■ QUESTION II.1.39

Typically a wedding is a _____ occasion, not a _____ one.

(A) superfluous . . . pious   (D) solemn . . . comic

(B) reprehensible . . . caustic   (E) futile . . . tedious

(C) private . . . stagnant

ANSWER

(D)   This sentence needs an adjective to describe a wedding, and another one that tells you what a wedding is not. So we are looking for two words that are opposite in meaning. The only choice that fits both conditions is (D).

A wedding is "solemn," but it is not "comic."

Choice (A) is not appropriate because a wedding is not a "superfluous" (exceeding what is sufficient or necessary) situation. In addition, a wedding is a "pious" time, so it is inaccurate to say that it is not such a time.

Choice (B) is incorrect because a wedding is not "caustic," nor can it be described as "reprehensible" (deserving blame or censure) because this word can only be used to describe people or their actions.

Choice (C) is only partially correct. A wedding may or may not be a "private" occasion but "stagnant" (foul from lack of movement) is inappropriate to describe a wedding, and is not the opposite of "private."

Choice (E) is incorrect. A wedding is not usually considered a "futile" or "hopeless" occasion.

■ QUESTION II.1.40

Rather than trying to _____ , one should try to _____ .

(A) abolish . . . destroy   (D) hurt . . . harm

(B) instigate . . . temper   (E) console . . . comfort

(C) demolish . . . enhance

ANSWER

(C)   The word "rather" implies a contrast of words within the sentence. So we are looking for two words that are the opposite of each other. (C) "demolish . . . enhance" is the only choice that meets this condition. "Demolish" means "to tear down" and "enhance" means "to improve."

Choice (A)'s words are synonyms of each other: "abolish" and "destroy" mean the same thing.

Choice (B) is incorrect because "instigate" means "to provoke" and is not the opposite of "temper," which means "to modify." "Hurt" and "harm" are synonymous words, and therefore choice (D) is incorrect. Likewise, "console" and "comfort" are close in meaning, and not antonyms; therefore, choice (E) is incorrect.

■ QUESTION II.1.41

The frightened mother _____ her young daughter for darting in front of the car.

(A) implored

(D) reproved

(B) extorted

(E) abolished

(C) exhorted

ANSWER

(D)   A key word in this problem is "for." It is important to find the option that works the best with this word, as well as making the most sense semantically in the sentence. To fit both of these qualifications, "reproved" is the best choice.

One "reprimands . . . " for, but typically, one "implores . . . " to, "extorts . . . " from, "exhorts . . . " to, and "abolishes . . . " from. Furthermore, a frightened mother would reprimand her daughter for disobeying street rules and running in front of a car. The mother would not (A) "implore" (beg) her daughter for doing a dangerous action. This makes no sense. Nor would the mother (B) "extort" (obtain by force) her daughter in this situation. (C) "exhorted" (urge, advise) and (E) "abolished" (to do away with) are not semantically correct in the sentence.

■ QUESTION II.1.42

The doctoral candidate was _____ as she sought to make the results of her research _____ to her committee.

(A) objective . . . lucid

(D) hypocritical . . . flagrant

(B) disdainful . . . complacent

(E) candid . . . subtle

(C) discerning . . . obscure

ANSWER

(A)   There is a cause-and-effect relationship in this sentence. The first blank needs an adjective to describe a manner of speaking, and the second blank needs an adjective to describe the effect that this manner of speaking has on an audience. The best answer is (A) "objective . . . lucid." The best way to describe the candidate would be "objective" (dealing with facts without personal feelings or prejudices), which would have the effect of making her research "lucid" (easily understood) to the committee.

Choices (B) "disdainful" (to look down upon), (C) "discerning" (distinguishing one thing from another), and (D) "hypocritical" (two-faced, deceptive) are not appropriate to the context of the sentence. Choice (E) "candid" (honest, truthful, sincere) is a possibility, but candidness could not cause "subtlety" (understatement, sophistication, cunning).

■ QUESTION II.1.43

The computer is a(n) _____ tool, for if one neglects to save a file, it cannot be recalled.

(A) ominous

(D) difficult

(B) complicated

(E) unforgiving

(C) essential

ANSWER

(E)   The way the word "for" is used in this sentence makes it synonymous with the word "because" and creates a cause-and-effect relationship. Some quality of a computer causes the effect described in the second half of the sentence. Furthermore, the second half of this sentence cites an example to support the assertion made in the first part of the sentence. The computer is "unforgiving" (E), because if one neglects to save a file, that file is lost. It cannot be recalled.

(A) "ominous" (threatening), (B) "complicated," (C) "essential," and (D) "difficult" do not express the idea of no reprieve for a mistake as does (E) "unforgiving."

■ QUESTION II.1.44

> Even though the dog seemed _____ , it was actually _____ .
>
> (A) furtive . . . eloquent   (D) benign . . . prodigal
>
> (B) stoic . . . auspicious   (E) servile . . . peripheral
>
> (C) prodigious . . . innocuous

ANSWER

(C)   The key words in this sentence are "even though the dog seemed," which means that the speaker perceived the dog a certain way, but that was not the way it actually was; therefore, (C) is the best answer. A "prodigious" (enormous) dog is not usually perceived as "innocuous" or "harmless."

Choices (A), (B), (D), and (E) are wrong because they all contain words that would be unusual if used to describe an animal. "Eloquent" (forceful in speech) and "prodigal" (extravagant) are only used to describe people, and "auspicious" (positive) and "peripheral" (unimportant) can only be used to describe ideas or inanimate objects.

■ QUESTION II.1.45

To _____ the action required _____ from an official of the company.

(A) rescind . . . enigma   (D) facilitate . . . ineffectiveness

(B) refute . . . colophon   (E) solicit . . . apathy

(C) defer . . . permission

ANSWER

(C)   We are looking for a verb to describe an "action" and a noun upon which it is conditional. (C) is the best answer because "to defer" (put off until another time) an action already in service might require "permission" from someone in authority ("an official of the company").

Choice (A) is wrong because "to rescind" (repeal, cancel) an action would not require an "enigma" (a puzzle).

(B) is incorrect because "to refute" (prove to be false) would not require a "colophon" (a small design or inscription). (D) is not right because "to facilitate" (bring about) an action does not require "ineffectiveness," but rather effectiveness.

Choice (E) is wrong because to take the initiative to "solicit" (try to bring about) an action does not indicate "apathy" (unconcern), but rather concern.

■ QUESTION II.1.46

John's _____ only _____ the problem of the impending deadline.

(A) immunity . . . derided   (D) virtue . . . hackneyed

(B) indolence . . . augmented   (E) incessance . . . disparaged

(C) stanza . . . mitigated

ANSWER

(B) A person's "indolence" (laziness) would certainly serve to "augment" an impending deadline. (B) is the best answer.

(A) "immunity" (safety) and "derided" (ridiculed) have no meaning when substituted into the sentence.

(C) "stanza" (a section of a poem) does not fit well into the sentence, although "mitigated" (made milder) might belong if the first answer were appropriate. The way the sentence is worded, (C) is the wrong answer.

(D) "virtue" (moral excellence) might fit the sentence, but "hackneyed" (banal, overused) is not appropriate. John's "incessance" (E) or "never stopping" might be a good choice for the first part of the sentence, but it is clear that "disparaged" (speak badly of) does not fit well.

■ QUESTION II.1.47

> The gold-studded costume appeared _____ when compared to the _____ of the flannel suit.
>
> (A) chaste . . . gaudiness   (D) ornate . . . simplicity
>
> (B) laconic . . . opulence   (E) feudal . . . raucousness
>
> (C) reserved . . . savoir-faire

ANSWER

(D) The phrase "when compared to" suggests that we are looking for two words that describe opposite qualities. Certainly a flannel suit is in many ways opposite to a gold-studded costume. The best answer is (D) "ornate" (elaborately decorated) is the most effective way of describing a "gold-studded costume," and "simplicity" (lack of complication) is a good way of describing a "flannel suit," especially when compared to a "gold-studded costume."

(A) "chaste" (virtuous, pure) is an incorrect description of something that is "gold-studded," and "gaudiness" (garishness, flashiness) is not an appropriate choice to describe a "flannel suit."

(B) "laconic" (terse) is an inappropriate way to describe a suit; "laconic" is used to describe people, so (B) is incorrect.

(C) "reserved" (restrained in actions or words) is not the way to compare a "gold-studded costume" to the "savior-faire" (knowing how to act) of a "flannel suit." (C) makes no sense when substituted into the sentence.

(E) "feudal" (having the characteristics of feudalism) is a meaningless choice in the sentence.

■ QUESTION II.1.48

He had a blind temper. He _____ fights over _____ remarks.

(A) enjoyed . . . valid   (D) initiated . . . innocuous

(B) refuted . . . plausible   (E) provoked . . . provocative

(C) assessed . . . benign

ANSWER

(D) The first sentence describes a person who does not intelligently control his temper ("blind temper"). Choice (D) is the best answer because someone who "initiates" (starts) fights over "innocuous" (innocent) remarks is not rational. In all choices, the adjective is appropriate for the sentence; therefore, we are concerned with the verb assigned to "fights."

Choice (A) is wrong because although the verb "enjoyed" is plausible, someone with a bad temper wouldn't necessarily fight over a "valid" remark.

Choice (B) "refuted" (prove false by argument) is not something someone with a "blind temper" would do.

Choice (C) is incorrect because "assessed" (evaluated) is a word associated with a rational person.

Choice (E) is possible because a man who can't control his temper might "provoke" fights, but it is also possible that any mild tempered person might fight over a "provocative" (aggravating) remark.

■ QUESTION II.1.49

In contrast to her _____ personality, she was known to vacillate on certain important issues.

(A) tranquil   (D) conspicuous

(B) austere   (E) provocative

(C) determined

ANSWER

(C) The key phrase here is "in contrast to." This means we are looking for an adjective that is the opposite of "vacillate." The best answer is (C) "determined" (firm, resolute), which is contrary to "vacillate" (to incline first to one course or opinion and then another, waver). The meaning of the sentence would be clear: "In contrast to her determined personality, she was known to change her mind on certain issues." The remainder of the adjectives, (A) "tranquil" (peaceful, harmonious), (B) "austere" (harsh, strict), (D) "conspicuous" (easy to see, noticeable), and (E) "provocative" (tempting, irritating) are incorrect, because they do not contradict "vacillate."

■ QUESTION II.1.50

After carefully evaluating the painting, the art critics unanimously agreed that the work had been done by a _____ and should be _____ .

(A) progeny . . . refurbished   (D) prodigal . . . nullified

(B) charlatan . . . repudiated   (E) fanatic . . . purchased

(C) neophyte . . . qualified

ANSWER

(B) We are looking for two words that are compatible—a noun and a verb that are related in a meaningful cause-and-effect way. (B) is the most logical choice. If a "charlatan" (imposter) paints a painting, then it should be "repudiated" (rejected), because the painting would have no value.

(A) has little meaning, because if a "progeny" (talented child) paints a painting, then why should it be "refurbished" (made new)?

(C) is incorrect because a "neophyte" (beginner) may paint a painting, but then it would be unusual for art experts to examine it, and there would be no reason for them to "qualify" it.

(D) is obviously incorrect in the context of the sentence, because of "prodigal" (someone lavish and wasteful) probably would not spend time painting, or doing anything meaningful.

(E) is also incorrect because a "fanatic" is an extremist and art experts would not necessarily recommend "purchasing" (buying) a painting from such a person.

■ QUESTION II.1.51

The _____ of the companies was inevitable since neither could profit without the assets of the other. This showed _____ behavior on the part of the owners.

(A) merger . . . prudent   (D) hiatus . . . monotonous

(B) pivot . . . exemplary   (E) diversity . . . fundamental

(C) antagonism . . . beneficial

ANSWER

(A)   The first sentence must provide an example that proves the quality set forth in the second sentence. The best answer is (A) "merger . . . prudent." The companies had to "merge" (combine, unite) because they needed each other's profits. This showed "prudent" (foresighted, sensible) behavior.

Choice (B) "pivot" (a fixed pin on which something turns) . . . "exemplary" (commendable) is incorrect, because although "exemplary" is an appropriate choice, "pivot" is semantically incorrect.

Choice (C) "antagonism" (hostility) . . . "beneficial" (helpful, advantageous) is also wrong, because the words "neither could profit without the assets of the other" imply that the companies needed each other; therefore, "antagonism" is not semantically correct within the context of the sentence.

(D) "hiatus" (break, lapse in continuity) . . . "monotonous" (one-tone, boring) has no meaning when inserted into the sentence.

(E) "diversity" (variety) . . . "fundamental" (basic) are incorrect, because they do not fit into the context of the sentence.

◼ QUESTION II.1.52

He was eagerly interested and wanted to participate in the experiment; but he was ultimately _____ on account of his age.

(A) dissuaded   (D) acclimated

(B) accommodated   (E) resigned

(C) reconciled

ANSWER

(A) The semicolon followed by the word "but" in this sentence suggests that the second half of the sentence will somehow contradict the first. Since we know he was eager to participate, we must choose the word that means he was NOT encouraged to do so; therefore, "dissuaded" (persuaded not to do something) is the best choice for the context of the sentence.

(B) "accommodated" and (C) "reconciled" are synonyms referring to bringing into agreement. These two words are not appropriate within the sentence because they are not contextually accurate with the use of "but."

Both (D) "acclimated" (to accustom to a new climate or situation) and (E) "resigned" (to give up) do not make any sense when inserted into the sentence.

◼ QUESTION II.1.53

Some people believe that flying saucers exist. As far as Jaclyn is concerned, this theory is a (an) _____ and has to be proven.

(A) obituary   (D) kaleidoscope

(B) travesty   (E) enigma

(C) irony

ANSWER

(E)   To choose a correct answer for this question, we would have to find a noun that describes something that "has to be proven." An "enigma" (mystery, secret, perplexity) is something that is unknown and has to be proven, just like the existence of flying saucers mentioned in the first sentence.

Choices (A) "obituary" (notice of a person's death), (B) "travesty" (parody, burlesque), and (C) "irony" (something contradictory, sarcastic) do not need to be proven, and so do not fit logically into the sentence.

(D) "kaleidoscope" (an instrument or toy that forms patterns through the use of mirrors) is the worse choice because as a material object it can never be "proven."

■ QUESTION II.1.54

Eric felt _____ after his _____ remark, but it was too late to retract it.

(A) respite . . . inadvertent   (D) tentative . . . extravagant

(B) irrational . . . incautious   (E) insensitive . . . premeditated

(C) remorse . . . disparaging

ANSWER

(C)   The best answer is "remorse" (regret for one's actions) . . . "disparaging" (degrading, belittling). We have to find a verb and an adjective that would fit the context of the sentence. What was Eric's feeling about his remark and what kind of remark was it that would cause him to want to "retract" (take back) what he said? That Eric felt "remorse" for a "disparaging" remark is the best choice for the sentence.

(A) "respite" (temporary delay) and "inadvertent" (heedless, unintentional) is an incorrect choice; although "inadvertent" is a fitting adjective, "respite" has no semantic integrity in this sentence.

(B) "irrational" (incapable of reasoning) and "incautious" (not careful) is incorrect. Although "incautious" would be a good choice, "irrational" makes no sense in the sentence.

(D) "tentative" (hesitant, uncertain) and "extravagant" (excessive) are incorrect. Both words are not logical for inclusion in the sentence.

(E) "insensitive" (not caring) and "premeditated" (carefully planned) are wrong. If Eric's remark was "premeditated," he would not want to retract it, even if it was "insensitive."

■ QUESTION II.1.55

Residents of the town, who normally wouldn't agree on anything, now _____ to _____ the construction of a wood-fired power plant that would cause air pollution.

(A) proceeded . . . defend   (D) alternated . . . establish

(B) dispersed . . . hamper   (E) mobilized . . . resist

(C) assembled . . . endorse

ANSWER

(E)   The combination "normally . . . now" suggests that the present situation is opposite to a habitual one. Since the residents normally don't agree, the correct answer would have the residents of the town agreeing on something. Furthermore, since air pollution is something negative, the verb would suggest opposition to it. Choice (E) "mobilized . . . resist" is the only answer that satisfies both conditions.

Choice (A) is not correct because although the first word satisfies the conditions, the residents of the town would not "defend" air pollution.

Choice (B) is not correct because although the residents might normally "disperse" (break up) on this issue, we are looking for the opposite now.

Choice (C) is wrong because although "assembled" satisfies the condition for the residents getting together, they wouldn't "endorse" air pollution in their town.

Choice (D) is incorrect because the residents of the town wouldn't "alternate" (take turns) getting together or "establish" a construction which causes air pollution.

■ QUESTION II.1.56

Zane Grey was able to _____ fictionalize the life of western cowboys even though he lived thousands of miles away in New York and probably never visited these western locales.

(A) benevolently   (D) frivolously

(B) authentically   (E) incoherently

(C) prosaically

ANSWER

(B)   The phrase "even though" in this sentence tells us that the state described in the second half of the sentence exists despite its contradictory relationship to something mentioned in the first half. Since the fact that Grey lived far away would imply that he would NOT be able to write about the West, we must look for a word that suggests the opposite, or that he wrote WELL about it. Therefore, (B) "authentically" (realistically) would be the best choice.

Choice (A) "benevolently" is incorrect; although Grey could describe cowboys in a kind way, that does not fit the context of the sentence where we are looking for a word that signifies the opposite of knowing little about a subject.

Choice (C) "prosaically" (in an ordinary way) is incorrect because it does not fit into the context of the sentence.

Choice (D) "frivolously" put into the sentence would mean that Grey made fun of the cowboys, and that is not implied in the sentence.

Choice (E) "incoherently" is wrong because it would mean that Grey did not know what he was writing about, and the sentence implies that the opposite was true.

■ QUESTION II.1.57

The scientist was horrified when all the new data he compiled for his experiment _____ his previous results.

(A) nullified   (D) validated

(B) suppressed   (E) consecrated

(C) instigated

ANSWER

(A)   "Horrified" is a very strong adjective describing negative emotions. We are looking for a word to fit into the second half of the sentence that would cause this extreme emotion. "Nullified" (cancelled) is correct because if all the scientist's data was "nullified" by the new data, then the results of his experiment would be incomplete. This is a good reason to be "horrified" (appalled, dismayed).

(B) is a possibility because having data "suppressed" (held back) is bad for a scientist, but not as terrible as having it cancelled, and since the scientist is described as being "horrified," this is not the best answer.

(C) "instigated" (provoked) is wrong because the word makes the sentence meaningless.

(D) is incorrect because if the new data "validated" (made acceptable) the old data, then the scientist would be thrilled, not horrified.

Choice (E) is wrong because "consecrated" (make sacred) is not a word associated with a scientific experiment.

■ QUESTION II.1.58

She took a _____ first step onto the unstable ladder.

(A) skeptical   (D) haggard

(B) tentative   (E) wanton

(C) limber

ANSWER

(B)   We are looking for an adjective to describe what kind of step she would take to climb an "unstable ladder." The best answer is "tentative" (B) (hesitant, uncertain). Certainly, one would only climb something unstable in a hesitant or uncertain way.

Choice (A) is wrong because "skeptical" (doubtful) relates more to an attitude than an action.

Choice (C) "limber" (flexible, pliant) is obviously wrong in the context of the sentence. No one in their right mind would climb in a limber way up an unstable ladder.

Choice (D) is wrong because "haggard" (tired looking, fatigued) describes how a person feels, not the way he would climb a ladder. It is used to describe an emotion not an action.

Choice (E) "wanton" (unruly, excessive) is not contextually accurate, because it does not describe how a person would climb a ladder.

■ QUESTION II.1.59

Facsimile, or fax, machines became common equipment in offices because they were _____ and more _____ than express mail and telex.

(A) faster . . . efficient   (D) valid . . . impeccable

(B) trivial . . . supported   (E) sporadic . . . torpid

(C) effusive . . . salutary

ANSWER

(A)   The best answer is (A) "faster . . . efficient," because we are looking for two adjectives that describe why fax machines replaced express mail and telex.

(B) "trivial" (minor importance) and "supported" do not make any sense in the sentence.

(C) "effusive" (gushing) and "salutary" (beneficial) are not appropriate as reasons why fax machines replaced mail and telex.

(D) "valid" (true) and "impeccable" (faultless) do not logically fit into the sentence.

(E) "sporadic" (happening occasionally) and "torpid" (lacking vigor, dull) are negative adjectives, and if placed in the sentence would mean that fax machines ran on an occasional basis and were dull. This makes little sense.

■ QUESTION II.1.60

> In ancient Greek mythology, the gods and goddesses would _____ before they came to Earth. Sometimes they would appear as animals, and at other times, as plants.
>
> (A) rant   (D) articulate
>
> (B) metamorphose   (E) saunter
>
> (C) venerate

ANSWER

(B)   The clue to completing this statement is the information given in the second sentence: "Sometimes they would appear as animals, and at other times, as plants."

Choice (B) "metamorphose" (change form) is the answer that describes this condition.

"Rant" (to speak in a loud, pompous manner) is possible, but doesn't address the conditions in the second sentence. Therefore, (A) is incorrect.

(C) "venerate" (revere) is wrong, because one must venerate something and there is no object for this verb in this sentence.

(D) "articulate" (to speak distinctly) is logically incorrect when substituted into the sentence.

(E) "saunter" (walk at a leisurely pace, stroll) may describe how the gods and goddesses would walk before they came to Earth, but it does not relate to the conditions set up in the second sentence.

■ QUESTION II.1.61

A notary public is sometimes hired by a lawyer to _____ the _____
of certain signatures.

(A) constrain . . . watermarks   (D) efface . . . consonance

(B) disdain . . . sanctity   (E) abrade . . . matrix

(C) verify . . . veracity

ANSWER

(C)   For this sentence, one must simply choose the words that make the most
logical sense in the sentence based on knowledge of the function of a notary
public, as well as two words that are directly related to one another. For these
reasons, the best choice is (C). "Verify" and "veracity" have the same Latin root
word meaning "true," and it makes sense to say that a notary public is hired to
"verify" (authenticate, confirm) the "veracity" (truthfulness) of signatures.

The remainder of the options (A) constrain. . . . watermarks, (B) disdain . . .
sanctify, (D) efface . . . consonance, and (E) abrade . . . matrix, make no sense
when substituted into the sentence.

■ QUESTION II.1.62

The waitress was _____ because her _____ attitude insured that she
would not receive a tip from the diners.

(A) lethargic . . . cryptic   (D) contrite . . . insolent

(B) nostalgic . . . esoteric   (E) antagonistic . . . prudent

(C) fortuitous . . . incongruous

ANSWER

(D)   The key words in this sentence are "not receive a tip from the diners."
This means we have to find a word that describes a negative quality in a waitress
which would displease the customers enough that they would not tip her, and
then a word to describe how she felt "because" (cause/effect) she did not get

tipped due to her own actions. "Contrite" (regretful, sorrowful) and "insolent" (rude, disrespectful) fit these qualifications, so (D) is the best answer.

(A) "lethargic" (lazy), (B) "nostalgic" (homesick), and (C) "fortuitous" (fortunate) are not appropriate to describe how the waitress felt about not receiving a tip.

(E) "antagonistic" (hostile) is a possible way of describing how the waitress felt towards the diners when they didn't leave her a tip, but "prudent" (wise) is not the kind of attitude that would cause this situation. Had the waitress acted in a prudent manner, she probably would have received a tip.

■ QUESTION II.1.63

The sociologist interpreted _____ as being socially shared ideas about what is right and _____ as specific moral rules of behavior for a surrounding environment.

(A) culture . . . laws   (D) sanctions . . . folkways

(B) mores . . . technologies   (E) values . . . norms

(C) class . . . caste

ANSWER

(E)   This sentence is essentially a definition of the two nouns we are searching for, so the correct answer would be the two nouns that fit the definition provided. "Values" (socially shared ideas about what is right) in a particular environment, and "norms" (specific moral rules of behavior in a particular environment) are therefore the best answer. (A) "culture" (the thoughts and behaviors within an environment that are handed down from generation to generation) means more than just "shared ideas" and is therefore incorrect. "Laws" are norms that have been enacted through the formal process of government, and all "moral rules" are not "laws." (B) is incorrect because the words do not fit into the sentence definitions. "Mores" are strongly sanctioned norms, and "technologies" are practical solutions.

(C) "class" is a social level defined by economic factors such as occupation, income, and wealth. "Caste" is a social level into which people are born and where they must remain for life. These words do not fit into the definitions provided in the sentence.

(D) "sanctions" are rewards and punishments for adhering to or violating behaviors designated; and "folkways" are rules of behavior that are less strongly sanctioned. Thus, (D) is wrong because the words do not fit the definitions.

■ QUESTION II.1.64

The general was _____ ; he considered disagreement with any of his ideas _____ .

(A) provocative . . . euphonic

(B) elusive . . . compatible

(C) fallacious . . . austere

(D) intangible . . . reticent

(E) dogmatic . . . heretical

ANSWER

(E)   This sentence demands two words that are logically related. Any word that describes the general will have to relate semantically to how he "considered disagreement with any of his ideas." The best answer is (E) "dogmatic" (positive in stating matters of opinion) . . . "heretical" (dissent from a dominant opinion or theory). The general is forthright in stating his opinion, and anyone who disagrees is dissenting with the dominant opinion.

The remainder of the options, (A) "provocative" (tempting, irritating) . . . "euphonic" (pleasant sounding), (B) "elusive" (hard to catch, difficult to understand) . . . "compatible" (harmonious), (C) "fallacious" (misleading) . . . "austere" (harsh, severe, strict), and (D) "intangible" (immaterial) . . . "reticent" (silent, reserved, shy) are illogical choices for the context of the sentence.

■ QUESTION II.1.65

The westward _____ from the Midwest to California in the 1930s created a large population of _____ workers on the Western produce farms.

(A) influx . . . wandering

(B) movement . . . incapable

(C) expansion . . . lackadaisical

(D) highways . . . hopeful

(E) exodus . . . migrant

ANSWER

(E) This is a cause-and-effect sentence in which the action described in the first half of the sentence caused the quality of the workers described in the second half. Furthermore, the phrase "from the Midwest to California" should indicate that the first word shows movement out of an area. The word that fits this definition is "exodus"; therefore, (E) is the best choice. An exodus would cause a large incidence of migrant workers.

Choices (A) "influx" and (D) "highways" would not be appropriate answers.

Choice (B) "movement" is possible, but "incapable" is not meaningfully related to the rest of the sentence.

Choice (C) "expansion" would fit into the first part of the sentence, but "lackadaisical" (lacking spirit or zest) is not connoted by the sentence.

◼ QUESTION II.1.66

Police officers often face _____ situations where they must maintain their _____ .

(A) inhospitable . . . agility

(D) perilous . . . composure

(B) impossible . . . gallantry

(E) extraordinary . . . strength

(C) unequivocable . . . sternness

ANSWER

(D) The first part of the sentence asks for an adjective that describes the type of situation faced by a police officer. The second part of the sentence requires a word that describes a quality the police officers must maintain in the face of the chosen situation. The best answer is (D). Police officers often face "perilous" (dangerous) situations where they must maintain their "composure" (calmness).

Choice (A) is incorrect because although "inhospitable" (not fit for normal living) might be appropriate to the context, "agility" (ability to move quickly) is not a word used with "maintain," nor is it considered a quality of a person's character.

Choice (B) "impossible" is a possible choice for the first part, but "gallantry" is not meaningful to the context.

Choice (C) "unequivocable" (leaving no doubt, clear) is not an appropriate choice for the first part of the sentence. Police officers often face situations which call for judgments because they are not clear-cut.

Choice (E) is a possible answer, but not the best choice. Although police officers face "extraordinary" situations, they don't have to maintain their "strength" at all times.

■ QUESTION II.1.67

The reason that restaurants have their personnel introduce themselves by their first names is that the _____ of familiarity may _____ the customer's inclination to be critical of the service rendered or the meal received.

(A) appearance . . . reduce

(B) affliction . . . retard

(C) reality . . . prohibit

(D) growth . . . limit

(E) pleasure . . . deny

ANSWER

(A)   The correct answer is (A) "appearance . . . reduce." The persons in question remain strangers to each other but on the surface they share a first-name basis, which might reduce the customer's inclination to complain about the service or the food.

Choice (B) "affliction" (to cause pain and torment) is incorrect because it makes no sense that familiarity would cause affliction.

Choice (C) "reality" also has no semantic value when added to the sentence, and makes the ideas meaningless.

Choice (D) "growth" implies that the customer and the personnel will become friends and there is nothing in the context of the sentence that supports this.

Choice (E) "pleasure" may fit the sentence, but it is not possible for "pleasure" to "deny," only people can "deny."

■ QUESTION II.1.68

The heavy spring rains caused the rivers to rise and _____ the surrounding fields.

(A) imbibe

(D) inundate

(B) sedate

(E) acerbate

(C) impugn

ANSWER

(D)   The word "caused" should make us instantly aware of the cause-and-effect relationship in the sentence. We must think logically what would happen as a result of the action described in the first part of the sentence. It makes sense that rising rivers would (D) "inundate" (cover with a flood) the surrounding fields. The word "inundate" is basically a synonym for flood in this case.

(A) "imbibe" (drink, absorb), (B) "sedate" (quiet and dignified), (C) "impugn" (to attack by words or arguments), and (E) "acerbate" (irritate, exasperate) are not words that would be used to describe what excessive water would do to surrounding fields.

■ QUESTION II.1.69

_____ is a key variable in relation to achievement; talent, support, effort, and practice are all important, but the fact remains: those who _____ to succeed go the furthest.

(A) Potential . . . need

(D) Training . . . struggle

(B) Desire . . . want

(E) Education . . . hope

(C) Heredity . . . train

ANSWER

(B)   The best choice is "Desire . . . want." The first blank identifies a key variable in relation to achievement, and the second blank requires you to find a synonym of the word in the first blank. The key phrase here is "but the fact remains," which tells you that what follows will be a reiteration of the first sentence. All of the other choices [(A), (C), (D), and (E)] have potentially correct first words; it is the second word that we must consider.

(A) "need" is not a synonym for "potential," and is therefore incorrect.

(C) "train" has no relation to "heredity," and would be an incorrect choice for the context of the sentence.

(D) "struggle" is not an appropriate choice because it is not a synonym for "train."

(E) "Hope" is not correct because it is not contextually related to "education" in the sentence.

■ QUESTION II.1.70

The _____ of the young student gave way to _____ as the semester progressed.

(A) provinciality . . . anarchy   (D) insecurity . . . confidence

(B) animosity . . . amity   (E) beneficence . . . profundity

(C) resignation . . . coalescence

ANSWER

(D)   We are looking for a word that describes a student's initial feelings in the first part of the sentence. The second word would be an antonym because the sentence says that the initial feelings "gave way . . . as the semester progressed." The best answer is (D). The student was "insecure" (uncertain, shaky) in the beginning of the semester, but became "confident" (self-assured) as the semester progressed.

(A) "provinciality" (narrow in ideas, confined to a region) and "anarchy" (a social structure without government) is incorrect. The words are contextually inaccurate in this sentence.

(B) "animosity" (ill will, resentment) and "amity" (friendship) meet the criteria of being antonyms, but do not fit into the meaning of the sentence. It is unlikely that a student will start a semester feeling resentful; it is more credible that he/she will begin by feeling insecure about the courses, professors, etc.

(C) "resignation" (give up deliberately) and "coalescence" (merging, blending) are meaningless when inserted into the sentence.

(E) "beneficience" (beneficial quality) and "profundity" (deep intellectual insights) have no relationship to the meaning of the sentence.

■ QUESTION II.1.71

The bitter root, when properly cooked, was converted into a(n) _____ and nutritious food.

(A) palatable   (D) appealing

(B) dissonant   (E) decorous

(C) delightful

ANSWER

(A)   The best answer is (A) "palatable" (agreeable to the taste). The sentence implies that the "bitter root," when cooked, converts (changes) into a food that is then agreeable, not bitter. The key word here is "converted" which implies that something changed to its opposite, so we are looking for the antonym of "bitter."

(B) "dissonant" (discord) is not appropriate to the meaning of the sentence.

(C) "delightful" is not a word that is the opposite of "bitter" with regard to food.

(D) "appealing" (to arouse a sympathetic response) might be considered a possibility, but "palatable" is the most likely antonym of "bitter."

(E) "decorous" (proper, seemly, correct) has no meaningful relationship to food.

■ QUESTION II.1.72

The home team fans greeted their players with _____ , but treated their rivals with _____ .

(A) arrogance . . . urbanity

(B) reverie . . . defamation

(C) complacency . . . maliciousness

(D) alacrity . . . derision

(E) valor . . . discord

ANSWER

(D) The home team players will be "greeted" by a positive adjective, and the rivals will be "treated" with a negative adjective; therefore, the best answer is (D). The home team fans greeted their players with "alacrity" (enthusiasm, fervor), and the rivals were treated with "derision" (scorn, ridicule).

Choice (A) is incorrect because the fans would not greet their home team with "arrogance" (conceit).

"Reverie" (daydream) is not an appropriate word for the answer, so (B) is a bad choice.

(C) "complacency" (self-satisfied, smug) is not an adjective that describes how fans would greet their home team.

(E) "valor" (personal bravery, heroism) is not an appropriate choice for this sentence. It doesn't make any sense when added to the text.

■ QUESTION II.1.73

As the city grows and more suburbs are annexed, its parks will become _____ for its needs; therefore, land should be purchased to provide _____ parks in the outlying suburbs.

(A) insufficient . . . updated   (D) important . . . new

(B) depleted . . . more   (E) inadequate . . . additional

(C) deficient . . . larger

ANSWER

(E)   The sentence implies that the city is growing. Under this circumstance, there will not be enough parks for the amount of people; therefore, more land should be purchased in the suburbs that will provide room for more parks. The best word choice that meets the context of the sentence is (E) "inadequate" to describe the amount of parks, and "additional" to tell that many parks will be provided "in the outlying suburbs."

(A) "insufficient" (not sufficient) is a possibility, but "updated" does not work because we are told that there won't be enough parks, not that those that exist are out of date.

(B) "depleted" (exhausted) implies that the amount of parks will be used up and is not appropriate to the context of the sentence.

(C) "deficient" (lacking in something necessary) is an appropriate word to describe the parks, but "larger" does not fit the context because the sentence tells us that more parks are needed, not necessarily larger ones.

(D) "important" is not a proper choice for the context of the sentence, because the parks were important to the city even before growth occurred.

■ QUESTION II.1.74

The use of a pen with indelible ink will _____ a student's ability to _____ at a later time.

(A) preclude . . . erase   (D) deplete . . . digress

(B) hinder . . . slander   (E) enhance . . . ameliorate

(C) nullify . . . desecrate

ANSWER

(A)   The key word here is "indelible." An indelible pen is one that has permanent ink that can never be erased; therefore, the use of such a pen will "preclude" (make impossible) a student's ability to "erase" at a later time. (A) is the best choice.

(B) "hinder" (interfere) is possible, but whether a student uses an indelible pen does not affect the ability to "slander" (defame).

Choice (C) "nullify" (cancel, invalidate) is possible, but not when coupled with "desecrate" (violate a holy place).

Choice (D) "deplete" (reduce, empty) is not meaningful in the sentence.

Choice (E) "enhance" (improve) and "ameliorate" (to make better) are not semantically logical choices for the sentence.

■ QUESTION II.1.75

Committees are ineffective when they cannot agree upon what to do or just how to go about accomplishing it; this situation is a(n) _____ of faulty _____ of committee responsibility.

(A) factor . . . acceptance   (D) part . . . knowledge

(B) cause . . . guidelines   (E) example . . . direction

(C) result . . . specifications

ANSWER

(C)   The two parts of this sentence, although divided by a semicolon, are joined in a cause-and-effect relationship. The first part states a problem, and the second shows how that problem was caused. In fact, the first blank calls for a verb that shows this is a cause-and-effect sentence. Such a verb is "result," which suggests that one condition causes another. Since the stated problem is "ineffectiveness," we must choose a word that would fit into the sentence to describe a condition that would cause this. If the committees did not know their responsibilities, it is likely that they would be ineffective; therefore, "specifications" (a description of work to be done) is the best word for the sentence.

Choices (A) "factor," (D) "part," and (E) "example" are incorrect because the situation described affects the whole committee all of the time, and not just part of it or on certain occasions. (B) "cause" is incorrect because the situation is a result, not a cause of the faulty specifications.

■ QUESTION II.1.76

After winning the award, her once pleasant personality altered. She was now consistently _____ and _____ .

(A) arrogant . . . authoritative   (D) depraved . . . holy

(B) ambivalent . . . determined   (E) erratic . . . organized

(C) skeptical . . . gullible

ANSWER

(A)   This sentence requires you to find two adjectives that are the opposite of "pleasant personality." The key words are "once" and "altered." The best answer would be "arrogant" (acting superior to others, conceited) and "authoritative" (demanding obedience), because, being negative, these are opposite to a "pleasant" personality. Somebody who was once pleasant might win an award and become arrogant and authoritative.

Choice (B) "ambivalent" (undecided) makes no sense in relation to the context, even though "determined" (being single-minded in purpose) is possible.

Choice (C) "skeptical" (doubtful) and "gullible" (easily fooled) are not correct. "Depraved" (morally corrupt) and "holy" (D) make absolutely no sense in the context of the sentence.

Choice (E) "erratic" and "organized" are not correct choices. Although "erratic" (unpredictable, strange) is possible, "organized" is a poor choice.

■ QUESTION II.1.77

> The weekly program on public radio is the most _____ means of educating the public about pollution.
>
> (A) proficient   (D) capable
>
> (B) effusive   (E) competent
>
> (C) effectual

ANSWER

(C)   To find the correct word for this sentence, you must agree that public radio is the best way to reach a large audience. If that is true, then the word that logically fits is the one that supports this idea. "Effectual" (having the power to produce the exact effect or result) is the best choice.

(A) "proficient" (competency that is above average), (B) "effusive" (too emotional), (D) "capable" (able to produce results), and (E) "competent" (capable, fit, qualified) are words that refer to people and would not be used to describe the effects of a radio program.

■ QUESTION II.1.78

> The board members _____ the organization for the _____ measures it had adopted to save money during the recession.
>
> (A) extolled . . . hedonistic   (D) denounced . . . exhaustive
>
> (B) censured . . . expedient   (E) lauded . . . stringent
>
> (C) revered . . . frivolous

ANSWER

(E)   The best answer is (E) "lauded" (praised) and "stringent" (strict, severe). The most effective way of answering the question would be to look at the second part of the sentence and ask which word fits best with "measures it had adopted to save money during the recession." "Stringent" is the correct choice, because if the organization took "stringent measures" and saved money during a bad economy (recession), then the board would "laud" them.

(A) "extolled" (praised, commended) is correct for the first space, but "hedonistic" (pleasure seeking) does not fit the context of the sentence.

(B) "censured" (criticized or disapproved of) and "expedient" (speed up, make easier) do not fit into the sentence. The board would not "censure" the committee for "expedient" measures to save money.

(C) "revered" (worshipped) is an incorrect choice for the sentence. It is semantically meaningless.

(D) "denounced" (condemned) is an inappropriate choice if the committee tried "exhaustive" (thorough, complete) measures to save money.

■ QUESTION II.1.79

Although her bedroom at home was always in disarray, her office work space was _____ .

(A) aloof

(D) diligent

(B) meticulous

(E) insipid

(C) viable

ANSWER

(B) "Meticulous" (exacting, precise) is the best answer because the context of the sentence asks for a word that is opposite in meaning to "disarray" (to be out of order, disorganized). The key word here is "although," which implies that whatever follows the first thought will be contradictory in meaning.

(A) "aloof" (distant in interest, reserved) is incorrect because this is an adjective that is usually used to describe a person, not a work area.

(C) "viable" (capable of maintaining life, possible) is an inappropriate word choice as an antonym for "meticulous."

(D) "diligent" (hard-working) is a word that describes a person's characteristics, and is not a good choice for the sentence.

(E) "insipid" (uninteresting, bland) is not an adjective that meets the conditions of the sentence, as it is not a word that is opposite in meaning to "meticulous."

■ QUESTION II.1.80

The pitcher tried to _____ the wounded catcher through increased
_____ .

(A) tarry . . . spending

(B) offset . . . concentration

(C) mediate . . . dedication

(D) divulge . . . repugnance

(E) alleviate . . . preparation

ANSWER

(B) The best answer is "offset" (balance, compensate for) and "concentration." The sentence tells us that the catcher is wounded, and therefore the pitcher (who works as a team with the catcher) has to make up for this deficiency. "Offset" tells us that the pitcher will compensate for the catcher's injury by improving his own performance through "concentration."

(A) "tarry" (to delay) and "spending" make no sense when substituted into the context of the sentence.

(C) "mediate" (acting as an intermediary to settle a dispute) and "dedication" are not meaningful. The pitcher's increased dedication does not mediate a wounded catcher.

(D) "divulge" (reveal, disclose) is not an appropriate choice because it makes no sense when put into the sentence.

(E) "alleviate" (to make easier) is not the correct choice because "alleviate" is used in conjunction with a symptom or a circumstance, not a person.

■ QUESTION II.1.81

Despite the fact that they believed in different political philosophies, the politicians agreed to _____ on issues when their goals
were _____ .

(A) digress . . . ambivalent   (D) demur . . . provocative

(B) concede . . . controversial   (E) collaborate . . . compatible

(C) dissent . . . viable

ANSWER

(E)   The phrase "Despite the fact . . . " suggests that the results of the situation described in the sentence will be different than one would normally expect.
The second part of the sentence, after the word "when," shows the specific
conditions necessary for this unexpected condition to occur; therefore, (E) is
the best answer, because politicians from different political parties wouldn't
normally "collaborate" (cooperate) with each other, but they might only do so
if their goals were "compatible" (in agreement).

Choice (A) "digress" (stray from the subject) and "ambivalent" (undecided)
do not make any sense when substituted into the sentence.

(B) is only partially correct in that "concede" would fit in, but then "controversial" would not. Politicians wouldn't agree if their goals were controversial.

Choice (C) is incorrect because it is rare that people, even politicians, agree
to "dissent," or disagree, especially on issues that are "viable" (workable).

(D) is a possibility because politicians may agree to "demur," or object, to
"provocative" issues, but it is not the best answer. We are looking for a word
that is a strong synonym for "agree," and that word is "collaborate."

■ QUESTION II.1.82

The poet's _____ style caused the publisher to _____ its contract with her.

(A) sycophantical . . . coil   (D) enduring . . . acclaim

(B) slipshod . . . renew   (E) prosaic . . . praise

(C) uninspired . . . cancel

ANSWER

(C)   The word "caused" in this sentence is an immediate indication that the sentence contains a cause-and-effect relationship. We are looking for an adjective that describes the poet's style and a verb that tells how the publisher was affected by that style; therefore, the words must mirror one another. If the style is described negatively, the publisher must take negative actions, or vice versa. The best answer is (C), because an "uninspired" (not arousing) style is a negative quality for a poet and might provoke a publisher to "cancel" a contract.

Of the remaining options, (B) and (E) don't work because they are antithetical; one word is negative and the other is positive. (A) and (D) don't work because it is impossible either to "coil" or to "acclaim" a contract.

■ QUESTION II.1.83

American words and phrases have been added to the lexicon of French and Japanese cultures despite the displeasure of politicians and the _____ of purists.

(A) concession   (D) resolution

(B) neutrality   (E) denunciation

(C) endorsement

ANSWER

(E)   The correct answer is "denunciation," because we are looking for a word that supports "displeasure." The key word here is "and" between the phrase "displeasure of politicians" and "purists." This means that the attitude of the purists is similar to that of the politicians.

(A) is incorrect because "concession" (give in) is the opposite of displeasure.

(B) is wrong because "neutrality" suggests that the purists won't take a stand; however, the sentence tells us that the purists hold the same attitude as the politicians.

(C) "endorsement" is wrong because it is the opposite in meaning to "denunciation," and we are looking for a word that has a parallel connotation.

(D) is wrong because "resolution" (determination) is not logical to the context of the sentence.

■ QUESTION II.1.84

Evan is five feet five inches tall and inclines towards stoutness, but his erect bearing and quick movements tend to _____ this.

(A) emphasize   (D) camouflage

(B) conceal   (E) disavow

(C) denigrate

ANSWER

(D)   The word "but" in this sentence means that something will turn out differently than the originally described situation might lead us to expect. From the description of Evan as relatively short and large, it is a surprise that he is "quick" and that he has an "erect bearing." The word we are looking for is a verb that causes this disparity. (D) "camouflage" (disguise in order to conceal) is the best answer, because it implies that things are not as they seem or as we expect them to be.

"Emphasize" (A) (to stress) is wrong because it would have the opposite effect to that described in the sentence.

"Conceal" (B) (to remove from view) might be considered as a possibility, but it is not the best choice. His bearing and movements do not "hide" his appearance; they only disguise him.

(C) "denigrate" and (E) "disavow" are synonyms meaning "to deny." Evan's movements and bearing do not "deny" his appearance; they disguise him.

■ QUESTION II.1.85

Some people say that fashion is _____ . What is in style today is outdated tomorrow.

(A) illicit   (D) circuitous

(B) capricious   (E) idiosyncratic

(C) benign

ANSWER

(B)   The second sentence acts as a definition for the word that fits into the blank. "Capricious" (changing suddenly) is the best choice. "What is in style today is outdated tomorrow" means that fashion trends can change suddenly, or from day to day and this is described by the word "capricious."

(A) "illicit" (not licensed) and (D) "circuitous" (not being forthright or direct in language or action) are inappropriate choices.

(E) "idiosyncratic" (peculiar tendency of a person) and (C) "benign" (kindly) are words used to describe people—not things.

■ QUESTION II.1.86

Although they tried to implicate him, they could not. He stated _____ and unequivocally that he was not involved in the crime.

(A) categorically   (D) fallibly

(B) contritely   (E) ignominiously

(C) elatedly

ANSWER

(A)   "Categorically" (absolutely, unqualified) is the best choice. We are looking for a word that is related as a synonym to "unequivocally" (leaving no doubt, clear) because of the key word "and," which joins the word in the blank with the word "unequivocally." The sentence context implies that the man could not be implicated because he stated in a very clear, absolute way that he was not involved.

(B) "contritely" (remorsefully) is a poor choice because the man wouldn't feel remorse if he were not involved in the crime.

(C) "elatedly" (joyfully) is inappropriate because the man wouldn't feel joyful if someone were trying to implicate him in a crime.

(D) "fallibly" (being deceived) and (E) "ignominiously" (disgracefully) make no sense in the context of this sentence.

■ QUESTION II.1.87

The Civil War was the _____ of the inability of the North and South to _____ on an interpretation of the Constitution.

(A) epitome . . . concur

(B) climax . . . agree

(C) drama . . . unite

(D) chaos . . . harmonize

(E) finalization . . . cooperate

ANSWER

(B)   In this sentence we must find words that fit into the cause-and-effect relationship. Some inability of the North and South caused the Civil War. Many wars are caused by disagreements, so it makes sense that this was caused by an inability to "agree." The first blank can be filled by logically assuming that the two parties had been struggling for some time to interpret the Constitution, but that the situation had gotten worse and worse. In such a case, war would come as a crucial moment or "climax."

Options (C) and (D) are not viable because it does not make sense to say the "drama of the inability" or "the chaos of the inability."

Choices (A) and (E) come closer to being appropriate, but they lack the connotation of the great impact of war that "climax" suggests.

■ QUESTION II.1.88

If you are not a medical person, you may find it _____ to _____ a simple fracture from a sprain.

(A) necessary . . . ascertain   (D) difficult . . . distinguish

(B) easy . . . determine   (E) wont . . . figure

(C) illusory . . . analyze

ANSWER

(D)   The second half of this sentence requires a word that describes the action of making a choice. The first half shows how the action of making this choice would affect someone who is not a doctor. The best answer is (D) because to "distinguish" (to perceive or show the difference) implies an ability to make a choice, and such an action would be "difficult" for someone without medical training.

(A) Although "ascertain" (to learn by inquiry) is possibly a good answer, "necessary" does not fit the context of the sentence because "if" you are not a medical person, you probably will NOT find it necessary to tell a fracture from a sprain.

(B) "easy" is inappropriate, because if you are not a medical person, it would not be easy to diagnose a medical situation.

(C) "illusory" (based on misconception, illusion) and (E) "wont" (custom, habit) are not the correct answers within the context of the sentence.

■ QUESTION II.1.89

The spacecraft Voyager, which travelled to Jupiter, was _____ because it was the only space vehicle to _____ a recorded message from our planet to distant star systems.

(A) blasphemous . . . meander   (D) unique . . . transport

(B) egocentric . . . trek   (E) vital . . . copy

(C) profound . . . provoke

ANSWER

(D) The correct answer contains an adjective that supports the word "only" and a verb that shows how a "recorded message" goes to "distant star systems." "Unique" means "one of a kind" and is the best choice to describe "only space vehicle"; "transport" (to carry) is the best choice to describe how "a recorded message" is carried to "distant star systems."

(A) is not meaningful because "blasphemous" and "meander" cannot describe a spacecraft.

(B) "egocentric" (self-centered) describes a person, not an inanimate object such as a spacecraft.

(C) "profound" (knowledgeable) is also not a good way to describe a spacecraft, for while the message may have been profound, certainly a machine is not.

(E) "vital" (important) is a possibility, but not within the context of the sentence where we are looking for a word that means the spacecraft is the "only" one.

QUESTION II.1.90

The spelling and pronunciation of some English words are _____ because they don't follow _____ rules.

(A) infamous . . . prosaic

(D) hackneyed . . . verbose

(B) erratic . . . inevitable

(E) incoherent . . . prudent

(C) fallacious . . . hypothetical

ANSWER

(B) The use of the word "because" in this relationship creates a cause-and-effect relationship. We are looking for one adjective for "rules," which has a specific effect on "words," demonstrated in this sentence by an adjective. The use of the negative "don't" in the second half of the sentence, however, turns the word around to its opposite; therefore, the correct answer has two adjectives that are almost opposite in meaning. The best answer is (B) "erratic" (unpredictable, strange) and "inevitable" (sure to happen).

(A) is incorrect because words cannot be described as "infamous" (having a bad reputation).

(C) is not correct because although the words may be "fallacious" (misleading), the rules cannot be "hypothetical" (uncertain). These are not opposite in meaning.

(D) is wrong because although "hackneyed" (trite) may fit the first part of the sentence, "verbose" (wordy, talkative) does not fit into the second part. Rules may be "verbose," but that would not explain why the spelling and pronunciation of the English words are "hackneyed" (commonplace, trite).

(E) is a possibility, but not the best choice. Spelling and pronunciation may be "incoherent" (illogical) to some people, but not to all; "prudent" (wise) is not an acceptable way to describe spelling rules.

■ QUESTION II.1.91

Before an inventor can receive a patent, the U.S. Patent and Trademark Office _____ the application to verify that a _____ invention doesn't exist.

(A) investigates . . . distorted   (D) questions . . . probable

(B) scrutinizes . . . comparable   (E) analyzes . . . contrasting

(C) expedites . . . compatible

ANSWER

(B)   "Scrutinizes . . . comparable" is the correct answer because we are looking for a verb to describe the action of the Patent Office and an adjective to describe why an inventor wouldn't receive a patent. The inventor would receive the patent if a "comparable" (similar) type of invention "doesn't exist." All of the verbs except (C) could adequately fit into the sentence; therefore, it is the second word that makes the difference in the other choices: (A), (D), (E).

Choice (A) is wrong because if an inventor creates a "distorted" (to twist out of normal shape) invention, he would not necessarily receive a patent.

(C) "expedites" (to make easier) is incorrect because it does not imply that the Patent Office is created to look carefully at an application to "verify" (to confirm) that a similar one doesn't exist.

(D) is wrong because "probable" (possible) doesn't fit into the context of the sentence.

(E) "contrasting" (the opposite of) is incorrect because it would not matter if a contrasting invention exists.

■ QUESTION II.1.92

George Burns, the poet, spent most of his youth as a farmer; as a result, some of his poems reflect his _____ background.

(A) trite   (D) ominous

(B) slavish   (E) urbane

(C) provincial

ANSWER

(C)   Choice (C) "provincial" is the best answer because we are looking for a word that is related to "farmer," and "provincial" means "regional or unsophisticated." "As a result" creates a cause-and-effect relationship that tells us that the subject of some of Burns' poetry is directly related to his upbringing.

(A) "trite" (commonplace, overused) is incorrect because it is not semantically related to the meaning of the sentence.

(B) "slavish" (obedient) and (D) "ominous" (threatening) are not appropriate words to describe a farmer.

(E) "urbane" (city-like) is the opposite of anything having to do with farming and is not a viable choice.

■ QUESTION II.1.93

The salesperson's _____ voice was exceptionally annoying. Potential customers avoided going anywhere near her product.

(A) exorbitant   (D) strident

(B) uproarious   (E) egocentric

(C) docile

ANSWER

(D)   "Strident" is the best answer because we are looking for a word to describe a voice that is a synonym to "exceptionally annoying." A "strident" (harsh-sounding) voice is annoying to hear and would keep people away.

(A) "exorbitant" (excessive), (B) "uproarious" (making a great tumult), (C) "docile" (easily taught, led, or managed), and (E) "egocentric" (self-centered) are all incorrect because not only are none of them synonymous with "annoying," but they are also all words better used to describe a person than a voice.

■ QUESTION II.1.94

> Not all persons whose lives are _____ remain provincial; some have the intellectual and personal characteristics that enable them to develop a(n) _____ orientation to life.
>
> (A) confirmed . . . philanthropic   (D) restricted . . . cosmopolitan
>
> (B) limited . . . hedonistic   (E) restrained . . . fastidious
>
> (C) circumscribed . . . altruistic

ANSWER

(D)   The best answer is (D) "restricted" (limited) . . . "cosmopolitan" (belonging to all the world). In the first part of the sentence, the correct word would be one that describes a "provincial" life. The best answer is "restricted." The second part of the sentence requires a word that relates to the following key sentence clues: "Not all." This means that the second word required will be an antonym of "restricted." The best choice is "cosmopolitan" (at home anywhere in the world).

(A) "confirmed" (ratified) and "philanthropic" (doing charitable acts or deeds) have no relation to the meaning of the sentence.

(B) "limited" is a good choice for the first part of the sentence; however, "hedonistic" (living for pleasure) is not appropriate for the second part of the sentence.

(C) "circumscribed" (limit narrowly a range of options) is also a possibility for the first part of the sentence, but "altruistic" (unselfish) is inappropriate for the second part.

(E) "restrained" (prevented from doing something) may be correctly inserted into the sentence, but "fastidious" (difficult to please) is not a correct word for the sentence.

■ QUESTION II.1.95

The air around the overgrown boat dock reeked with the _____ odor of seaweed, damp, and dead fish.

(A) malodorous   (D) redolent

(B) rankling   (E) pungent

(C) flavorful

ANSWER

(A)   We are looking for an adjective that describes the "odor of seaweed, damp, and dead fish." In addition, the verb "reeked" (to give off or become permeated with a strong, disagreeable odor) indicates that this will be a rather disgusting smell. (A) "malodorous" (having a bad odor) is the best choice.

(B) "rankling" (to fester, to cause anger) does not meet the conditions set forth in the previous sentences.

(C) "flavorful" is wrong because we are looking for a very disagreeable smell, and this word suggests the opposite. For the same reason, (D) "redolent" (fragrant, aromatic) is incorrect.

(E) "pungent" having a sharp taste or smell is not a correct substitute in this sentence because a pungent odor is not necessarily negative.

■ QUESTION II.1.96

It is good advice to _____ any document that requires your signature.

(A) efface   (D) despoil

(B) mollify   (E) scrutinize

(C) broach

ANSWER

(E)   If a document requires your signature, then it is a good idea to (E) "scrutinize" (examine closely, study) it. (E) is the best answer because it is logical and makes the most sense.

(A) is wrong, because it would not be a good idea or "good advice" to "efface" (wipe out, erase) your signature on a document.

"Mollify" (B) (to soothe in temper) makes no sense in this sentence.

Choice (C) "broach" (introduce as a topic for a sentence or conversation) and choice (D) "despoil" (to strip of belongings) are meaningless in relation to the word "document."

■ QUESTION II.1.97

The _____ mob _____ all semblance of law and order.
(A) ubiquitous . . . avoided   (D) impetuous . . . hindered
(B) tyrannical . . . thwarted   (E) indifferent . . . salvaged
(C) unruly . . . relinquished

ANSWER

(C)   In this question, we are looking for an adjective to describe a mob and a verb that relates the mob to "law and order." The best answer is (C). The "unruly" (not submitting to discipline, disobedient) mob "relinquished" (abandoned) all semblance (appearance) of law and order. A "mob" is usually described as "a large, disorderly group of people"; therefore, "unruly" is the best word to use as an adjective.

(A) "ubiquitous" (ever present in all places, universal) is not an appropriate adjective to use in describing a mob; and although "avoided" may be appropriate, this answer is wrong.

(B) "tyrannical" (having absolute power) is a possible way of describing a mob; however, it is not the best choice. In addition, "thwarted" (frustrate) is not appropriate with "semblance."

(D) "impetuous" (rash, impulsive) . . . "hindered" (blocked) and (E) "indifferent" (unbiased) . . . "salvaged" (rescued from loss) cannot be used in the sentence because they do not make any semantic sense.

■ QUESTION II.1.98

The spectators were astounded by his _____ move. They had never seen anyone accomplish such a fearless maneuver.

(A) banal   (D) audacious

(B) truculent   (E) uncanny

(C) charismatic

ANSWER

(D)   We are looking for an adjective that describes the kind of move relating to a "fearless maneuver" that would "astound" spectators. The best answer is (D) "audacious" (fearless, bold).

(A) "banal" (common, petty, ordinary) is incorrect because it is the opposite in meaning to the word we are looking for. A maneuver that is common or ordinary would not "astound" spectators.

(B) "truculent" (aggressive) is an adjective that describes a person, not an action.

(C) "charismatic" (appealing, magnetic personality) is an adjective that might relate, but it is not the best choice, because, once again "charisma" is a word that often describes a personality, not an action.

(E) "uncanny" (of a strange nature, weird) does not fit with "fearless," and is not the correct choice.

■ QUESTION II.1.99

Not wanting to face the dire consequences of her actions, she _____ for as long as she could before she appeared before the committee.

(A) tarried   (D) vacillated

(B) waned   (E) disparaged

(C) stagnated

ANSWER

(A)   The sentence implies that she is reluctant to face "the dire consequences of her actions," and so we are looking for a word that would describe how she stretched the time "before she appeared before the committee." The best choice is (A) "tarried" (to go or move slowly, delay). (B) "waned" (grow gradually smaller) makes absolutely no sense when fitted into the sentence because a person cannot "wane."

(C) "stagnated" (motionless, dull, inactive) is a possibility, but is probably unlikely. People do not usually remain inactive when they know they have to do something.

(D) "vacillated" (fluctuated) makes some sense in the sentence but it is not as good a choice as "tarried," because it implies a choice between two options, which is not mentioned in the sentence.

(E) "disparaged" (belittled, undervalued) makes no sense when inserted into the sentence.

■ QUESTION II.1.100

In the early 1900s the chinchilla became almost _____ because of the _____ demand for its fur.

(A) prosaic . . . redundant   (D) extinct . . . prodigious

(B) obsolete . . . incidental   (E) hypothetical . . . unique

(C) banal . . . inadvertent

ANSWER

(D)   "Extinct" (no longer existing) and "prodigious" (exceptional, tremendous) are the best choices to complete this sentence. The word "because" makes us aware that we are looking for two words that relate logically to each other in a cause-and-effect relationship. Some quality of the chinchilla caused it to become a certain way. The chinchilla became almost "extinct" because of the "prodigious" demand for its fur; because so many people desired the chinchilla's fur, they almost wiped out the entire population of the animal.

(A) "prosaic" (tiresome, ordinary) is an inappropriate word to describe an animal.

(B) "obsolete" (no longer in use) is incorrect because "obsolete" refers to inanimate things, not people or animals.

(C) "banal" (common, petty, ordinary) is a word that is opposite in connotation to the meaning of the sentence.

(E) "hypothetical" (assumed, uncertain) is not meaningfully related to the context of the sentence.

UNIT 2: PASSAGE-BASED READING

The role that passage-based reading plays in the New SAT should be fully comprehended by anyone hoping to earn a top score. In the Critical Reading sections, passage-based reading questions outnumber Sentence Completions 5 to 2. Half of the more than one hundred verbal multiple-choice questions on the test measure your ability to extract meaning efficiently from prose passages. "Why," you must wonder, "would this much importance be attached to reading?" The reason is simple. Your ability to read at a strong pace while grasping a solid understanding of the material is a key factor in your high school performance and your potential college success. And your grasp of the SAT passages must go beyond simple comprehension. You'll need to be able to analyze and evaluate the passages and make inferences about the writers' meaning. Even your ability to understand vocabulary in context will come under scrutiny. "Can I meet the challenge?" you ask yourself. Yes, and preparation is the means!

CRITICAL READING PASSAGES AND QUESTIONS

There are three Critical Reading sections in the test (two 25-minute sections and one 20-minute section). More than two-thirds of the questions in each of these sections are based on short and long passages (the rest are Sentence Completion questions). The short passages are about one hundred words long and are typically followed by two questions. The long passages fall into two categories: 400- to 550-word passages followed by 7 or 8 questions and 700- to 850-word passages followed by as many as 13 or 14 questions. Both the short and long passages may appear as paired passages—two passages addressing the same topic or theme from different perspectives. Whatever the combination of short, long, or paired passages, they will form the basis for 17 to 20 Reading Comprehension questions per section.

The reading content of the passages will cover:

- the humanities (philosophy, the fine arts)

- the social sciences (psychology, archaeology, anthropology, economics, political science, sociology, history)

- the natural sciences (biology, geology, astronomy, chemistry, physics)

- narration (fiction, nonfiction)

Familiarize yourself with these basic departments of human expression and inquiry. As you read the sample passages, find out which interest you most. Because you can start anywhere in a given section, you may want to start with a reading passage that interests you and gives you the momentum needed to plow efficiently through the questions.

You will encounter four kinds of Reading Comprehension questions:

1. Synthesis/Analysis

2. Evaluation

3. Vocabulary-in-Context

4. Interpretation

Although you'll never be required to identify these question types, getting familiar with them as you review for the test and do practice questions will hone your reading skills and help make the test seem more manageable.

ABOUT THE DIRECTIONS

Make sure to study and learn the directions to save yourself time during the actual test. You should simply skim them when beginning the section. The directions will read similar to the following.

DIRECTIONS: Read each passage and answer the questions that follow. Each question will be based on the information stated or implied in the passage or its introduction.

A variation of these directions will be presented as follows for the double passage.

DIRECTIONS: Read the passages and answer the questions that follow. Each question will be based on the information stated or implied in the selections or their introductions, and may be based on the relationship between the passages.

IDENTIFYING PASSAGE AND QUESTION TYPES

ow are four short passages, each drawn from one of the content areas men-
d above (i.e., the humanities, social sciences, sciences, and narration). The

questions that follow have been designed to illustrate the four kinds of Reading Comprehension questions. The explanations of correct answer choices will suggest strategies for identifying and approaching each question type.

An in-depth explanation of the four question types occurs after the sample short passages.

Consult it as you try to identify the question types.

SHORT PASSAGE #1

1   A biologist has to look no further than cya-
    nobacteria to find an ecological illustration
    of the dangers posed by too much of a good
    thing. Also known as blue-green algae, cyano-
5   bacteria helps keep the atmosphere life-sus-
    taining; through photosynthesis, it produces
    more oxygen than all land plants combined.
    Phytoplankton, a kind of cyanobacteria that
    floats on the surface of lakes and oceans, is
10 the principle food source for many organisms.
    But too much blue-green algae can be toxic.
    When an excess of nitrates allows it to grow
    unchecked, cyanobacteria can start to blanket
    lakes and ponds with a smelly blue-green film
15 that kills off fish populations and even threat-
    ens human health.

The preceding passage is drawn from which of the following?

   (A) Humanities, (B) Social Sciences, (C) Natural Sciences, or (D) Nar-
       ration

1.   Based on the passage, the writer would most likely characterize cyano-
     bacteria as

     (A)   a necessary evil within the global environment.

     (B)   an important but potentially harmful organism.

     (C)   an insignificant contributor to the atmosphere.

     (D)   a powerful antidote to fresh and saltwater toxins.

     (E)   proof that too much of a good thing is not enough.

Question Type: Synthesis/Analysis

Explanation: Synthesis and analysis are complementary modes of thought. To analyze is to "break down" into parts; to synthesize is to "put together" to form a whole. Both the question stem and the answer choices indicate that the test taker is being asked to assess the author's general attitude toward cyanobacteria. We can only know how an author might be likely to "characterize" something (which would be an expression of attitude) if the passage provides enough clues about the author's attitude. These clues come in the form of specific word choices that can be identified (i.e., analyzed) within a text. Taken together—that is, synthesized—these word choices form an overall tone, which in turn can suggest a general attitude.

The author describes cyanobacteria as a "good thing" that "helps" make the air around us "life-sustaining" and that acts as the "principle food source" for many creatures. Together, the words in quotes suggest a positive attitude based on the conviction that blue-green algae has an important role to play. The author also describes the algae as potentially "toxic," "smelly," and capable of "killing" or "threatening." Again, the word choice establishes a tone—in this case, a tone that suggests the author's repugnance for the algae's "dark side." Choice (B) best captures the author's attitude toward cyanobacteria's positive and negative aspects. Choice (A) is incorrect because it disregards the author's positive attitude toward the algae. Choice (C) directly contradicts the author's assertion that the algae contributes more oxygen to the atmosphere than all other sources combined. Choice (D) is not correct because, although the notion of toxicity is introduced, cyanobacteria is described as a potential toxin, not a neutralizer of toxins. Choice (E) is incorrect because it completely contradicts the passage's opening statement while seeming to rephrase it in simpler terms.

2.   As used in the passage, the word "unchecked" (line 13) most nearly means

   (A)   unobserved.

   (B)   uncontrolled.

   (C)   unexplained.

   (D)   undisciplined.

   (E)   unexpected.

Question Type: Vocabulary-in-Context

Explanation: All vocabulary-in-context questions have the same format. A word or phrase from the passage is isolated, and the test taker is asked to choose best possible synonym based on how the word is used in the passage. The ences immediately preceding and immediately following the sentence that contains the vocabulary word are usually all the "context" you'll need to determine the contextual meaning of the word.

In the passage, the author states that an "excess of nitrates" may cause the cyanobacteria to "blanket" the body of water it inhabits. The words "excess" and "blanket" both suggest an overabundance—a state of affairs in which too much of something is resulting in the water being nearly or totally covered by the algae. The implication is that the cyanobacteria had not been controlled by the usual environmental factors that keep the algae's growth in check. The correct answer is (B). Choice (A) is not correct because the algae's growth has clearly been observed by biologists. Choice (C) is incorrect because the passage explains why the algae grows—because of an "excess of nitrates." Choice (D) is not correct because "undisciplined" is a human characteristic, and nothing in the passage warrants personifying the bacteria. Choice (E) is not correct because the passage itself states the circumstances under which cyanobacteria is expected to grow. Indeed, the passage is all about scientific expectations concerning cyanobacteria.

SHORT PASSAGE #2

1   The ancient Egyptian word *ka* perfectly illustrates the hazards of interpreting another culture purely in terms of one's own. The ancient Egyptians used the word *ka* to refer to a fun-
5   damental part of the self that is distinct from the physical body. Because the *ka* becomes a crucial factor in one's fate after death, it has often been translated as "soul" or "spirit." But this translation is misleading. After an individ-
10 ual's death, his or her *ka* required sustenance like a living person; it was not so much the essence of the person who had died as it was a stand-in who could act on behalf of the deceased, whom death had incapacitated. The *ka*
15 was more of a helper or guide who ministered to the real focus in the Egyptian conception of the afterlife: the mummified body.

The preceding passage is drawn from which of the following?

(A) Humanities, (B) Social Sciences, (C) Natural Sciences, or (D) Narration

3. The author assumes that the reader will recognize the "soul" as being each of the following EXCEPT

    (A) a part of the self distinct from the body.

    (B) a determining factor in life after death.

    (C) an essential part of the self.

    (D) an entity that does not require food.

    (E) a substitute for the dead body.

Question Type: Evaluation

Explanation: Writers are human. Like all of us, they possess prejudices, make assumptions, and sometimes even argue in the face of reason. Sometimes a writer's assumptions are justified; other times they need to be critically evaluated. A good reader doesn't just get at the writer's meaning; he or she notes and passes judgment on the arguments and assumptions the writer makes in the process of getting that meaning across.

In the preceding passage, the writer attempts to convince us that "soul" does not accurately translate the Egyptian word "ka." The writer then proceeds to detail all the nuances of the word "ka." The writer assumes that we will recognize differences between the meaning of the word "ka" and the meaning of "soul." However, the writer never defines "soul." He or she assumes we already have a rough-and-ready definition in our minds. The evaluation question asks us to piece together the writer's implicit definition of "soul"—the one it is assumed we already know—and identify the one choice that does not constitute an assumption. Choice (A) is not correct because the writer does in fact imply that "soul" and "ka" both designate noncorporeal parts of the self. Choice (B) is not correct because the writer cites the importance of the "ka" in regards to the afterlife as the primary reason that the "ka" has been equated with "soul," implying that the "soul" is important in the same way. Choice (C) is incorrect because, in the portion of the passage where the writer is implicitly contrasting "ka" with "soul," the writer says that the "ka" was NOT the "essence of the person," implying that "soul" does designate "an essential part of the self." Choice (D) is not correct for the same reason that (C) is not correct. Again, in that portion of the passage where "ka" and "soul" are implicitly contrasted, the writer asserts that the "ka" required sustenance, implying that the soul does NOT need nourishment. The correct answer is (E). The writer describes the "ka" as a stand-in (i.e., substitute) when implicitly detailing differences between "ka" and "soul." The writer never assumes that the "soul" functions as a "substitute."

SHORT PASSAGE #3

1 In the past few years, the status of comic
   books has risen dramatically. Long dismissed
   as childish fare, comic books—or "graphic
   novels"—are now embraced as serious art.
5 Poignant works such as Daniel Clowes' *Ghost
   World* have begun to receive the critical attention once reserved for serious fiction and
   poetry. Of course, the newfound legitimacy of
   comic books is due in no small part to a sea
10 change in their content. In the world of comic
   book art, the superhero battling evil has yielded to the flawed everyman slogging through
   an existence strangely like our own.

The preceding passage is drawn from which of the following?

   (A) Humanities, (B) Social Sciences, (C) Natural Sciences, or (D) Nar-
       ration

4.   It can be inferred from the passage that serious comic book readers pre-
      fer

   (A) characters that resemble real people.

   (B) comic books that blend traditions.

   (C) stories in which the superhero loses.

   (D) works with a supernatural element.

   (E) graphic novels that are critically acclaimed.

Question Type: Interpretation

Explanation: In the section entitled "ABOUT THE QUESTIONS," it states that
interpretation questions will ask you to "distinguish probable motivations and
effects or actions not stated outright in the essay." In the preceding passage, we
are told why comic books have begun to receive critical attention: it's because
they've gone from being tales of superheroes to real-life narratives.

   But in this simple assertion of cause and effect, something crucial concerning the change in content is implied rather than stated: serious critics and readers prefer stories about real people. The correct answer is (A). Answer choice
(B) is incorrect because the only implied comic book tradition in the passage
is the depiction of superheroes, which has been superseded by, not blended
with, the real-life content. Answer choice (C) is incorrect because no stories
about superheroes losing are mentioned. The passage does state that the "super-

hero battling evil has yielded to the flawed everyman," which suggests a plot in which a superhero is overthrown. But the writer is being figurative; he or she is not describing the plot of a specific comic book but the evolution of comic books *as though* it were a comic book with a doomed hero. Answer choice (D) completely contradicts the main thrust of the passage, which asserts readers' preference for realism over supernatural content. Choice (E) ignores the basic cause-and-effect argument of the passage: the new content resulted in the new-found legitimacy. Of course, critical acclaim often does generate interest. But, whereas nothing in the passage rules out this possibility, it never implies it.

Now that we have illustrated the four question types and the kinds of reasoning that might go into solving them, apply what you have learned to the following passage and two questions (most short passages are followed by two questions).

SHORT PASSAGE #4

1 Up in her bedroom window Sally Happer rest-
    ed her nineteen-year-old chin on the sill and
    watched Clark Darrow's ancient Ford turn into
    the driveway. Clark laboriously climbed the
5 drive's gentle incline, the wheels squeaking
    indignantly, and then with a terrifying expres-
    sion he gave the steering wheel a final wrench
    and deposited self and car approximately in
    front of the Happer steps. There was a plain-
10 tive heaving sound, a death-rattle, followed
    by a short silence; then the air was rent by a
    startling whistle. Sally gazed down sleepily.
    She started to yawn, but finding this quite im-
    possible unless she raised her chin from the
15 window-sill, changed her mind and continued
    silently to regard the car, whose owner sat at
    attention as he waited for an answer to his
    signal.

The preceding passage is drawn from which of the following?

    (A) Humanities, (B) Social Sciences, (C) Natural Sciences, or (D) Nar-
       ration

5. Which of the following reactions does Clark's arrival elicit from Sally?

    (A) Complete indifference

    (B) Mild disapproval

    (C) Feigned boredom

    (D) Sudden interest

    (E) Sleepy attention

6. The wheels of Clark's car "squeak indignantly" because

    (A) Sally's driveway is steep.

    (B) Clark is a poor driver.

    (C) Clark's car is decrepit.

    (D) Sally ignores the whistle.

    (E) the road is deeply rutted.

ABOUT THE QUESTIONS

As previously mentioned, there are four major question types that appear in the Critical Reading section of the SAT. The following explains what these questions will cover.

Question Type 1: Synthesis/Analysis

Synthesis/analysis questions deal with the structure of the passage and how one part relates to another part or to the text as a whole. These questions may ask you to look at passage details and from them, point out general themes or concepts. They might ask you to trace problems, causes, effects, and solutions or to understand the points of an argument or persuasive passage. They might ask you to compare or contrast different aspects of the passage. Synthesis/analysis questions may also involve inferences, asking you to decide what the details of the passage imply about the author's general tone or attitude. Key terms in synthesis/analysis questions are example, difference, general, compare, contrast, cause, effect, and result.

Question Type 2: Evaluation

Evaluation questions involve judgments about the worth of the essay as a whole. You may be asked to consider concepts the author assumes rather than factually proves and to judge whether the author presents a logically consistent case. Does he/she prove the points through generalization, citing an authority, use of example, implication, personal experience, or factual data? You'll need to be able to distinguish the supportive bases for the argumentative theme. Almost as a book reviewer, you'll also be asked to pinpoint the author's writing techniques. What is the style, the tone? Who is the intended audience? How might the author's points relate to information outside the essay itself? Key terms you'll often see in evaluation questions and answer choices are generalization, implication, and support.

Question Type 3: Vocabulary-in-Context

Vocabulary-in-context questions occur in several formats. You'll be given easy words with challenging choices or the reverse. You'll need to know multiple meanings of words. You'll encounter difficult words and difficult choices. In some cases, your knowledge of prefixes-roots-suffixes will gain you a clear advantage. In addition, connotations will be the means of deciding, in some cases, which answer is the best. Of course, how the term works in the textual context is the key to the issue.

Question Type 4: Interpretation

Interpretation questions ask you to decide on a valid explanation or clarification of the author's points. Based on the text, you'll be asked to distinguish probable motivations and effects or actions not stated outright in the essay. Furthermore, you'll need to be familiar with clichés, euphemisms, catch phrases, colloquialisms, metaphors, and similes and to explain them in straightforward language. Interpretation question stems usually have a word or phrase enclosed in quotation marks.

Keep in mind that being able to categorize accurately is not of prime importance. What is important, however, is that you are familiar with all the types of information you will be asked and that you have a set of basic strategies to use when answering questions. The remainder of this review will give you these skills.

ANSWERING CRITICAL READING QUESTIONS

You should follow these steps as you begin each critical reading passage. They will act as a guide when answering the questions.

STEP 1   Before you address the critical reading, answer all sentence completions within the given verbal section. You can answer more questions per minute in these short sections than in the reading; and because all answers are credited equally, you'll get the most for your time here.

Now, find the Critical Reading passage(s). If more than one passage appears, give each a brief overview. Attack the easiest and most interesting passages first. Critical Reading passages are not automatically presented in the order of least-to-most difficult. The difficulty or ease of a reading selection is an individual matter, determined by the reader's own specific interests and past experience; so what you might consider easy, someone else might consider hard, and *vice versa*. Again, time is an issue, so you need to begin with something you can quickly understand to get to the questions, where the pay-off lies.

STEP 2   First, read the question stems following the passage, making sure to block out the answer choices with your free hand. (You don't want to be misled by incorrect choices.)

In question stems, underline key words, phrases, and dates. For example:

1. In line 27, "stand" means:

2. From 1776 to 1812, King George did:

3. Lincoln was similar to Pericles in that:

The act of underlining takes little time and will force you to focus first on the main ideas in the questions, then in the essays.

You will notice that questions often note a line number for reference. Place a small mark by the appropriate lines in the essay itself to remind yourself to read those parts very carefully. You'll still have to refer to these lines upon answering the questions, but you'll be able to find them quickly.

STEP 3A   If you are addressing a short passage, read it with an eye toward formulating its main idea or concept in a concise sentence. A firm grasp of the passage's focus and purpose will make most questions about the passage seem straightforward.

Short Passage #3 in the preceding "Identifying Passage and Question Types" could be summarized thus:

Today's comic books are more respected, largely because they portray real people instead of superheroes.

See how readily you can provide one-sentence summaries for the other Short Passages in this review section.

STEP 3B   If you are addressing a long passage and it is not divided into paragraphs, read the first 10 lines. If the passage is divided into manageable paragraphs, read the first paragraph. Make sure to read at a moderate pace because fast skimming will not be sufficient for comprehension and slow, forced reading will take too much time and yield too little understanding of the overall passage.

In the margin of your test booklet, using two or three words, note the main point of the paragraph/section. Don't labor long over the exact wording. Underline key terms, phrases, or ideas when you notice them. If a sentence is particularly difficult, don't spend too much time trying to figure it out. Bracket it, though, for easy reference in the remote instance that it might serve as the basis for a question.

You should proceed through each paragraph/section in a similar manner. Don't read the whole passage with the intention of going back and filling in the main points. Read carefully and consistently, annotating and underlining to keep your mind on the context.

Upon finishing the entire passage, quickly review your notes in the margin. They should give you main ideas and passage structure (chronological, cause and effect, process, comparison/contrast). Ask yourself what the author's attitude is toward his/her subject. What might you infer from the selection? What might the author say next? Some of these questions may appear, and you'll be immediately prepared to answer.

STEP 4   Start with the first question and work through to the last question. The order in which the questions are presented follows the order of the passage; so going for the "easy" questions first, rather than answering the questions consecutively, will cost you valuable time in searching and backtracking.

Be sure to block the answer choices for each question before you read the question itself. Again, you don't want to be misled.

If a line number is mentioned, quickly re-read that section. In addition, circle your own answer to the question *before* viewing the choices. Then, carefully examine each answer choice, eliminating those that are obviously incorrect. If you find a close match to your own answer, don't assume that it is the best answer, as an even better one may be among the last choices. Remember, in the SAT, only one answer is correct, and it is the *best* one, not simply one that will work.

Once you've proceeded through all the choices, eliminating incorrect answers as you go, choose from among those remaining. If the choice is not clear, re-read the question stem and the referenced passage lines to seek tone or content you might have missed. If the answer is not readily obvious now and you have reduced your choices by eliminating at least one, then simply choose one of the remaining and proceed to the next question. Place a small mark in your test booklet to remind you, should you have time at the end of this test section, to review the question and seek a more accurate answer.

Now, let's tackle a natural sciences passage. Read the passage, and then answer the questions that follow using the skills gained through this review.

The following article was written by a physical chemist and recounts the conflict between volcanic matter in the atmosphere and airplane windows. It was published in a scientific periodical in 1989.

(*Reprinted by permission of* American Heritage Magazine, *a division of Forbes Inc., Copyright © Forbes Inc., 1989.*)

1 Several years ago the airlines discovered a new kind of problem—a window problem. The acrylic windows on some of their 747s were getting hazy and dirty-looking. Suspicious travelers thought the airlines might have stopped cleaning them, but the windows were not dirty; they were inexplicably deterio-
5 rating within as little as 390 hours of flight time, even though they were supposed to last for five to ten years. Boeing looked into it.

  At first the company thought the culprit might be one well known in modern technology, the component supplier who changes materials without telling the customer. Boeing quickly learned this was not the case, so there followed an
10 extensive investigation that eventually brought in the Air Transport Association, geologists, and specialists in upper-atmosphere chemistry, and the explanation turned out to be not nearly so mundane. Indeed, it began to look like a grand reenactment of an ancient Aztec myth: the struggle between the eagle and the serpent, which is depicted on the Mexican flag.

15 The serpent in this case is an angry Mexican volcano, El Chichon. Like its reptilian counterpart, it knows how to spit venom at the eyes of its adversary. In March and April of 1982 the volcano, in an unusual eruption pattern, ejected millions of tons of sulfur-rich material directly into the stratosphere. In less than a year, a stratospheric cloud had blanketed the entire Northern Hemisphere.
20 Soon the photochemistry of the upper atmosphere converted much of the sulfur into tiny droplets of concentrated sulfuric acid.

  The eagle in the story is the 747, poking into the lower part of the stratosphere in hundreds of passenger flights daily. Its two hundred windows are made from

an acrylic polymer, which makes beautifully clear, strong windows but was
25   never intended to withstand attack by strong acids.

The stratosphere is very different from our familiar troposphere environment.
Down here the air is humid, with a lot of vertical convection to carry things
up and down; the stratosphere is bone-dry, home to the continent-striding jet
stream, with unceasing horizontal winds at an average of 120 miles per hour. A
30   mist of acid droplets accumulated gradually near the lower edge of the stratosphere, settling there at a thickness of about a mile a year, and was able to wait
for planes to come along.

As for sulfuric acid, most people know only the relatively benign liquid in a
car battery: 80 percent water and 20 percent acid. The stratosphere dehydrated
35   the sulfuric acid into a persistent, corrosive mist 75 percent pure acid, an extremely aggressive liquid. Every time the 747 poked into the stratosphere—on
almost every long flight—acid droplets struck the windows and began to re-
act with their outer surface, causing it to swell. This built up stresses between
the softened outer layer and the underlying material. Finally, parallel hairline
40   cracks developed, creating the hazy appearance. The hazing was sped up by the
mechanical stresses always present in the windows of a pressurized cabin.

The airlines suffered through more than a year of window replacements before the acid cloud finally dissipated. Ultimately the drops reached the lower
edge of the stratosphere, were carried away into the lower atmosphere, and fi-
45   nally came down in the rain. In the meantime, more resistant window materials
and coatings were developed. (As for the man-made sulfur dioxide that causes
acid rain, it never gets concentrated enough to attack the window material. El
Chichon was unusual in its ejection of sulfur directly into the stratosphere, and
the 747 is unusual in its frequent entrance into the stratosphere.)

50   As for the designers of those windows, it is hard to avoid the conclusion that
a perfectly adequate engineering design was defeated by bad luck. After all, this
was the only time since the invention of the airplane that there were acid droplets of this concentration in the upper atmosphere. But reliability engineers, an
eminently rational breed, are very uncomfortable when asked to talk about luck.
55   In principle it should be possible to anticipate events, and the failure to do so
somehow seems like a professional failure. The cosmos of the engineer has no
room for poltergeists, demons, or other mystic elements. But might it accom-
modate the inexorable scenario of an ancient Aztec myth?

1. Initially, the company thought the hazy windows were a result of

    (A) small particles of volcanic glass abrading their surfaces.

    (B) substandard window material substituted by the parts supplier.

    (C) ineffectual cleaning products used by the maintenance crew.

    (D) a build-up of the man-made sulfur dioxide that also causes acid rain.

    (E) the humidity.

2. When first seeking a reason for the abraded windows, both the passengers and Boeing management exhibited attitudes of

    (A) disbelief.   (D) pacifism.

    (B) optimism.   (E) disregard.

    (C) cynicism.

3. In line 12, "mundane" means

    (A) simple.   (D) ordinary.

    (B) complicated.   (E) important.

    (C) far-reaching.

4. In what ways is El Chichon like the serpent on the Mexican flag, knowing how to "spit venom at the eyes of its adversary" (line 16)?

    (A) It seeks to poison its adversary with its bite.

    (B) It carefully plans its attack on an awaited intruder.

    (C) It ejects tons of destructive sulfuric acid to damage jet windows.

    (D) It angrily blankets the Northern Hemisphere with sulfuric acid.

    (E) It protects itself with the acid rain it produces.

5. The term "photochemistry" in line 20 refers to a chemical change caused by

    (A) the proximity of the sun.

    (B) the drop in temperature at stratospheric altitudes.

    (C) the jet stream's "unceasing horizontal winds."

    (D) the vertical convection of the troposphere.

    (E) the amount of sulfur present in the atmosphere.

6.   Unlike the troposphere, the stratosphere

   (A) is extremely humid because it is home to the jet stream.

   (B) contains primarily vertical convections, which cause air particles to rise and fall rapidly.

   (C) is approximately one mile thick.

   (D) contains powerful horizontal winds resulting in an excessively dry atmosphere.

   (E) contains very little wind activity.

7.   In line 36, "aggressive" means

   (A) exasperating.   (D) assertive.

   (B) enterprising.   (E) surprising.

   (C) prone to attack.

8.   As the eagle triumphed over the serpent in the Mexican flag,

   (A) El Chichon triumphed over the plane as the 747s had to change their flight altitudes.

   (B) the newly designed window material deflected the damaging acid droplets.

   (C) the 747 was able to fly unchallenged by acid droplets a year later as they drifted away to the lower atmosphere.

   (D) the reliability engineers are now prepared for any run of "bad luck" which may approach their aircraft.

   (E) the component supplier of the windows changed materials without telling the customers.

9.   The reliability engineers are typified as people who

   (A) are uncomfortable considering natural disasters.

   (B) believe that all events are predictable through scientific methodology.

   (C) accept luck as an inevitable and unpredictable part of life.

   (D) easily accept their failure to predict and protect against nature's surprises.

   (E) are extremely irrational and are comfortable speaking about luck.

   The questions following the passage that you just read are typical of those in the Critical Reading section. After carefully reading the passage, you can begin to answer these questions. Let's look again at the questions.

1.   Initially, the company thought the hazy windows were a result of

(A)   small particles of volcanic glass abrading their surfaces.

(B)   substandard window material substituted by the parts supplier.

(C)   ineffectual cleaning products used by the maintenance crew.

(D)   a build-up of the man-made sulfur dioxide that also causes acid rain.

(E)   the humidity.

As you read the question stem, blocking the answer choices, you'll note the key term "result," which should alert you to the question category, *synthesis/ analysis*. Argument structure is the focus here. Ask yourself what part of the argument is being questioned: cause, problem, result, or solution. Careful reading of the stem and perhaps mental rewording to "_____ caused hazy windows" reveals cause is the issue. Once you're clear on the stem, proceed to the choices.

The word "initially" clues you in to the fact that the correct answer should be the first cause considered. Answer choice (B) is the correct response, as "substandard window material" was the *company's* first (initial) culprit, as explained in the first sentence of the second paragraph. They had no hint of (A) a volcanic eruption's ability to cause such damage. In addition, they were not concerned, as were the *passengers*, that (C) the windows were not properly cleaned. Answer (D) is not correct since scientists had yet to consider testing the atmosphere. Along the same lines, answer choice (E) is incorrect.

2.   When first seeking a reason for the abraded windows, both the passengers and Boeing management exhibited attitudes of

(A)   disbelief.   (D)   pacifism.

(B)   optimism.   (E)   disregard.

(C)   cynicism.

As you read the stem before viewing the choices, you'll know you're being asked to judge or *evaluate* the tone of a passage. The tone is not stated outright, so you'll need to rely on your perception as you re-read that section, if necessary. Remember, questions follow the order of the passage, so you know to look after the initial company reaction to the windows, but not far after, as many more questions are to follow. Now, formulate your own word for the attitude of the passengers and employees. "Skepticism" or "criticism" works well.

If you can't come up with a term, at least note if the tone is negative or positive. In this case, negative is clearly indicated since the passengers are distrustful of the maintenance crew and the company mistrusts the window supplier. Proceed to each choice, seeking the closest match to your term and/or eliminating words with positive connotations.

Choice (C) is correct because "cynicism" best describes the skepticism and distrust with which the passengers view the cleaning company and the company views the parts suppliers.

Choice (A) is not correct because both Boeing and the passengers believed the windows were hazy; they just didn't know why.

Choice (B) is not correct because people were somewhat agitated that the windows were hazy—certainly not "optimistic."

Choice (D), "pacifism," has a rather positive connotation, which the tone of the section does not.

Choice (E) is incorrect because the people involved took notice of the situation and did not disregard it. In addition to the ability to discern tone, of course, your vocabulary knowledge is being tested. "Cynicism," should you be unsure of the term, can be viewed by its root, "cynic," which may trigger you to remember that it is negative and, therefore, appropriate in tone.

3.   In line 12, "mundane" means

(A) simple.   (D) ordinary.

(B) complicated.   (E) important.

(C) far-reaching.

This question obviously tests *vocabulary-in-context*. Your strategy here should be to view line 12 quickly to confirm usage, to block answer choices while devising your own synonym for "mundane"—perhaps "common"—and then to view each choice separately, looking for the closest match. Although you might not be familiar with "mundane," the choices are all relatively simple terms. Look for contextual clues in the passage if you can't define the term outright. While the "component supplies" explanation is "mundane," the Aztec myth is not. Perhaps you could then look for an opposite of mythical: "real" or "down-to-earth" comes to mind.

Choice (D), "ordinary," fits best as it is clearly the opposite of the extraordinary Aztec myth of the serpent and the eagle, which is not as common as a supplier switching materials.

Choice (A), "simple," works contextually, but not as an accurate synonym for the word "mundane;" it does not deal with "mundane's" "down-to-earth" definition.

Choice (B), "complicated," is inaccurate because the parts switch is anything but complicated.

Choice (C), "far-reaching," is not better as it would apply to the myth rather than the common, everyday action of switching parts.

Choice (E), "important," does not work either, because the explanation was an integral part of solving the problem.

Had you eliminated (B), (C), and (E) due to contextual inappropriateness, you were left with "ordinary" and "simple." A quick re-reading of the section, then, should clarify the better choice. But, if the re-reading did not clarify the better choice, your strategy would be to choose one answer, place a small mark in the booklet, and proceed to the next question. If time is left at the end of the test, you can then review your answer choice.

4.   In what ways is El Chichon like the serpent on the Mexican flag, know-
      ing how to "spit venom at the eyes of its adversary" (line 16)?
      (A)   It seeks to poison its adversary with its bite.
      (B)   It carefully plans its attack on an awaited intruder.
      (C)   It ejects tons of destructive sulfuric acid to damage jet windows.
      (D)   It angrily blankets the Northern Hemisphere with sulfuric acid.
      (E)   It protects itself with the acid rain it produces.

As you view the question, note the word "like" indicates a comparison is be-
ing made. The quoted simile forms the comparative basis of the question, and you must *interpret* that phrase with respect to the actual process. You must care-fully seek to duplicate the tenor of the terms, coming close to the spitting action in which a harmful substance is expelled in the direction of an object similar to the eyes of an opponent. Look for key words when comparing images. "Spit," "venom," "eyes," and "adversary" are these keys.

In choice (C), the verb that is most similar to the serpent's "spitting" venom is the sulfuric acid "ejected" from the Mexican volcano, El Chichon. Also, the jet windows most closely resemble the "eyes of the adversary" that are struck by El Chichon. Being a volcano, El Chichon is certainly incapable of injecting poison into an adversary, as in choice (A), or planning an attack on an intruder, as in choice (B).

In choice (D), although the volcano does indeed "blanket the Northern Hemi-sphere" with sulfuric acid, this image does not coincide with the "spitting" im-age of the serpent.

Finally, in choice (E), although a volcano can indirectly cause acid rain, it cannot produce acid rain on its own and then spew it out into the atmosphere.

5.   The term "photochemistry" in line 20 refers to a chemical change caused
      by
      (A)   the proximity of the sun.
      (B)   the drop in temperature at stratospheric altitudes.
      (C)   the jet stream's "unceasing horizontal winds."
      (D)   the vertical convection of the troposphere.
      (E)   the amount of sulfur present in the atmosphere.

Even if you are unfamiliar with the term "photochemistry," you probably
know its root or its prefix. Clearly, this question fits in the *vocabulary-in-context*
mode. Your first step may be a quick reference to line 20. If you don't know the
term, context may provide you a clue. The conversion of sulfur-rich *upper* atmosphere into droplets may help. If context does not yield information, look at
the term "photochemistry," itself. "Photo" has to do with light or sun, as in pho-
tosynthesis. Chemistry deals with substance composition and change. Knowing
these two parts can take you a long way toward a correct answer.

Answer choice (A) is the correct response, as the light of the sun closely
compares with the prefix "photo." Although choice (B), "the drop in temperature," might lead you to associate the droplet formation with condensation, light
is not a factor here; nor is it in choice (C), "the jet stream's winds"; choice (D),
"the vertical convection"; or choice (E), "the amount of sulfur present."

6.   Unlike the troposphere, the stratosphere
      (A)   is extremely humid because it is home to the jet stream.
      (B)   contains primarily vertical convections, which cause air particles to
            rise and fall rapidly.
      (C)   is approximately one mile thick.
      (D)   contains powerful horizontal winds resulting in an excessively dry
            atmosphere.
      (E)   contains very little wind activity.

"Unlike" should immediately alert you to a *synthesis/analysis* question, asking you to contrast specific parts of the text. Your margin notes should take you
right to the section contrasting the atmospheres. Quickly scan it before considering the answers. Usually you won't remember this broad type of comparison
from your first passage reading. Don't spend much time, though, on the scan
before beginning to answer, as time is still a factor.

This question is tricky because all the answer choices contain key elements/
phrases in the passage, but again, a quick, careful scan will yield results. Answer (D) proves best, as the "horizontal winds" dry the air of the stratosphere.

Choices (A), (B), (C), and (E) are all characteristic of the troposphere, while only the acid droplets accumulate at the rate of one mile per year within the much larger stratosphere. As you answer such questions, remember to eliminate incorrect choices as you go; don't be misled by what seems familiar, yet isn't accurate—read all the answer choices.

7.   In line 36, "aggressive" means

    (A)   exasperating.   (D)   assertive.

    (B)   enterprising.   (E)   surprising.

    (C)   prone to attack.

Another *vocabulary-in-context* surfaces here; yet, this time, the word is probably familiar to you. Again, before forming a synonym, quickly refer to the line number, aware that perhaps a secondary meaning is appropriate as the term already is a familiar one. Upon reading the line, you'll note "persistent" and "corrosive"—both strong terms, the latter being quite negative in its destruction. Now, form an appropriate synonym for aggressive—one that has a negative connotation. "Hostile" might come to mind. At this point you are ready to view all choices for a match.

Using your vocabulary knowledge, you can answer this question. "Hostile" most closely resembles choice (C), "prone to attack," and is therefore the correct response. Choice (A), "exasperating," or irritating, is too weak a term, while choices (B), "enterprising," and (D), "assertive," are too positive. Choice (E), "surprising," is not a synonym for "aggressive."

8.   As the eagle triumphed over the serpent in the Mexican flag,

    (A)   El Chichon triumphed over the plane because the 747s had to change their flight altitudes.

    (B)   the newly designed window material deflected the damaging acid droplets.

    (C)   the 747 was able to fly unchallenged by acid droplets a year later because they drifted away to the lower atmosphere.

    (D)   the reliability engineers are now prepared for any run of "bad luck" which may approach their aircraft.

    (E)   the component supplier of the windows changed materials without telling the customer.

This question asks you to compare the eagle's triumph over the serpent to another part of the text. "As" often signals comparative relationships; so you are forewarned of the *synthesis/analysis* question. You are also dealing again with a simile; so, of course, the question can also be categorized as *interpretation*. The eagle-serpent issue is a major theme in the text. As you will soon discover in the answer choices, you are being asked what this general theme is. Look at the stem keys: eagle, triumphed, and serpent. Ask yourself to what each corresponds. You'll arrive at the eagle and the 747, some sort of victory, and the volcano or its sulfur. Now that you've formed that corresponding image in your own mind, you're ready to view the choices.

Choice (C) is the correct choice because we know the statement "the 747 was able to fly unchallenged . . . " to be true. Not only do the remaining choices fail to reflect the eagle-triumphs-over-serpent image, but choice (A) is inaccurate because the 747 did not "change its flight altitudes."

In choice (B), the windows did not deflect "the damaging acid droplets."

Furthermore, in choice (D), "the reliability engineers" cannot be correct because they cannot possibly predict the future and, therefore, cannot anticipate what could go wrong in the future.

Finally, we know that in (E) the window materials were never changed.

9.   The reliability engineers are typified as people who
   (A)   are uncomfortable considering natural disasters.
   (B)   believe that all events are predictable through scientific methodology.
   (C)   accept luck as an inevitable and unpredictable part of life.
   (D)   easily accept their failure to predict and protect against nature's surprises.
   (E)   are extremely irrational and are comfortable speaking about luck.

When the question involves such terms as type, kind, example, or typified, be aware of possible *synthesis/analysis* or *interpretation* issues. Here the question deals with implications: what the author means but doesn't state outright. Types can also lead you to situations which ask you to make an unstated generalization based on specifically stated details. In fact, this question could even be categorized as *evaluation* because specific detail to generalization is a type of argument/essay structure. In any case, before viewing the answer choices, ask yourself what general traits the reliability engineers portray. You may need to check back in the text for typical characteristics. You'll find the engineers to be rational unbelievers in luck. These key characteristics will help you to make a step toward a correct answer.

Choice (B) is the correct answer because the passage specifically states that the reliability engineers "are very uncomfortable when asked to talk about luck" and believe "it should be possible to anticipate events" scientifically. The engineers might be uncomfortable, as in choice (A), but this is not a main concern in the passage.

Choice (C) is obviously incorrect, because the engineers do not believe in luck at all, and choice (D) is not correct because "professional failure" is certainly unacceptable to these scientists.

There is no indication in the passage that (E) the scientists are "irrational and are comfortable speaking about luck."

DRILLS

Now, use what you have learned to answer the following questions.

DIRECTIONS: Read each passage and answer the questions that follow. Each question will be based on the information stated or implied in the passage.

A variation of the directions will be presented as follows for the double passage.

DIRECTIONS: Read the passages and answer the questions that follow. Each question will be based on the information stated or implied in the selections or their introductions, and may be based on the relationship between passages.

SHORT PASSAGES

Questions II.2.1 and II.2.2 are based on the following passage.

1   "Beauty is in the eye of the beholder." While this statement may be true, some works of art tend to remain beautiful in the eyes of many "beholders," eventually passing the test of time. Although such masterpieces are obviously unique and famous in their own right, they share certain qualities. Pablo Picasso's abstract
5   cubist-inspired *Three Musicians* can be interpreted only through an understanding of his style—angular shapes that represent feet, tiny five-pronged objects that symbolize hands, masks that hide faces. Even the most experienced art lover can look at this painting and be unsure as to what he sees. But—comprehend it or not—he is likely to be intrigued by it. Equally appealing is impressionist
10   Claude Monet's painting of a Japanese bridge over a pond full of water lilies. Even a brief glance leaves the admirer with no doubt as to what he is viewing. Yet each painting is a masterpiece. Each indefinably attracts the viewer, drawing his eyes—and perhaps his very soul—to them. To look at it is to become it, at least fleetingly. Like all true masterpieces, each work has stood the test of
15   time, alluring critics and admirers over decades if not centuries. Each in its own

way expresses an understanding or an experience common to mankind—not just of a certain era, but of all eras.

▓ QUESTION II.2.1

The primary purpose of this passage is to

(A) depict the differences between cubism and impressionism.

(B) discuss similarities between the works of Picasso and Monet.

(C) show that different people see beauty in different things.

(D) define what makes a work of art a masterpiece.

(E) demonstrate that Picasso and Monet each had a unique style.

ANSWER

(D) Choice (D) is the correct answer. The focus of the passage is on the characteristics of masterpieces—the fact that each is unique but all share certain qualities. Although the paragraph does address differences between the cubist style of Picasso and the impressionistic style of Monet to show that each is unique, conveying that point is not the paragraph's primary purpose. Therefore, Choices (A) and (E) are wrong. And the paragraph does discuss traits that all masterpieces share; however, it does not focus specifically on similarities between Picasso and Monet, as Choice (B) indicates. The paragraph opens with the idea reflected in Choice (C), indicating "beauty is in the eye of the beholder." However, proving this point is not the paragraph's primary purpose.

■ QUESTION II.2.2

Which of the following is NOT indicated in this passage as a characteristic of all masterpieces?

(A) Each is unique, distinct from all other works.

(B) They hold appeal for people over a period of many years.

(C) They are mysterious, and therefore difficult to understand or interpret.

(D) They relate to the lives of everyone.

(E) They have a way of drawing the viewer to—and into—them.

ANSWER

(C) Choice (C) is the correct answer. Keep in mind that your purpose here is to find the choice that does *not* apply to masterpieces. The description of Monet's work ("Even a brief glance leaves the admirer with no doubt as to what he is viewing.") reveals that not every masterpiece is difficult to understand or interpret. Choice (A) is wrong because the passage says "masterpieces are obviously unique and famous in their own right." Choice (B) is incorrect because the passage indicates "each work has stood the test of time, alluring critics and admirers over decades if not centuries . . . not just of a certain era, but of all eras." Choice (D) is wrong because the passage says, "Each in its own way expresses an understanding or an experience common to mankind." And "Each indefinably attracts the viewer, drawing his eyes—and perhaps his very soul—to them" proves Choice (E) wrong.

Questions II.2.3 and II.2.4 are based on the following passage.

1   Most female idols—models, television and movie stars, and popular musicians—are much thinner than the average person. But because these divas seem ideal—what every teenage girl and every woman wants to be—many women of all ages have a poor body image and continually strive to lose weight. Often
5   the result is destructive dieting behaviors, sometimes to the extreme of bulimia or anorexia nervosa. Teenage girls as well as women unrealistically seek the androgynous look by which they define beauty. They have trouble grasping the fact that real beauty lies not in how many pounds they weigh, nor in what size of clothes they wear. Of course one should eat wholesome foods and maintain
10 a weight that falls in the salubrious range. However, focusing so much on diet and weight to the detriment of other things is clearly imprudent. Eating too little

may very well result in a thin body; however, the consumption of too few necessary vitamins and minerals results in thinning hair; jaundiced, wrinkled skin;
and loss of energy, among other things. Clearly, a woman with such features
15 may be thin, but she certainly isn't beautiful. Far more comely is the female
who likes herself, who focuses less on herself than on others and on the world
around her. She may not be so svelte that her hip bones protrude; but the sheen
of her hair, the glow of her skin, and the enthusiasm with which she approaches
life make her far more beautiful than any cadaverous model or movie star.

◼ QUESTION II.2.3

In line 10, "salubrious" means

(A) attractive.   (D) undisputed.

(B) definitive.   (E) healthy.

(C) popular.

ANSWER

(E)   Choice (E) is the correct answer. If you are unfamiliar with the word,
try determining its meaning in context. This question requires considering vocabulary in context. Re-read the sentence containing the term. Develop your
own synonym for "salubrious" and then look for the choice that has the closest meaning. You are looking for a word that describes a weight range that
coordinates with the wholesome diet proposed in the first half of the sentence.
Choice (E), "healthy," fits best because it is a synonym of "wholesome" and is
an appropriate adjective for weight range. Although the author does find a person who eats a wholesome diet attractive, Choice (A), "attractive" is not a dictionary synonym for "salubrious," and it does not work as well as an objective
descriptor of weight range. Choice (B) "definitive" is incorrect because it does
not specify the weight range; for example, a "definitive" range could refer to
an unhealthy span as well as a healthy one. Choice (C) is incorrect because the
author's point is that females should focus not on what is popular but on what
is healthy. And Choice (D) is incorrect because there is no "undisputed" weight
range; any range—healthy or unhealthy—may be disputed by some people.

■ QUESTION II.2.4

Which of the following women would the author be most likely to find attractive?

(A) The thin young rock star who exercises frequently and eats only one meal per day.

(B) The overweight young lady who eats robustly and tries hard to please others.

(C) The pretty teenager who is within the average weight range but is constantly striving to lose weight.

(D) The thin young woman who eats as much as she can hold, in an effort to be in the average weight range.

(E) The teenager who is slightly overweight and is eating healthy meals to lose weight but focuses primarily on social activities.

ANSWER

(E) Choice (E) is the correct answer. Although the paragraph does not say anything about overweight people, it is clear that people who are underweight, those who do not eat healthily, and those who do not focus on others are not attractive to the author. Choice (E) describes a person who is eating healthy meals in an effort to lose weight—which goes along with the author's emphasis that "one should eat wholesome foods and maintain a weight that falls in the salubrious range." And the person described in Choice (E) "focuses primarily on social activities," thus corresponding to the author's comment: "Far more comely is the female who likes herself, who focuses less on herself than on others and on the world around her…. the enthusiasm with which she approaches life make(s) her far more beautiful than any cadaverous model or movie star." The clues indicating that Choice (A) is wrong include "thin," and "eats only one meal per day." Although it is normally healthy to exercise frequently, a thin person who eats only one meal per day may be exercising for unhealthy reasons—perhaps out of an obsession to become even thinner. Choice (B) is incorrect because an overweight person is not within a "salubrious" (healthy) weight range; her "eating robustly" tells you she is perhaps over-eating rather than eating "wholesomely." And "trying hard to please others" does not imply a healthy self-image, so this person may not "like herself." Choice (C) describes the very concept that the paragraph opposes. The author clearly believes that a healthy teenager who is within an average weight range should stay that way, rather than trying to lose weight. Choice (D) is wrong because the person described is not eating healthily and does not have a positive self-image. The paragraph does not say that no one should be thin; it does speak out against unhealthy efforts to become underweight.

Questions II.2.5 and II.2.6 are based on the following passage.

1   "Do what I say, not what I do!" seems to be a common parenting philosophy. However, it's clearly not a successful one. Time and time again, studies have proven that children are much more likely to imitate their parents' behavior than to heed their advice. Mingling with the crowd at the mall, or sitting on a park
5   bench and observing families can do much to verify the truth of this research. A father screams at his son to stop shouting. A mother spanks her toddler for hitting his little friend. Clearly, parent and child are mimicking one another, and the child is simply behaving as the parent has taught him or her—albeit inadvertently in most cases. More effective are the parents who model the be-
10 haviors they expect of their children. A child who receives respect and consid- eration from his or her parents is likely to treat others with the same regard. Obviously, all children misbehave, as a way of testing their limits; however, the child whose parents follow rules similar to the ones they establish for him or her is more likely to see such behaviors as acceptable—as the "correct" way to
15 behave. Discipline with the goal of teaching the child self-control is much more effective than punitive discipline. And modeling a more acceptable alternative behavior works better than reinforcing the misbehavior by acting as immaturely as the child. "Like father, like son" may be a realistic adage—and the results can be heartening or disastrous.

■ QUESTION II.2.5

The parents who are most likely to gain the approval of the author of this passage are those who:

(A) teach their children to do what they say, not what they do.

(B) teach their children to teach different people in different ways.

(C) teach their children to defend themselves when they are at- tacked.

(D) serve as role models for their children.

(E) allow their children to be a part of everything they do.

ANSWER

(D)   Choice (D) is the correct answer. The author emphasizes the importance of parents "modeling the behaviors they expect of their children," and following the same rules they set for their children. Choice (A) is incorrect because the paragraph begins by stating that the approach of "Do what I say, not what I do" is an unsuccessful one. And the author clearly disapproves of parents who exhibit negative behaviors (e.g., shouting and hitting) but punish their children for engaging in those same behaviors. The passage does not address parents teaching children to treat different people differently or to defend themselves when attacked; therefore, choices (B) and (C) are incorrect. And although the passage implies that parents should be an active part of their children's lives, it does not state that children should be a part of everything the parents do; thus, Choice (E) is wrong.

■ QUESTION II.2.6

> In lines 6–7, the author describes specific incidents in order to
>
> (A) elicit pity for the children.
>
> (B) exemplify negative parenting behaviors.
>
> (C) show the reader how enjoyable it can be to observe people in public places such as parks and malls.
>
> (D) make the reader aware of the variety of ways parents discipline their children.
>
> (E) convey the effectiveness of corporal punishment.

ANSWER

(B)   Choice (B) is the correct answer. The author uses these examples to support his point that children mimic their parents' behaviors, even when they are punished for those behaviors. Choice (A) is incorrect because nothing in the passage indicates that the author pities even the children whose parents punish them. Although suggesting that the reader observe parents and children at the park or the mall, the author does not indicate that the experience is a pleasant one; thus, Choice (C) is incorrect. Choice (D) is incorrect because the author uses these specific incidents to exemplify the negative behaviors that children mimic—not to demonstrate the variety of disciplinary methods. And Choice (E) is wrong because the passage does not defend corporal punishment (spanking);

in fact, the author is critical of the parent who spanks a child as punishment for hitting.

Questions II.2.7 and II.2.8 are based on the following passage.

1 His shoulders shook so violently that I thought his body was going to fall apart, just as surely as his heart had broken. He hid his face in his hands; water steadily streamed from between his thin fingers. The blue veins seemed ready to burst through the thin skin on the backs of his hands. His wispy white hair was com-
5 pletely unkempt. His entire demeanor bespoke his grief. Only the casket kept his poor weary body from melting to the floor.

■ QUESTION II.2.7

The word "unkempt" (line 5) means

(A) disjointed.   (D) coiffed.

(B) invisible.   (E) antiquated.

(C) in disarray.

ANSWER

(C)   Choice (C) is the correct answer. You are looking for a word that goes along with the rest of the description of this man who obviously was not thinking about his appearance, including his hair. Choice (C) "in disarray" (disorderly) is an appropriate choice. Choice (A) "disjointed" (thrown out of orderly function; incoherent) does not fit in this context. And although the man's hair was "wispy" (thin, straw-like), it was not "invisible" (not to be seen). Choice (D) is wrong because the other clues—concerned his distraught state—do not in any way indicate that his hair was "coiffed" (neatly arranged by combing, bruching, or curling). And although the description may lead the reader to believe the man was aged, no clues imply that his hair or hairstyle was "antiquated" (old or obsolete).

◼ QUESTION II.2.8

The passage infers that the man was most likely

(A) dead   (D) frustrated.

(B) in mourning.   (E) angry.

(C) frightened.

ANSWER

(B)   Choice (B) is the correct answer. The man's intense crying, the fact that "his entire demeanor bespoke his grief" and the statement that "only the casket kept his poor weary body from melting to the floor" are all clues that his emotion probably had something to do with the death of the person in the casket. Therefore he was in "in mourning" (in a state of grief over a death). Choice (A) is incorrect because the man himself was obviously alive, and although the man was definitely in a highly emotional state, nothing in the passage indicates that was (C) "frightened" (afraid) or (D) "frustrated" (discouraged) or (E) "angry" (feeling strong displeasure or ire).

Questions II.2.9 and II.2.10 are based on the following passage.

1   With the convenience of today's technology, we are readily accessible at all times. Leaving the house or the office no longer means leaving the phone; our cell phones are as mobile as we are. And being away from our mailboxes no longer means having no access to mail; electronic correspondence is as close
5   as the nearest connected computer, which may be right at the side of the wireless laptop owner. So it is possible to be available to anyone, anytime, anywhere. However, with this unlimited accessibility comes the inability to escape the complaints of clients or coworkers, orders from a too-demanding boss who wants us to take care of matters immediately, or messages from family members
10 who like to think we are at their disposal. Our free time is no longer free. Our "own time" is no longer our own. Technological progress enhances others' accessibility to us, but—in a world where leisure time is already at a premium—it serves only to stifle our own access to privacy.

◾ QUESTION II.2.9

According to this passage, which of the following is limited by technological progress?

(A) ability to communicate

(B) use of the post office

(C) use of telephones

(D) right to privacy

(E) freedom of speech

ANSWER

(D)   The last sentence says, "Technological progress . . . serves only to stifle our own access to privacy." And the entire passage focuses on the fact that because of modern-day technology we are accessible "to anyone, anytime, anywhere." Choice (A) is incorrect because phones and the Internet, by their own nature, encourage communication rather than limiting it. And although the passage does mention that "being away from our mailboxes no longer means having no access to mail," it does not indicate that technology limits our use of the post office. So choice (B) is wrong. Choice (C) is incorrect because the passage includes cell phones as one of the technological devices that make us readily accessible, so phone use certainly isn't limited by technological progress. And no mention is made of limitations on the freedom of speech; therefore, choice (E) is incorrect.

◾ QUESTION II.2.10

What does "at a premium" mean in line 12?

(A) expensive   (D) unappreciated

(B) insured   (E) plentiful

(C) scarce

ANSWER

(C)   Even if you are unfamiliar with this phrase, looking at the context will help you understand the meaning. It may help to make up your own meaning, based on what the rest of the sentence and passage say, and then find the choice that most closely fits our definition. You could say, "Technological progress enhances others' accessibility to us, but—in a world where leisure time is already scarce—it serves only to stifle our own access to privacy." So choice (C) is appropriate. Although in a different context the phrase might mean "expensive," it does not fit here; thus, choice (A) is wrong. If you selected choice (B), you might have been thinking of "premium" in terms of insurance, but that meaning does not fit in this context. Choices (D) and (E) are incorrect because their meanings contradict the message of the passage.

Questions II.2.11 and II.2.12 are based on the following passage.

1   Today, plastic credit cards and debit cards are almost more common than paper money and coins. Although plastic is a relatively new invention, the concept of credit is over 3,000 years old. In those days, Babylonians, Assyrians, and Egyptians could settle one-third of a debt with cash and two-thirds with a
5   "bill of exchange." In 1730 Christopher Thornton first allowed his customers in London to make weekly payments for the furniture they bought from him. And in the eightenth and nineteenth centuries, tallymen accepted weekly payments for clothing and other articles, using one side of a wooden stick to keep a tally of how much a customer owed and the other side to record how much that cus-
10   tomer had paid. In the 1920s, Americans used shopper's plates, in stores that issued them, as a kind of promissory note allowing them a month to pay for their purchases. It was not until the 1950s that Diner's Club and American Express issued the first credit cards. But use of such "plastic money" was quite limited until 1970, when government standards for the magnetic strip were established
15   and credit cards gradually gained widespread acceptance. Today—only a few decades later—peple can go shopping and make unlimited purchases without having a penny in their pockets—and often without having the assets to pay for them anytime in the near future.

■ QUESTION II.2.11

People have been able to use credit to acquire the things they want

(A) only in the past century.

(B) for thousands of years.

(C) only since the invention of plastic.

(D) since the government began regulating the use of the magnetic strip.

(E) since Diner's Club and American Express began issuing credit cards.

ANSWER

(B) Lines 2 and 3 say, "the concept of credit is over 3,000 years old." And then the passage explains the use of credit by people who lived in those days, in the 1700s, and on through the centuries until the present time. The passage outlines the historical progress of the use of credit through choice (A) the past century, choice (C) the invention of plastic, choice (D) the governmental regulation of the plastic strip, and choice (E) the issuance of credit cards by Diner's Club and American Express; however, none of these marked the beginning of the use of credit.

■ QUESTION II.2.12

The word "promissory" in line 11 means

(A) having to do with money matters; financial.

(B) personally signed.

(C) containing or conveying a promise or assurance.

(D) listing the items purchased on credit.

(E) listing the assets of the consumer.

ANSWER

(C)   If you are not familiar with the meaning of the word "promissory" (containing or conveying a promise or assurance) or the phrase "promissory note" (written promise to pay in an agreed-upon manner at a fixed or determinable future time to a specified individual or bearer), you should look at the use of the word in context. The passage compares shopper's plates to promissory notes, allowing consumers a month to pay for their purchases. In other words, by accepting a shopper's plate (or promissory note), the consumer was promising to pay for the item(s) within a month. Choice (A) is wrong, primarily because "financial" and "promissory" are not synonyms. Although a promissory note often is related to financial matters, by definition it is not limited to finances. Choice (B) is wrong also; although a promissory note usually requires a signature, this is not a part of the definition of "promissory." And although a listing of the purchased items and/or a list of the consumer's assets may be involved in the business agreement between buyer and seller, neither is by definition required in a promissory note. Therefore, choices (D) and (E) are wrong.

Questions II.2.13 and II.2.14 are based on the following passage.

1   Pandas are currently at risk of becoming extinct. For centuries bamboo—their exclusive food source—was plentiful in pandas' native southern Asia. However, as the Asian population has expanded, heretofore plentiful bamboo forests have steadily decined. Cities have grown up, and people have occupied an increas-
5 ing amount of space; bamboo forests have been cut down for timber and to make way for agricultural projects. Pandas have been forced to retreat. Not only has the size of their natural habitat drastically decreased; their food supply has become limited to only a few small mountainous regions, which supply a relatively small amount of bamboo. To add to the panda's plight, a few decades
10 ago a severe bamboo die-off occurred, and any starving pandas survived only because they were rescued and taken to zoos. Today, an estimated 1,000 pandas still exist in the wild. These numbers are rapidly dwindling, not only because of the decreasing supply of bamboo but also because of poaching, a practice that is still quite common despite the fact that it is illegal.

■ QUESTION II.2.13

The author implies that the potential extinction of the panda is primarily the result of

(A) man's actions.

(B) the natural decline of the bamboo supply.

(C) man's need to hunt pandas to make up for the decreasing food supply.

(D) pandas' reluctance to stay in their natural habitat.

(E) changing weather patterns.

ANSWER

(A)   Pandas are becoming extinct primarily as a result of people taking up bamboo forests to build cities, cutting down bamboo forests for timber and to make room for agricultural growth, and poaching. Although the severe bamboo die-off a few decades ago did add to the panda's extinction, nothing in the passage indicates that the effects of this natural phenomenon were as drastic as these actions of humans; thus, choice (B) is incorrect. Choice (C) is wrong because the passage does not indicate that man needed to hunt pandas to make up for a decreasing food supply. The pandas were forced from their natural habitat, rather than being reluctant to stay there; thus, choice (D) is wrong. And the passage says nothing abut changing weather patterns, so choice (E) is incorrect.

■ QUESTION II.2.14

In line 9, "plight" most nearly means

(A) escape.   (D) fear.

(B) promise.   (E) predicament.

(C) starvation.

ANSWER

(E)   One definition of "plight" is "predicament" or "dilemma." Although the dictionary indicates that "plight" can also mean "promise," choice (B) is incorrect because this definition does not fit in the context here because the passage is discussing the unfortunate situation of pandas. "Plight" does not mean "escape," "starvation," or "fear"; therfore, choices (A), (C), and (D) are incorrect.

Questions II.2.15 and II.2.16 are based on the following passage.

1   Until the early 1900s, Americans were not extremely concerned about their futures as they became older. The major source of economic security was farming, and the extended family cared for the elderly. However, the Industrial Revolution brought an end to this tradition. Farming gave way to more progressive
5   means of earning a living and family ties became looser; as a result, the family was not always available to take care of the older generation. The Great Depression of the 1930s exacerbated these economic security woes. So in 1935 Congress, under the direction of President Franklin D. Roosevelt, signed into law the Social Security Act. This act created a program intended to provide
10 continuing income for retired workers at least 65 years old, partially through the collection of funds from Americans in the work force. Much organization was required to get the program underway, but the first monthly Social Security checks were issued in 1940. Over the years the Social Security Program has metamorphosed into benefits not only for workers but also for the disabled and
15 for survivors of beneficiaries, as well as medical insurance benefits in the form of Medicare.

      Today there is some concern that Social Security is not so "secure." Rumors and prediction contend that by 2012, if not sooner, the system will be running in the red, distributing more money in benefits that it is taking in. Life expectancy
20 is lengthening while birth rates are declining, so the number of people receiving benefits is steadily increasing while the number of workers contributing to the Social Securitiy coffers is declining. Fifty years ago, the ratio of workers to Social Security beneficiaries was approximately 16 to 1. In 1998 it was 3 to 1. Theories about how to solve this problem are plentiful, but what ap-
25 proach would be most effective—and what the government decides to do—remains to be seen.

QUESTION II.2.15

The primary purpose of this passage is to

(A) criticize the Social Security Program.

(B) praise the Social Security Program.

(C) offer alternatives to the Social Security Program.

(D) provide background information about the Social Security Program.

(E) warn about the potential failure of the Social Security Program.

ANSWER

(D)   The passage traces the development of the Social Security Program from its inception to current speculations about related problems. Although it does acknowledge the existence of concerns that the program currently faces some problems, the passage is not critical; thus, choice (A) is incorrect. At the same time, it does not praise the program, although it does present reasons behind the creation of Social Security. So choice (B) is wrong. Choice (C) is incorrect because the passage does not offer alternatives to the program. And although the passage does acknowledge the predictions and rumors that the system may soon be operating "in the red" and that problems are imminent, it does not include any warnings as to the potential failure of the program. Therefore, choice (D) is not appropriate.

■ QUESTION II.2.16

The passage indicates that the Social Security Program is experiencing problems at least partly because

(A) the people in charge of the program have managed the money poorly.

(B) not enough people have made large enough contributions.

(C) more people are living longer, and fewer people are having children.

(D) too many people are depending on Social Security benefits rather than setting aside their own private retirement funds.

(E) the program has expanded to include more benefits than it can afford to support.

ANSWER

(C)   As you consider this question, you must be careful to focus on the passage itself rather than thinking about things you may have read elsewhere or about your own opinion The last paragraph says, "Life expectancy is lengthening while birth rates are declinining, so the number of people receiving benefits is steadily increasing while the number of workers contributing to the Social Security coffers is declining." Therefore, choice (C) is correct. Choice (A) is not correct because the passage says nothing to indicate poor management of the money. The passage does indicate, "Rumors and predictions contend that by 2012, if not sooner, the system will be running in the red, distributing more money in benefits that it is taking in." However, nothing in the passage addresses the size of contributions that some people have made; therefore, choice (B) is incorrect. Since no mention is made of private retirement funds, choice (D) is wrong. The passage does mention, "Over the years the Social Security Program has metamorphosed into benefits not only for wokers but also for the disabled and for survivors of beneficiaries, as well as medical insurance benefits in the form of Medicare." However, it does not indicate that this expansion is the source of the woes facing the Social Security Program; thus, choice (E) is not the correct choice.

Questions II.2.17 through II.2.20 are based on the following passages.

Passage 1

1   The opponents of drug testing in the workplace like to cite our supposed constitutional right to privacy. I hate to be the bearer of bad tidings, but there is no constitutional guarantee to privacy, and in fact no mention of privacy at all in that great document. That argument aside, however, it seems untoward to
5   suggest that anyone's right to privacy, constitutionally endowed or otherwise, is sufficient excuse to hide a crime. Would these same citizens protect the privacy of a producer and purveyor of child-porn? I doubt it. I readily admit that the whole drug testing question has problems. For example, impairment from licit or illicit drugs seems a silly distinction, and in fact, most drug tests performed
10 for employers only measure the presence of the illicit variety. But this does not mean you throw the baby out with the bath water. Drug testing weeds out employees who will probably become a burden in the future, and no one can claim exemption from the law, in the name of privacy or anything else.

Passage 2

    Those who claim that Americans do not have a constitutional guarantee to
15 privacy are correct in the literal sense but completely mistaken at the same time. Although constitutional literalists will tell you that the word is not mentioned in our great guiding document, even most of this ilk will readily admit that much falls under the "inalienable rights" category that is not expressly listed elsewhere in the constitution. I would argue that if ever there was an implicit
20 right in this country it would certainly be to our privacy. However, I would also agree with the proponents of drug testing at some level. Although I firmly believe that privacy is one of our inalienable rights, public safety is certainly important too, especially in our age. I would argue that there are some American workers whose bodily fluids should be tested in order to protect us all. The fast
25 food employee only risks his own precious skin running the fry machine while impaired, and therefore I would argue that he or she should not be tested in the name of sacred privacy; but I am all for testing the person who drives a train full of hazardous material that could poison thousands and damage the environment for years to come if he or she makes a mistake.

QUESTION II.2.17

The author of Passage 1 draws a false analogy between child pornography and drug use. Which of the following best describes this false analogy?

(A) One offense is against others and one offense is a so-called victimless crime, hurting only the perpetrator.

(B) One offense is a felony and the other a misdemeanor.

(C) One offense affects adults and the other affects children.

(D) One offense is socially deviant and the other is not.

(E) It is difficult to define which drugs are illicit.

ANSWER

(A) Both offenses have misdemeanor and felony variations (B), and both can affect children as well as adults (C). (D) is perhaps true but less so than (A). (E) is irrelevant.

QUESTION II.2.18

The arguments in Passage 1 and Passage 2 overlap. Which of the following best describes where these writers agree?

(A) Drug testing warrants a violation of anyone's privacy.

(B) Drug use is illegal and should remain illegal.

(C) Because drug use is illegal, that fact alone warrants the invasion of privacy for a drug test.

(D) All employers should have the right to test their employees.

(E) The right to privacy cannot always preclude drug testing.

ANSWER

(E) Only the writer of Passage 1 holds the views in (A) and (C) and, by inference, (D). Neither writer makes the claim in (B).

◼ QUESTION II.2.19

The author of Passage 1 says that there is not a constitutionally guaranteed right to privacy. The author of Passage 2 admits that the word "privacy" is not in that document but that Americans have the right to privacy nevertheless. Which of the following best describes the second writer's reasoning?

(A) One must read between the lines of the Constitution rather than merely interpreting it literally.

(B) The right to privacy falls under the First Amendment right to free speech.

(C) It goes without saying that we have a right to privacy because this is something that Americans have always believed.

(D) Privacy need not be listed in the Constitution as a specific right because we know our rights and don't need a document to tell us what they are.

(E) The term "inalienable rights" is a categorical designation that includes many rights not expressly listed in the Constitution, including the right to privacy.

ANSWER

(E)   The writer of Passage 2 makes this claim in line 5.

■ QUESTION II.2.20

Which of the following best describes the relationship of Passage 1 to Passage 2?

(A) Passage 2 refutes the need for drug testing on the grounds that we have an inalienable right to privacy.

(B) Passage 2 refutes the primary claim of Passage 1 regarding our right to privacy, but it also qualifies the acceptance of drug testing at the expense of privacy relative to public safety.

(C) Passage 2 refutes the argument in Passage 1 point by point.

(D) Passage 2 uses the Constitution to bolser the argument for drug testing made in Passage 1.

(E) Passage 2 agrees completely with the argument of Passage 1 with the exception of the right to privacy.

ANSWER

(B)   Only choice (B) is correct.

Questions II.2.21 and II.2.22 are based on the following passage.

1   As a boy, he used to sit at his grandfather's feet and listen to his stories. The old man had grown increasingly nostalgic for the days of his own youth, and he would tell him about far off places and of his adventures. Now the boy was a man, and although he did not consider himself old, he too found himself telling
5 his sons about the trees he had climbed and the bicycle wrecks and the minor misbehavior he was prone to in school. He also found that he missed his grand-father more than ever these days, although the old man had been gone for eight years now. He wondered why he would feel this way at this point in his life: his own aging, his children reaching his age when he listened to those old stories,
10 or maybe something he did not yet recognize.

■ QUESTION II.2.21

The main idea in this passage is:

(A) a man's memories of his grandfather.

(B) a man's recognition that he is aging.

(C) a story about this man's grandfather and the stories he told him long ago.

(D) a man's stories about his sons.

(E) a man's recognition that he misses his grandfather and wonders what that might mean.

ANSWER

(E)   The last two sentences in the passage state the answer overtly.

■ QUESTION II.2.22

Judging by the tone of this passage and any other hints you can find, why is the speaker now missing his grandfather more than ever?

(A) He is lonely and simply misses the old man.

(B) He is reminded of those times because his sons are the same age he was when his grandfather told him stories.

(C) The anniversary of his grandfather's death is near.

(D) His sons look like his grandfather.

(E) He feels old.

ANSWER

(B)   The author mentions telling the same kinds of stories to his sons, but there is no mention that he is lonely, that the anniversary of his grandfather's death is approaching, or that his sons look like his grandfather. He also expressly states that he does not feel old.

Questions II.2.23 and II.2.24 are based on the following passage.

1   The customary way to provide a framework for one's thoughts is to compare the age of the universe to the length of one earth day, but the scientist Francis Crick suggests that perhaps a better comparison would be to equate the age of the earthy using the earthly week. On such a scale, the age of the universe since
5   the big bang would be two or three weeks, and the oldest microscopic fossils would have been alive a single day. Modern man, *homo sapiens sapiens*, would have appeared in the last 10 seconds, and agriculture would have been with us for only the last two seconds.

     Twenty-first century humans, take heed: we assume that our technological
10   power imbues us with a special status in the history of all things, but we have not been here all that long and our earthly tenure is always in doubt on such a scale. Indeed, one might wonder if our many inventions are but acts of hubris. We cannot control nature, for nature is the context within which we find ourselves, and time is her primary agent to keep us humble.

■ QUESTION II.2.23

Given the metaphors the author mentions as the "framework for one's thoughts," such a framework is meant to

(A) show how old the universe really is in a form we can comprehend.

(B) give us a cosmic context within which to view the brevity of human existence.

(C) provide an accurate picture of human history.

(D) make us think small.

(E) give the reader hope for the human race because we are the dominant species.

ANSWER

(B)   The metaphors the author mentions are smaller measures of time (a day and a week) to compare the length of human existence and human accomplishments (agriculture) to the age of the universe.

■ QUESTION II.2.24

In the second paragraph, the reader summarizes his intentions in this passage, which are

(A) to give us a cosmic context within which to understand our individual existence on earth.

(B) to demean human accomplishments.

(C) to give us a context within which to understand our technological accomplishments, an understanding that we cannot ultimately control nature.

(D) to offer a warning that we will destroy our environment if we are not careful with technology.

(E) to inspire us to the kinds of technological innovations that will let us live forever.

ANSWER

(C)   The second paragraph discusses human technological innovation relative to the timescale he set up in the first paragraph.

LONG PASSAGES

Both of the following selections discuss the authors' early education at home. Passage 1 was written by Artur Rubinstein; Passage 2 was written by Vladimir Nabokov.

Passage 1

1 My new life started right away. Heinrich Barth, the senior piano professor of the Imperial and Royal Academy, accepted me, on Joachim's recommendation. Moreover, he agreed to teach me without any remuneration, and to take charge of all money matters on my behalf—such as gathering the contributions of the
5 other four subscribers and paying from the fund all my living expenses, other lessons, and so on. Things looked pretty good at that moment, and my near future seemed assured and in excellent hands.

The question of my schooling was a very important one, and Joachim, Barth and my mother had many discussions about it. Finally, they agreed not to send
10 me to a *Realgymnasium*, deciding instead that it would be better for me to be

tutored at home. It was not easy to find the right person for such a task, which entailed preparing me for yearly examinations at the *Gymnasium* and following the school's full curriculum.

15 Eventually they found a Dr. Theodor Altmann, a man who would assume the great responsibility for my education all by himself, and I was taken by Professor Barth to my first lesson at nine o'clock one morning, The lessons were to be for two hours every day.

So this was the unforgettable day when I met Theodor Altmann! He appeared to me to be tall (I was still small, of course), a heavy-set, rather fat man around 20 forty, with a huge, round face, his nose ridden by a steel-rimmed pince-nez held by a black ribbon. His hair was cropped in the German fashion; but a warm and intelligent twinkle in his eye made me love him right away.

At this point I must express my heart's gratitude to this wonderful man. My dear, dear Theodor Altmann—you began by giving me lessons like any other 25 normal teacher. We would start with German history, geography, Latin, and oh, the dreaded and hated mathematics. You were brilliant at introducing all these different subjects to me, and I was eager to absorb every word you said. You used precise, clear terms to express your thought, and it was delightful and exciting to listen to you.

30 As to mathematics—my lack of interest in it was a real calamity! You used to get angry, even going to complain to Professor Barth—but to no avail. The great Pythagoras and Euclid and the sublime science of algebra were a deadly bore to me! "Why do you make me verify their great theories?" I would protest in despair. "I give them full credit!" After a few stormy lessons, though, I saw through 35 an unmistakable twinkle in your eye a sympathy and a secret understanding of my ordeal. You knew well that my ignorance of higher mathematics was not going to paralyze the real course of my future. From that point on, thanks to you, life became a constant joy in learning. You revealed to me the philosophers of all time—Plato and Socrates, Aristotle, and later Kant and Schopenhauer. We 40 read Nietzsche's *Also Sprach Zarathustra* together, and I was impressed by the beauty of his prose—less by the trend of his thought, although his first book, *The Birth of Tragedy,* where he points so clearly to the distinction between music and the other fine arts, found me completely in accord. When it came to history, you abandoned very soon the dryness of the textbook, and took me on 45 a journey over centuries of human experience, showing me the results of frailty upon our own time, and the greed for power, the wickedness of men.

The next moment, you would open my eyes to the beauty of living in all its incessant variety, to the infinite possibilities of life, and at the same time foster my encourage for facing it.

50   The books you gave me to read became my best friends forever; thanks to
you I made the acquaintance of Goethe, Heine, Kleist, Balzac, Maupassant,
Dostoevsky, Gogol, and Tolstoy. At the age of eleven I was deeply stirred by
them. Yes, you treated me like a grownup, and you listened with indulgence and
apparent interest to my interjections or opinions—tolerating even my sharply
55 expressed criticisms.

Thank you for all this, my dear Theodor Altmann, from the bottom of my
hcart.

Passage 2

The close of Russia's disastrous campaign in the Far East was accompanied
by furious internal disorders. Undaunted by them, my mother, with her three
60 children, rcturned to St. Petersburg after almost a year of foreign resorts. This
was in the beginning of 1905. State matters required the presence of my father
in the capital; the Constitutional Democratic Party, of which he was one of
the founders, was to win a majority of seats in the First Parliament the following year. During one of his short stays with us in the country that summer, he
65 ascertained, with patriotic dismay, that my brother and I could read and write
English but not Russian (except KAKAO and MAMA). It was decided that the
village schoolmaster should come every afternoon to give us lessons and take
us for walks.

With a sharp and merry blast from the whistle that was part of my first sailor
70 suit, my childhood calls me back into that distant past to have me shake hands
with my delightful teacher. Vasily Martinovich Zhernosekov had a fuzzy brown
beard, a balding head, and china-blue eyes, one of which bore a fascinating
excrescence on the upper lid. The first day he came he brought a boxful of tre-
mendously appetizing blocks with a different letter painted on each side; these
75 cubes he would manipulate as if they were infinitely precious things, which
for that matter, they were (besides forming splendid tunnels for my trains). He
revered my father who had recently rebuilt and modernized the village school.
In old-fashioned token of free thought, he sported a flowing black tie carelessly
knotted in a bowlike arrangement. When addressing me, a small boy, he used
80 the plural of the second person—not in the stiff way servants did, and not as
my mother would do in moments of intense tenderness, when my temperature
had gone up or I had lost a tiny train-passenger (as if the singular were too thin
to bear the load of her love), but with the polite plainness of one man speaking
to another whom he does not know well enough to use "thou." A fiery revo-
85 lutionary, he would gesture vehemently on our country rambles and speak of
humanity and freedom and the badness of warfare and the sad (but interesting, I
thought) necessity of blowing up tyrants, and sometimes he would produce the
then popular pacifist book *Doloy Oruzhie*! (a translation of Bertha von Suttner's

Die Waffen Nieder!), and treat me, a child of six, to tedious quotations; I tried
90 to refute them: at that tender and bellicose age I spoke up for bloodshed in angry defense of my world of toy pistols and Arthurian knights. Under Lenin's
regime, when all non-Communist radicals were ruthlessly persecuted, Zhernosekov was sent to a hard-labor camp but managed to escape abroad, and died
in Narva in 1939.

■ QUESTION II.2.25

We can infer from the *second* narrator's penchant for "bloodshed"
and "toy pistols" (lines 90–91) that

(A) Zhernosekov's recommended book was a hawkish demand for
arms.

(B) Zhernosekov exploited the narrator's sympathy for Communism.

(C) he was listening to quotes from a book on disarmament.

(D) his teacher was trying to persuade him to support Lenin.

(E) his teacher found him too immature for intelligent debate.

ANSWER

(C)   According to Nabokov, a six-year-old boy is inclined to be "bellicose,"
or warlike. He raises the subject when describing how, at that age, he was inclined to refute passages that his teacher read to him from a contemporarily
popular pacifist book; therefore, (C) is the best answer.

We can assume that if the teacher, Zhernosekov, was reading from a pacifist
book, he was not "hawkish," so (A) is incorrect.

Since he was sent to a hard-labor camp for non-Communist radicals, (B) is
incorrect; and since this imprisonment occurred during Lenin's regime, (D) is
incorrect as well. The very fact that the teacher engaged young Nabokov in debate testifies to the assumption of equality, not immaturity.

■ QUESTION II.2.26

> Both narrative passages portray teachers who
>
> (A) come from the "old-school" notion of cold authoritarianism.
>
> (B) treat their charges as intellectual equals.
>
> (C) limit their instruction to particular technical skills.
>
> (D) constantly refer controversial issues back to the students' parents.
>
> (E) ultimately had to bow before the superior intellect of the pupil.

ANSWER

(B)   Both passages contain glowing remembrances of teachers who treated their pupils as intellectual equals, despite their difference in age; so (B) is the correct response.

(A) is incorrect as neither teacher assumes an authoritative role, nor does either report back to the parents (D) for justification. Equality of intellect seems mutual in both instances, not inverse superiority (E). Both teachers display a range of skills, mostly in humanistic studies; so (C) is incorrect.

■ QUESTION II.2.27

> Rubinstein's reference to "the sublime science of algebra" (line 32)
>
> (A) is employed ironically, since his talents lay elsewhere.
>
> (B) is indicative of the universal respect he had for learning.
>
> (C) demonstrates his native mathematical leanings.
>
> (D) is only said to pacify his teacher, who insisted he study it.
>
> (E) is paradoxical, given his preference for other aspects of mathematics.

ANSWER

(A)   Although Rubinstein displayed a great intellectual interest in a broad variety of fields of knowledge, mathematics was not one of these. He goes so far as to describe his lack of interest in it as a real calamity. Following this statement, the phrase "the sublime science of algebra" can only be ironic; so (A) is the correct answer.

Since he did not enjoy studying mathematics, (C) and (E) are obviously incorrect. Although he did have many interests, his distaste for math proved that his respect for learning was not quite "universal" (B). Rubinstein made his dislike of math quite clear to his teacher, and did not try to hide it; so (D) is incorrect.

◼ QUESTION II.2.28

Rubinstein responded to the philosopher Nietzsche because

(A) of the mathematical precision of Nietzsche's arguments.

(B) of their mutual interest in the arts, especially music.

(C) Theodor Altmann had demonstrated Nietzsche's correctness.

(D) of his attraction to the formal study of logic.

(E) *Also Sprach Zarathustra* made a case for the arts.

ANSWER

(B)   Nietzsche's *Birth of Tragedy* touched the chord of music in Rubinstein. It is not cited as formally "logical" (D) nor "mathematical" (A), which would only have repelled Rubinstein. Nietzsche's *Zarathustra* only appealed to Rubinstein because of its style, not its content (E). Altmann's sympathies (C) for Nietzsche are not discussed.

QUESTION II.2.29

The education of the respective narrators

(A) is virtually identical, given their mutually exact levels of maturity.

(B) tends to be more scientifically oriented in Rubinstein's narrative.

(C) differs insofar as the political orientation in Rubinstein's narrative supports a conservative point of view.

(D) demonstrates the extreme care with which handicapped children were tutored.

(E) acknowledges a liberty with which gifted children received private instruction.

ANSWER

(E)   Both narrators speak with gratitude of the special education they received. Both were gifted as children, and this caused their parents to seek a unique education for them, which would allow them to take full advantage of their talents and interests. They both had private instruction in which they worked individually with one teacher rather than attending school; therefore, (E) is correct.

Both narrators are gifted, not handicapped (D); and each received a liberal tutor's instruction, although at different age levels and maturity, causing (A) to be wrong. Rubinstein preferred humanities to science (B), and his education was liberal, not conservative (C).

◼ QUESTION II.2.30

> The manner in which the respective narrators addressed unpopular or unpleasant topics
>
> (A) reveals a degree of outspoken freedom on each of their parts.
>
> (B) demonstrates the utter subservience of students to their teachers.
>
> (C) shows a defiance on the part of Rubinstein, but timidity on the part of Nabokov.
>
> (D) suggests that the political climate in each case was repressive.
>
> (E) reveals timidity on the part of Rubinstein, but defiance on the part of Nabokov.

ANSWER

(A) Both Rubinstein and Nabokov expressed their youthful opinions openly with their teachers; there was no timid subservience (B) or repression (D). Nabokov was forthright in defense of his toy guns, making (C) incorrect. Rubinstein attacked mathematics with a certain candor, and so (E) is incorrect as well.

QUESTION II.2.31

> Nabokov's simultaneously "tender and bellicose" (line 90) age
>
> (A) reflects his mature reaction to his teacher's pacifist views.
>
> (B) tries to convey the complexity of the youth's mind.
>
> (C) captures the father's strong influence on his son's opinions.
>
> (D) expresses the warlike instincts of young children.
>
> (E) indicates the degree to which his mother had nurtured him.

ANSWER

(D) When Nabokov describes a six-year-old boy as "tender and bellicose," he is speaking with a fond memory of childish innocence. We know this partially because his symbols of war are Arthurian knights and toy pistols—two aspects of childish fantasy; therefore, (D) is correct.

He specifically speaks of his reaction to his teacher's pacifist views as childish, so (A) is incorrect. He represents his views as tender and innocent, not "complex." There is no mention that his father is warlike (C), and there is no mention of his mother at all (E).

■ QUESTION II.2.32

Through his guided studies in history and literature, Rubinstein came to see

(A) that humanity is beneficent and kindly in nature.

(B) the value of a practical, businesslike approach to everyday life.

(C) that mathematics would play a relatively unimportant role in his life.

(D) men's lives as blending good and evil, baseness and beauty.

(E) only the inherent evil in man, the dark side of human nature.

ANSWER

(D)   Rubinstein came to see the totality of life (lines 43–49) through Altmann's lessons, not merely its extremes of good (A) and evil (E). There is no mention of any business instinct (B) in him. Rubinstein had always known that mathematics would not play an important role in his life.

QUESTION II.2.33

Rubinstein's use of the phrase "dryness of the textbook" (line 44)

(A) betrays his intrinsic hatred of all academic discipline.

(B) suggests that his real problem lay in respecting any form of authority.

(C) stands in opposition to the method of his beloved teacher.

(D) stresses the basic difference in teaching strategies between Altmann and Zhernosekov (in Nabokov's narrative).

(E) merely reminds us how little he cared for reading.

ANSWER

(C)   Altmann enriched education beyond the textbook, so (C) is the correct answer. Altmann was an authority figure and an enforcer of academic discipline who was beloved by Rubinstein, denying (B) and (A). A youthful and passionate reader, Rubinstein negates (E) by the testimony of his list of authors (lines 51–52). Both teachers used similar strategies with their charges, so (D) is wrong.

QUESTION II.2.34

The word "rambles" in Nabokov's narrative (line 85) is used

(A) to suggest the illogical nature of Zhernosekov's instruction.

(B) as a metaphor for the tangents on which their debates would wander.

(C) to imply that "forbidden" topics often entered into discussions.

(D) to indicate that teacher and pupil did not confine their interactions to a fixed classroom.

(E) to suggest the politically opposite viewpoints teacher and pupil maintained.

ANSWER

(D) Nabokov uses the word "rambles" literally to state that he and his teacher went on walks in the country as they were engaged in lessons; therefore, (D) is correct. There is no mention that the instruction was illogical (A). There seemed to be no fixed plan to Nabokov's education: everything was important enough to be discussed and learned, so nothing could be considered tangential (B) and nothing was taboo (C). Although teacher and pupil may have had disagreements, and they did discuss volatile subjects (E), this could not be described as "rambling."

■ QUESTION II.2.35

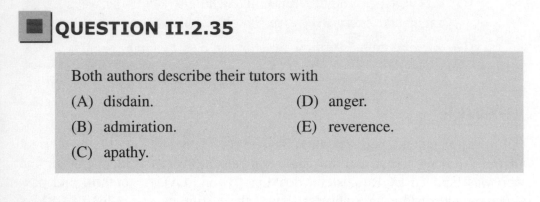

Both authors describe their tutors with

(A) disdain.   (D) anger.

(B) admiration.   (E) reverence.

(C) apathy.

ANSWER

(E) Reverence is the correct response because this is the sense one gets after reading both passages. Both authors have fond and respectful feelings about their teachers. So (A) and (D) are not correct. From their descriptions, we sense that the narrators revere these men; admiration (B) could be used to describe the author's tone, but it does not fully describe the emotion as vehemently as it is expressed. (C) is also incorrect because it suggests that there was no feeling behind the descriptions and this is just not the case.

■ QUESTION II.2.36

It can be inferred from the passages that both authors felt

(A) privileged to have received such an extensive education.

(B) resentful for having had to endure a horrible childhood.

(C) different because of their unique circumstances.

(D) that there was nothing exceptional about their youth.

(E) their education provided them with nothing but trivial knowledge.

ANSWER

(A) Both authors seem to be thankful that they received the education they did from the tutors they had. Resentful (B) does not describe the attitude of the authors. Although it is possible that their unique education made them feel "different," they make no specific mention of this. Through their expression of feeling privileged, they also seem to be saying that their youth was exceptional; so (D) is incorrect. The authors were very positive in the passages and did not express triviality about their education (E).

The following selections are excerpts from two presidential inaugural speeches. Passage 1 is from John F. Kennedy; Passage 2 was delivered by Franklin D. Roosevelt.

Passage 1

1   Let every nation know, whether it wishes us well or ill, that we shall pay any price, bear any burden, meet any hardship, support any friend, oppose any foe to assure the survival and the success of liberty.

This much we pledge—and more.

5   To those old allies whose cultural and spiritual origins we share, we pledge the loyalty of faithful friends. United, there is little we cannot do in a host of co-operative ventures. Divided, there is little we can do, for we dare not meet a powerful challenge at odds and split asunder.

To those new states whom we welcome to the ranks of the free, we pledge
10 our word that one form of colonial control shall not have passed away merely to

be replaced by a far more iron tyranny. We shall not always expect to find them supporting our view. But we shall always hope to find them strongly supporting their own freedom, and to remember that, in the past, those who foolishly sought power by riding the back of the tiger ended up inside.

15   To those people in the huts and villages of half the globe struggling to break the bonds of mass misery, we pledge our best efforts to help them help themselves, for whatever period is required, not because the Communists may be doing it, not because we seek their votes, but because it is right. If a free society cannot help the many who are poor, it cannot save the few who are rich.

Passage 2

20   This is pre-eminently the time to speak the truth, the whole truth, frankly and boldly. Nor need we shrink from honestly facing conditions in our country today. This great nation will endure as it has endured, will revive, and will prosper.

So first of all let me assert my firm belief that the only thing we have to fear is 25 fear itself—nameless, unreasoning, unjustified terror, which paralyzes needed efforts to convert retreat into advance.

In every dark hour of our national life a leadership of frankness and vigor has met with that understanding and support of the people themselves which is essential to victory. I am convinced that you will again give that support to 30 leadership in these critical days.

In such a spirit on my part and yours we face our common difficulties. They concern, thank God, only material things. Values have shrunken to fantastic levels; taxes have risen; our ability to pay has fallen; government of all kinds is faced by serious curtailment of income; the means of exchange are frozen in 35 the currents of trade; the withered leaves of industrial enterprise lie on every side; farmers find no markets for their produce; the savings of many years in thousands of families are gone.

More important, a host of unemployed citizens face the grim problem of existence, and an equally great number toil with little return. Only a foolish optimist 40 can deny the dark realities of the moment.

Yet our distress comes from no failure of substance. We are stricken by no plague of locusts. Compared with the perils which our forefathers conquered because they believed and were not afraid, we have still much to be thankful for. Nature still offers her bounty, and human efforts have multiplied it. Plenty 45 is at our doorstep, but a generous use of it languishes in the very sight of the supply.

Primarily, this is because the rulers of the exchange of mankind's goods have failed through their own stubbornness and their own incompetence, have admitted their failure and abdicated. Practices of the unscrupulous money-changers
50 stand indicted in the court of public opinion, rejected by the hearts and minds of men.

■ QUESTION II.2.37

In line 3, "liberty" most nearly means

(A) privilege.   (D) freedom.

(B) familiarity.   (E) cooperation.

(C) emancipation.

ANSWER

(D)   In the broad sense in which it is employed here, liberty most nearly means freedom, the absence for necessity or constraint in thought or action. (A) and (B) are also synonyms for liberty, but make little sense in this context. (C) implies the removal of bondage, which is an added connotation not mentioned by the author. (E) Cooperation is not a definition for liberty.

■ QUESTION II.2.38

In lines 12–13, the use of "supporting" in two ways emphasizes the

(A) idea that liberty itself is more important than the form it takes.

(B) struggle between freedom and tyranny.

(C) power that countries can wield in alliance with one another.

(D) desire of the speaker to influence the politics of weaker countries.

(E) importance the speaker places on individual freedom.

ANSWER

(A)   The double use of the word is meant to imply that the author will not be selfish in defending only the liberty of Americans. He suggests that even if they don't agree with our ideals, he hopes that they will be active in defending their own. This supports answer (A), as it implies a non-selfish, non-judgmental love for liberty.

(B) and (C) are both discussed by the author, but do not relate to this portion of the passage. In this sentence the author is not talking about influencing the politics of other countries; he hopes, instead, that they are defending their own interests.

(E) is wrong since the author does not speak of liberty as it relates to individuals.

QUESTION II.2.39

In lines 13–14, the phrase "in the past . . . ended up inside" is a reference to

(A) nations of the past who built great empires through cooperative efforts.

(B) the importance of remembering all those who have lost their lives defending liberty.

(C) the importance of remembering the struggles and hardships that the first free societies fought in order to preserve liberty.

(D) the importance of remembering that those who tried to gain by following despotic governments in the past eventually lost their freedom.

(E) the valor of nations that declared their independence against overwhelming odds.

ANSWER

(D)   The metaphor clearly states that following something inherently bloodthirsty, such as a despot or a tiger, will lead to being consumed by the stronger power. With this understanding of the metaphor, (A), (B), and (C) are seen to be incorrect. While (E) may express an idea similar to the one implied by the metaphor, the word "valor" makes it incorrect because the author describes such nations as "foolish."

■ QUESTION II.2.40

The statement "If a free society . . . save the few who are rich" (lines 18–19) suggests that the author believes that

(A) supporting the poor is the function of government in a free society.

(B) protecting liberty abroad is a necessary component of a free society.

(C) suppressing communism is the goal of a free society.

(D) democracy is synonymous with a free society.

(E) defending liberty is not a valid reason to go to war.

ANSWER

(B)   This summation restates the author's main idea: It is the duty of a strong nation to support liberty the world over. (A) could be taken to be literally correct; however, the author speaks not of supporting the poor, but of helping them to help themselves.

(C) and (E) are both in direct opposition to other sections of the passage. The author states that neither imitating nor suppressing the Communists is the reason for helping other nations, and he states that no burden is too great to ensure liberty. (D) is incorrect since the author never mentions democracy.

■ QUESTION II.2.41

In line 22, the word "endure" most nearly means

(A) exist.   (D) confirm.

(B) linger.   (E) flourish.

(C) withstand.

ANSWER

(C)   Throughout this passage, it becomes obvious that the author is speaking to a nation facing huge problems and dangers; therefore, "withstand" is correct because it means to oppose with firm determination and to resist successfully. If this resistance were possible, it would lead to the nation reviving and prospering—enduring. Both (A) and (B) are synonyms but they mean to continue and do not imply opposition or resistance. (D) and (E) are incorrect because they bear no relation to the word "endure."

■ QUESTION II.2.42

> The author of Passage 2 uses the phrase "the only thing we have to fear is fear itself" (lines 24–25) to suggest that
>
> (A) the problems of which he speaks are illusory and inconsequential.
>
> (B) the dire problems of which he speaks can be overcome if a strong effort is put forth.
>
> (C) once the unscrupulous people in power are exposed that the economy will improve.
>
> (D) the nation will eventually prosper despite the grim present outlook.
>
> (E) speaking the truth will lead to greater prosperity.

ANSWER

(B)   The author is eloquently saying that no circumstances warrant fear if they are directly confronted. (A) makes no sense because the author describes the problems in detail and they are very concrete. (C), (D), and (E) are all points made by the author elsewhere in the speech, but have little to do with this particular phrase.

■ QUESTION II.2.43

In lines 31–37 the author most likely describes "our common difficulties" in order to

(A) illustrate the near impossibility of conquering these problems.

(B) back up his earlier statement about the importance of speaking the whole truth.

(C) portray the powers of observation that a leader must possess.

(D) show that farmers are the hardest hit by economic difficulties.

(E) point out that these difficulties are merely transitory in nature.

ANSWER

(B)   The author is directly stating the grim reality of which he speaks. (A) and (E) stand in direct opposition to the author's ideas. (C) may be true, but is of only slight—if any—relevance here. (D) is incorrect since the author states that many, besides farmers, are experiencing hard times.

■ QUESTION II.2.44

The author of Passage 2 most likely mentions "the perils which our forefathers conquered" (line 42) in order to

(A) escape from present misery by drawing on the past.

(B) put current hardships in an historical context to show that no problem is insurmountable.

(C) illustrate that despite hardship, conditions could be much worse than they are.

(D) draw strength from the fact that our forefathers were able to overcome adversity.

(E) remind his audience that perils have existed in every age and will continue to exist.

ANSWER

(C)   The complete sentence this quote is taken from reads, "Compared with the perils which our forefathers conquered because they believed and were not afraid, we have still much to be thankful for." That he mentions they have much to be thankful for shows he is using the comparison to prove that their forefathers were much worse off; so by projection, their own troubles could be much worse than they were.

The author never suggests that they escape from their problems (A), but that they try to solve them. The author is showing how different the problems were from their forefathers', not trying to put them in the same context (B). Although (D) and (E) state part of the author's purpose, they both leave out the sense of comparison that is implicit in the quote.

■ QUESTION II.2.45

The overall tone of Passage 2 can be said to be one of

(A) hopeless fatalism.   (D) cautious optimism.

(B) desperate fear.   (E) frank honesty.

(C) grim acceptance.

ANSWER

(D)   The author believes that hardship will be overcome by facing the grim conditions that exist. (A) and (B) ignore the hope displayed by the author. (C) is closer; however, the narrator does not encourage his listeners to accept the grim situation, but to take steps to change it. The author speaks of the importance of honesty (E), but as a means of combating the dire circumstances. This is just one characteristic of the overall tone.

QUESTION II.2.46

The authors of both passages are concerned with

(A) the ability of their nation to thrive despite any adverse conditions.

(B) the ability of their nation to overcome economic hardship.

(C) what it means to be free.

(D) the role of the president in a democratic society.

(E) the role of their nation on a global scale.

ANSWER

(A)   In both passages the authors describe problems that a nation may have to face, either from within or without, but they also speak of the strength and courage available to face these problems. Both authors state that their nation can endure any hardship. (B) is a concern only in the second passage. (C) Passage 1 discusses the importance of freedom, but not its meaning, and passage 2 does not mention it at all. (D) is not addressed in either passage; and (E) is a concern only in the first passage.

QUESTION II.2.47

Which statement best describes the contrast between the intended audience for the two passages?

(A) Passage 1 addresses the whole free world, while Passage 2 addresses only one nation.

(B) Both passages address only one nation.

(C) Both passages address the free world.

(D) It is impossible to generalize about the intended audiences from the information given.

(E) Passage 1 addresses a much smaller audience than Passage 2.

ANSWER

(A) Both passages are concerned mainly with their own nation; but the first passage, in relating one nation to the rest of the world, addresses "every nation." The first passage addresses the whole world, while in Passage 2 the author is speaking directly to the citizens of his "great nation," therefore making (B), (C), and (E) incorrect. There is ample evidence to infer the intended audience of both passages, so (D) is incorrect.

◼ QUESTION II.2.48

Lines 18–19 of Passage 1 echoes what theme from Passage 2?

(A) A strong nation has to have the capacity to help those who are struggling to survive.

(B) A thriving nation must protect the rich.

(C) A free society must completely support the poor.

(D) A clearly defined class structure is necessary if a nation is to survive.

(E) A nation must be prosperous if it is to influence world events.

ANSWER

(A) Both passages speak of helping those less well-off. The first speaks of those in developing countries, and the second speaks of those hard hit by a faltering economy in their own country. (B) and (C) are blindly literal interpretations that pay no attention to the context in which they are framed. (D) has no basis in either passage. (E) could be inferred to be true, but it is not a theme of Passage 2.

■ QUESTION II.2.49

Both passages mention which of the following as being important to the success of a nation as they describe it?

(A) Unity among peoples or countries

(B) Powerful leadership

(C) A strong foreign policy

(D) A willingness to protect liberty at all costs

(E) The ability to overcome material difficulties

ANSWER

(A)   Both authors speak of the importance of understanding and support that is gained through unity. Passage 2 says that leadership must be frank and vigorous, but no mention is made of being powerful; so (B) is incorrect. (C) and (D) are preoccupations of only Passage 1, while (E) is only a concern in Passage 2.

In this passage, John Donne discusses the philosophical similarities between Earth and Man.

1   It is too little to call man a little world; except God, man is diminutive to nothing. Man consists of more pieces, more parts, than the world; than the world
doth, nay, than the world is. And if these pieces were extended and stretched
out in man as they are in the world, man would be the giant and the world the
5 dwarf; the world but the map, and the man the world. If all the veins in our
bodies were extended to rivers, and all the sinews to veins of mines, and all
the muscles that lie upon one another to hills, and all the bones to quarries of
stones, and all the other pieces to the proportion of those which correspond to
them in the world, the air would be too little for this orb of man to move in,
10 the firmament would be but enough for this star. For as the whole world hath
nothing to which something in man doth not answer, so hath man many pieces
of which the whole world hath no representation. Enlarge this meditation upon
this great world, man, so far as to consider the immensity of the creatures this
world produces. Our creatures are our thoughts, creatures that are born giants,
15 that reach from east to west, from earth to heaven, that do not only bestride all
the sea and land, but span the sun and firmament at once: my thoughts reach all,
comprehend all.

Inexplicable mystery! I their creator am in a close prison, in a sick bed, anywhere, and any one of my creatures, my thoughts, is with the sun, and beyond
20 the sun, overtakes the sun, and overgoes the sun in one pace, one step, everywhere. And then as the other world produces serpents and vipers, malignant and
venomous creatures, and worms and caterpillars, that endeavor to devour that
world which produces them, and monsters compiled and complicated of divers
parents and kinds, so this world, ourselves, produces all these in us, producing
25 diseases and sicknesses of all those sorts; venomous and infectious diseases,
feeding and consuming diseases, and manifold and entangled diseases made
up of many several ones. And can the other world name so many venomous, so
many consuming, so many monstrous creatures, as we can diseases, of all these
kinds? O miserable abundance, O beggarly riches! How much do we lack of
30 having remedies for every disease when as yet we have not names for them?

But we have a Hercules against these giants, these monsters: that is the physician. He musters up all the resources of the other world to succor this, all nature
to relieve man. We have the physician but we are not the physician. Here we
shrink in our proportion, sink in our dignity in respect of very mean creatures
35 who are physicians to themselves. The hart that is pursued and wounded, they
say, knows an herb which, being eaten, throws off the arrow: a strange kind of
vomit. The dog that pursues it, though he is subject to sickness, even proverbi-
ally knows his grass that recovers him. And it may be true that the drugger is as
near to man as to other creatures; it may be that obvious and present simples,
40 easy to be had, would cure him; but the apothecary is not so near him, nor the
physician so near him, as they too are to other creatures. Man hath not that
innate instinct to apply these nature medicines to his present danger, as those
inferior creatures have. He is not his own apothecary, his own physician, as
they are. Call back therefore thy meditation again, and bring it down. What's
45 become of man's great extent and proportion, when himself shrinks himself and
consumes himself to a handful of dust? What's become of his soaring thoughts,
his compassing thoughts, when himself brings himself to the ignorance, to the
thoughtlessness of the grave? His diseases are his own, but the physician is not,
he hath them at home, but he must send for the physician.

QUESTION II.2.50

Donne finds an ironic contrast

(A) among the venomous creatures of this world.

(B) between Hercules and the physician.

(C) between the hart and the dog.

(D) between man's confinements and man's thoughts.

(E) between apothecaries and physicians.

ANSWER

(D)   Lines 18–21 describe how a confined man may still enjoy imaginative freedom and dominance of the universe. Apothecaries and physicians (line 43) are not contrasted; they are both admired as benefactors of man, denying (E) and by extension (B), since physicians are directly compared to the Greek hero (lines 31–32). He describes the venomous creatures (A) as a cohesive group, and he draws a comparison between the hart and the dog (C).

QUESTION II.2.51

The word "simples" (line 39) means

(A) uncomplicated possessions.

(B) foolish people.

(C) direct procedures.

(D) remedies.

(E) mathematical formulas.

ANSWER

(D)   Donne speaks of "simples" as easy to be had and sure to cure an illness; so, in context, "simples" are remedies, prescriptions from a druggist. The rest of the options are possible meanings for "simple," but none of them bear any relation to this passage.

■ QUESTION II.2.52

In his opening discussion, Donne inverts

(A) microscopic organisms with cosmic giants.

(B) the relation between maps and geographic locations.

(C) the magnitude of men with that of Earth.

(D) the proportions of sinews and muscles.

(E) the relationship of hills to stones.

ANSWER

(C) The breadth of men and Earth are given inverse proportions in Donne's conceit (lines 2–3); (A) is a strong distractor only if the reader superimposes "microcosmic" onto the image of man that Donne has not. World and map are inverted (line 5), not geography and map, and only in contrast to man as the world, choice (B). Both (D) and (E) are incorrect based on misreading analogies; Donne speaks of sinews, muscles, hills, and stones, but only to support his original inversion of the size of man and the size of the Earth.

■ QUESTION II.2.53

Phrases like "O miserable abundance, O beggarly riches!" (line 29) reveal

(A) Donne's contradictory style.

(B) Donne's inability to see the positive aspects of life.

(C) the effects of venom on the human constitution.

(D) the poet's use of oxymoron in describing a union of opposites.

(E) how much happier beasts are than men.

ANSWER

(D) An "oxymoron" is a figure of speech in which opposite or contradictory ideas are combined. This is what Donne does when he combines the antonyms, "miserable" and "abundance," and "beggarly" and "riches." (A) is insufficient to explain the reversals Donne posits throughout the passage as an explanation of his mystical humanism. The contradictions are not important to the style but to the content of Donne's work. All of paragraph one is grandly positive and assertive, denying choices (B) and (C). The disposition of beasts (E) does not arise until the final paragraph (lines 35–38).

■ QUESTION II.2.54

The nature of the "very mean creatures" (line 34)

(A) tends to raise man's estimate of himself.

(B) provides the proper study for science.

(C) prohibits their adapting to change or struggle.

(D) shows man to be comparatively inept at healing himself.

(E) raises the dignity of the physician's skill.

ANSWER

(D)   Ironically, the "mean creatures" prove more able to heal themselves than man; so we "shrink in proportion," negating (A) and (E), as well as contradicting (C) (see lines 41–43). (B) is never discussed.

QUESTION II.2.55

For Donne, the ultimate negation of the power of thought is

(A) sleep.

(B) unscientific speculation.

(C) death.

(D) simple nature.

(E) imaginary concern with "monsters."

ANSWER

(C)   Death is explicit in the phrase "the thoughtlessness of the grave" (line 48). (D) is incorrect since nature provokes thought (lines 33–44). (E) The abil-

ity to create imaginary "monsters" is a tribute to the power of thought. (A) and
(B) are never addressed as subjects.

■ QUESTION II.2.56

When Donne says that "he hath them at home" (line 49), the
"them" refers to

(A) man's imaginings.   (D) creatures.

(B) man's illnesses.   (E) medicines.

(C) the physicians.

ANSWER

(B)   The complete sentence from which this is taken states, "His diseases
are his own . . . he hath them at home." So, taken in context, (B) is obviously
correct. Man nurtures his diseases, his own destruction, at home. Grammatical
(and logical) scrutiny should dismiss (C) and (E) quickly; (A) and (D) are almost synonymous—and wrong.

■ QUESTION II.2.57

The "diseases and sicknesses" (line 25) of men

(A) are sent as a punishment for human pride.

(B) are produced by men themselves.

(C) are no worse than the venomous beasts in nature.

(D) baffle the physicians who try to cure them.

(E) are merely metaphors for Donne's troubled times.

ANSWER

(B)   In lines 24–25, Donne explicitly states that " . . . ourselves, produces
all these in us, producing diseases and sicknesses of all those sorts . . . " So (B)
is the correct answer. Donne does not dwell on "pride" (A) or on his "troubled
times" (E).

Donne speaks of the physicians as curing the diseases, not being baffled by them (D). Donne does draw similarities between diseases and beasts of nature (C), but does not say one is "worse" than another.

■ QUESTION II.2.58

When Donne says, "my thoughts reach all, comprehend all" (lines 16–17), he confirms

(A) his earlier estimation of the power of poetry.

(B) his prior comparison of man with God.

(C) the pride and conceit that he says lead to downfall.

(D) his contrasting ideas on the creatures of this world.

(E) his claim that the world is literally populated by giants.

ANSWER

(B)   Among the defining qualities of God are omniscience and omnipresence. Donne's metaphysics elevate man to godlike proportions. Only later does he qualify his meditation and find man inferior to the simple beasts, (D). "If these pieces were extended" (line 3) is a concession to metaphor, not a literal belief in giants, choice (E). (C) might be inferred by the Biblical or literary reader of Donne; it is not stated. (A) is not addressed in the passage.

■ QUESTION II.2.59

Donne's command to "bring it down" (line 44)

(A) means he wishes to simplify the language.

(B) forces us to reassess the position of man in the universe.

(C) symbolizes the lack of morals and compassion in the world.

(D) suggests that the sphere of heaven be made available on Earth.

(E) warns us that we are too materialistic in our values.

ANSWER

(B)   The first part of Donne's meditation glorifies mankind, making it seem larger than the Earth. When he admonishes us to "bring it down," he is showing us how disease and death can quickly make man seem much smaller and "forcing us to reassess the position of man in the universe" (B). He does not simplify his language (A). He never addresses our morals (C) or our "materialistic . . . values" (E). Nor does he mention the sphere of heaven (D).

In this excerpt from Jules Verne's Twenty Thousand Leagues Under the Sea, *we are presented with a danger on board the* Nautilus, *Captain Nemo's legendary submarine.*

1   The next day, the 22nd of March, at six in the morning, preparations for departure were begun. The last gleams of twilight were melting into night. The cold was great, the constellations shone with wonderful intensity. In the zenith glittered that wondrous Southern Cross—the polar bear of Antarctic regions. The
5   thermometer showed 12° below zero, and when the wind freshened it was most biting. Flakes of ice increased on the open water. The sea seemed everywhere alike. Numerous blackish patches spread on the surface, showing the formation of fresh ice. Evidently the southern basin, frozen during the six winter months, was absolutely inaccessible. What became of the whales in that time? Doubt-
10   less they went beneath the icebergs, seeking more practicable seas. As to the seals and morses, accustomed to life in a hard climate, they remained on these icy shores. The creatures have the instinct to break holes in the ice-fields and to keep them open. To these holes they come for breath; when the birds, driven away by the cold, have emigrated to the north, these sea mammals remain sole
15   masters of the polar continent. But the reservoirs were filling with water, and the *Nautilus* was slowly descending. At 1,000 feet deep it stopped; its screw beat the waves, and it advanced straight towards the north at a speed of fifteen miles an hour. Towards night it was already floating under the immense body of the iceberg. At three in the morning I was awakened by a violent shock. I sat up
20   in my bed and listened in the darkness, when I was thrown into the middle of the room. The *Nautilus*, after having struck, had rebounded violently. I groped along the partition, and by the staircase to the saloon, which was lit by the luminous ceiling. The furniture was upset. Fortunately the windows were firmly set, and had held fast. The pictures on the starboard side, from being no longer
25   vertical, were clinging to the paper, whilst those of the port side were hanging at least a foot from the wall. The *Nautilus* was lying on its starboard side perfectly motionless. I heard footsteps, and a confusion of voices; but Captain Nemo did not appear. As I was leaving the saloon, Ned Land and Conseil entered. . . .

We left the saloon. There was no one in the library. At the centre staircase,
30   by the berths of the ship's crew, there was no one. I thought that Captain Nemo

must be in the pilot's cage. It was best to wait. We all returned to the saloon.
For twenty minutes we remained thus, trying to hear the slightest noise which
might be made on board the *Nautilus*, when Captain Nemo entered. He seemed
not to see us; his face, generally so impassive, showed signs of uneasiness. He
35 watched the compass silently, then the manometer; and, going to the plani-
sphere, placed his finger on a spot representing the southern seas. I would not
interrupt him; but, some minutes later, when he turned towards me, I said, using
one of his own expressions in the Torres Straits:

"An incident, Captain?"

40   "No, sir; an accident this time."

"Serious?"

"Perhaps."

"Is the danger immediate?"

"No."

45   "The *Nautilus* has stranded?"

"Yes."

"And this has happened—how?"

"From a caprice of nature, not from the ignorance of man. Not a mistake has
been made in the working. But we cannot prevent equilibrium from producing
50 its effects. We may brave human laws, but we cannot resist natural ones."

Captain Nemo had chosen a strange moment for uttering this philosophical
reflection. On the whole, his answer helped me little.

■ QUESTION II.2.60

Why do the birds fly to the north in lines 13–15?

(A) The only type of cold that they can endure is in the North Pole.

(B) Extreme cold allows them to hibernate until the summer months.

(C) The seals and morses, seeking supremacy in the land, drive the birds away.

(D) The birds flee to the warmer climates of the north.

(E) The cold drives the birds into a panic, and they fly in the wrong direction.

ANSWER

(D)   The passage states that the *Nautilus* was in the "Antarctic regions," and that the birds who flew to the north were "driven away by the cold." It becomes clear from this that the birds fly north from the freezing South Pole to reach warmer climates.

The scene takes place on the opposite end of the world from the North Pole (A); so going north will not bring the birds to a place of extreme cold in order to "hibernate" (B). Although the seals and morses remain behind, they do not seek to drive the birds away (C). The passage does not imply that the birds were flying about in a blind panic (E).

▪ QUESTION II.2.61

What is meant when the narrator informs us that the *Nautilus* has "stopped" in line 16?

(A) The *Nautilus* has completely ceased to move.

(B) The *Nautilus* has paused only briefly before descending further.

(C) The *Nautilus* no longer descends, but continues to move.

(D) The *Nautilus* halts only long enough to fill its reservoirs with much-needed water.

(E) The *Nautilus* never ended its descent completely; it only slowed down its continuing descent.

ANSWER

(C) The passage states that "the reservoirs were filling with water, and the *Nautilus* was slowly descending. At 1,000 feet deep it stopped; its screw beat the waves, and it advanced straight towards the north at a speed of fifteen miles an hour"; therefore, even though the *Nautilus* stopped descending, it continued to run straight towards the north. Because of this, it did not completely cease to move (A), nor did it descend any further (B). Its reservoirs were filled to allow the *Nautilus* to descend; there was no reason for them to be filled after the vessel had finished its descent (D). We have already shown that the Nautilus did indeed halt its descent (E).

▪ QUESTION II.2.62

In line 22–23, "luminous" most nearly means

(A) extravagant.

(B) glowing.

(C) enormous.

(D) artificial.

(E) damaged.

ANSWER

(B) "Luminous" means brilliant, shining, or glowing. This is exemplified by the fact that the saloon "was lit by the luminous ceiling." While the other selections may or may not have applied to the saloon's ceiling, these qualities were not included in the use of the word "luminous."

■ QUESTION II.2.63

What is the message of Nemo's "philosophical reflection" in lines 48–50?

(A) Nature despises the artificial creations of mankind.

(B) Were it not for man's fallibility, anything would be possible.

(C) Despite man's perfection of the sciences, he may still succumb to the whims of Nature.

(D) Human beings are unable to complete a great project without including some terrible, fatal flaw.

(E) Man is ignorant only because Nature makes him so.

ANSWER

(C) The key word here is the "caprice," or whim, of Nature, to which all of Nemo's excellent planning falls victim. Nemo does not mention that Nature has any particular vendetta against man's accomplishments; it is a mere whim that the tides have turned against them (A). Nemo is sure to note that it is not the "ignorance of man" or a "mistake" that has endangered them; therefore, human fallibility of any sort [(B) and (D)] is not an issue here. Once again, Nemo does not feel that man's ignorance is important here; nor does he suggest that Nature would cause a state of ignorance (E).

■ QUESTION II.2.64

What is the narrator's overall attitude toward Captain Nemo?

(A) Contempt   (D) Confusion

(B) Respect   (E) Condescension

(C) Anger

ANSWER

(B)   It is clear from several factors that the narrator has a great deal of re-spect for Captain Nemo. Not only did he wait anxiously for Nemo's arrival to fix matters, but when the captain did arrive, the narrator "would not interrupt him," but held his tongue until Nemo turned specifically to him. The narrator never considers Nemo in a tone of contempt (A), anger (C), or condescension (E). Although the narrator is sometimes unsure of Nemo's motives, he does not express a state of overall confusion when regarding the captain (D).

■ QUESTION II.2.65

Why does Nemo feel the need to qualify the narrator's sugges-tion that the *Nautilus*'s situation be considered an "incident" (lines 39–40)?

(A) Nemo always corrects the narrator, no matter what the latter suggests.

(B) Nemo believes their current situation is of a significantly dif-ferent character from what they experienced in the Torres Straits.

(C) Nemo considers "accidents" to be far more important than "in-cidents."

(D) Nemo fears that they will never survive their current situation and therefore changes the narrator's choice of definition.

(E) Nemo blames himself for his folly in bringing them into dan-gerous, uncharted territory.

ANSWER

(B)   The narrator uses the word "incident" in his conversation with Nemo to refer directly back to Nemo's own use of the word to describe an occurrence in the Torres Straits. Nemo's need to correct the narrator shows that he feels the narrator is incorrect in his assumption that the current situation is similar to whatever occurred in the Torres Straits.

There is no indication in the passage that Nemo constantly corrects the narrator (A), nor that "accidents" are normally of a graver nature than "incidents," although such may coincidentally be the case (C). Nemo never suggests that an "accident" is irreparable (D), nor does he reprimand himself for their current crisis (E).

QUESTION II.2.66

The narrator notes that Nemo's face is normally "so impassive" (line 34) in order to

(A) show how Nemo's current visage emphasizes the gravity of their situation.

(B) stress Nemo's arrogance to others whom he feels are beneath his station.

(C) explain why Nemo's expression is so uneasy.

(D) show why others are never able to approach Nemo intimately.

(E) reiterate Nemo's inability to deal with a crisis situation.

ANSWER

(A)   The narrator is concerned that Nemo's apparent uneasiness bodes a serious problem merely because Nemo's countenance does not normally reflect his internal emotions. The narrator does not imply that this is a measure of Nemo's arrogance (B), nor that the captain is unable to communicate with others intimately (D). Nemo's normally stoic expression does not in itself explain his present uneasiness (C). There is no indication in the passage that Nemo is unable to deal with a crisis situation (E).

■ QUESTION II.2.67

What is the most likely reason that the narrator seeks Captain Nemo after he leaves the saloon?

(A) He is angry and wishes to chastise Nemo for his ineptitude.

(B) He wants to do a favor for Ned Land and Conseil, who were looking for Nemo.

(C) He wants Nemo to repair the furniture in the saloon.

(D) He knows that Nemo is the only person capable of rectifying the situation.

(E) He is afraid that Nemo may have been injured in the collision.

ANSWER

(D)   It is apparent from his later questioning of Nemo that the narrator has absolutely no idea what has happened to the *Nautilus*, much less any idea how to go about rectifying the situation; he clearly believes Nemo has the ability to right the matter.

There is no indication in the passage that the narrator is angry at Nemo (A), nor that he has any interest at the present in repairing the saloon furniture (C). The narrator was curious about Nemo's locale before he met Ned Land and Conseil; he is obviously seeking the captain for his own reasons (B). That the narrator decided to wait for Nemo's arrival in the saloon indicates he probably did not imagine that the captain was injured (E).

In the following passage Martin Luther King
presents his vision of racial unity.

1   We cannot walk alone. And as we walk, we must make the pledge that we
shall always march ahead. We cannot turn back. There are those who are asking the devotees of civil rights, "When will you be satisfied?" We can never
be satisfied as long as the Negro is the victim of unspeakable horrors of police
5 brutality. We can never be satisfied as long as our bodies, heavy with the fatigue
of travel, cannot gain lodging in the motels of the highways and the hotels of the
cities. We can never be satisfied as long as the Negro's basic mobility is from a
smaller ghetto to a larger one. We can never be satisfied as long as our children
are stripped of their selfhood and robbed of their dignity by signs stating "For
10 Whites Only."

We cannot be satisfied as long as a Negro in Mississippi cannot vote and a Negro in New York believes he has nothing for which to vote. No, no, we are not satisfied and will not be satisfied until "justice rolls down like water and righteousness like a mighty stream."

15   I am not unmindful that some of you have come here out of great trials and tribulations. Some of you have come fresh from narrow jail cells. Some of you have come from areas where your quest for freedom left you battered by the storms of persecution and staggered by the winds of police brutality. You have been the veterans of creative suffering. Continue to work with the faith that un-
20 earned suffering is redemptive.

Go back to Mississippi, go back to Alabama, go back to South Carolina, go back to Georgia, go back to Louisiana, go back to the slums and ghettoes of our northern cities, knowing that somehow this situation can and will be changed. Let us not wallow in the valley of despair.

25   I say to you today, my friends, even though we face the difficulties of today and tomorrow, I still have a dream. It is a dream deeply rooted in the American dream. I have a dream that one day this nation will rise up and live out the true meaning of its creed: "We hold these truths to be self-evident, that all men are created equal."

30   I have a dream that one day on the red hills of Georgia, the sons of former slaves and the sons of former slaveowners will be able to sit down together at the table of brotherhood. I have a dream that one day even the state of Mississippi, a state sweltering with the heat of injustice, sweltering with the heat of oppression, will be transformed into an oasis of freedom and justice.

35   I have a dream that my four little children will one day live in a nation where they will not be judged by the color of their skin but by the content of their character.

I have a dream that one day in Alabama, with its vicious racists, with its Governor having his lips dripping with the words of "interposition" and "nul-
40 lification"—one day right there in Alabama little black boys and black girls will be able to join hands with little white boys and little white girls as brothers and sisters.

I have a dream that one day "every valley shall be exalted, every hill and mountain shall be made low; the rough places will be made plain, and the
45 crooked places will be made straight; and the glory of the Lord shall be revealed, and all flesh shall see it together."

This is our hope. This is the faith that I go back to the South with. With this faith, we will be able to hew out of the mountain of despair a stone of hope.

With this faith we will be able to transform the jangling discords of our nation
50 into a beautiful symphony of brotherhood. With this faith, we will be able to
work together, to play together, to struggle together, to go to jail together, to
stand up for freedom together, knowing that we will be free one day. . . .

■ QUESTION II.2.68

In line 39, the word "interposition" most nearly means

(A) a mixing, a conglomeration.

(B) a lofty height or position.

(C) a coming together, a union.

(D) a uniting.

(E) an intervention.

ANSWER

(E)   The word "interposition" means an intervention or a mediation. Answer
(E) most nearly satisfies that definition.

A conglomeration is not an intervention or a coming between, but a mixing;
(A) would not be the best choice. One who intervenes does not necessarily
have to be in a lofty position; (B) is not, therefore, the best answer. Perhaps the
person who chose this answer selected it merely because both the word being
considered and the answer contained the letters "position."

After an intervention, there may be a coming together (C) or a uniting (D),
but interposition does not necessarily ensure this result; (C) and (D) are not,
therefore, the best answers.

QUESTION II.2.69

In lines 13–14, the words "justice rolls down like water and righteousness like a mighty stream" can best be described as

(A) onomatopoeic words.

(B) an alliterative expression.

(C) an understatement.

(D) an analogy.

(E) a fantasy.

ANSWER

(D)   In lines 13–14, the words "justice rolls down like water and righteousness like a mighty stream" can best be described as a comparison, or an analogy (D).

Since an onomatopoeic word is formed by making an imitation of the sound associated with the object or action and these words don't sound like water or a stream, onomatopoeic (A) is not the best answer.

An alliterative expression repeats the same sound at the beginning of each word; this has not been done in the phrase, "justice rolls down like water and righteousness like a mighty stream." It is not alliterative, so (B) is incorrect. Using terms like "mighty stream" and "righteousness" are not understatements; (C) should not be selected. The words in question do not describe a fantasy, but a vision capable of being fulfilled. (D) should not be selected since it expresses this quotation as being a fantasy.

QUESTION II.2.70

The Southern states, the slums, and the ghettos in the fourth paragraph were listed

(A) in order to show that though the United States is large, racial inequality is limited to two main areas.

(B) in order to name the areas from which most of the audience came.

(C) in order to single out areas where political leaders were most biased.

(D) to warn those areas of the violence planned.

(E) to remind people in those areas that even though times may be rough, they should not give up.

ANSWER

(E) The Southern states, the slums, and the ghettos in the fourth paragraph were listed to inspire hope; even if those areas were desolate at this time, King had faith that in the future things would change. (E) is the best answer.

Unfortunately, racial bias and inequality are not just evident in two areas; (A), then, was an inadequate answer.

The audience did not necessarily come only from the areas listed above; (B) is not the best answer.

Biased political leaders are not restricted to slums, ghettos, and Southern states; (C) is not the best choice. King did not plan violence; so answer (D) is not appropriate.

QUESTION II.2.71

King reminded the audience that "unearned suffering is redemptive" in lines 19–20. The best explanation for this statement is that

(A) some suffering is earned; it is deserved.

(B) some suffering is justified; it is purifying, as such.

(C) unearned suffering is cruel and unforgivable.

(D) unearned suffering is desirable.

(E) some undeserved suffering is freeing and releasing.

ANSWER

(E) King reminded the audience that "unearned suffering is redemptive" in line 20. He said this to give them hope and to make their suffering a little easier to bear. The best explanation for this statement is that King was suggesting that some undeserved suffering may actually be freeing and releasing. (E) is the best choice.

King makes no reference to the fact that some of the suffering endured was earned or deserved. (A) is not the best choice. King does not see suffering as being justified; so (B) is incorrect. King does not advocate unforgiveness; (C) is incorrect. King does not advocate followers seeking to suffer for no reason; he does not see unearned suffering as something to be sought or desired; (D) is incorrect.

QUESTION II.2.72

King compares his audience to those who had fought in great battles by calling them

(A) veterans.   (D) flesh.

(B) battered.   (E) devotees.

(C) staggered.

ANSWER

(A) In line 19, King uses the phrase " . . . the veterans of creative suffering." King best compared his audience to those who had fought in great battles by calling them (A) veterans. It is true that the audience may have been (B) battered, but that does not necessarily go along with war alone; victims of other situations may be battered; (B) should not be chosen. The audience may be oppressed and may stagger, but this does not necessarily relate to war; staggered (C) is not a good choice. Flesh (D) does not describe people; so (D) should not be selected. A devotee (E) may or may not relate to war; (E) should not be chosen.

■ QUESTION II.2.73

> The "old saying" that best fits lines 35–37 is
>
> (A) "A soft answer turneth away wrath."
>
> (B) "You can't judge a book by its cover."
>
> (C) "Birds of a feather flock together."
>
> (D) "Let sleeping dogs lie."
>
> (E) "A good name is rather to be chosen than great riches."

ANSWER

(B) The "old saying" that best fits lines 35–37 is (B), "You can't judge a book by its cover." King is looking forward to the day when people are judged by their character and not by their skin color; (B) is the answer to be chosen.

Although (A) is an oft-repeated statement and even though it does fit some of King's speeches, it does not fit in this context; (A) should not be chosen.

Judging little children by their skin color does not relate to "birds of a feather flock(ing) together;" (C) should not be chosen.

Not disturbing the situation, or "let(ting) sleeping dogs lie," does not relate to the color of the children's skin; (D) does not fit. "A good name is rather to be chosen than great riches" has nothing to do with judging children by their skin color; (E) is not the best answer.

QUESTION II.2.74

King used the analogy of winds for police brutality because winds

(A) rise up and then die.

(B) turn first one way and then another.

(C) are easy to protect oneself against.

(D) can be harnessed and used, as by a windmill.

(E) can be a damaging and a fearful obstacle, when strong.

ANSWER

(E)   The word "brutality" implies dangerous and destructive forces. King used the analogy of winds for police brutality because winds when strong can be damaging and a fearful obstacle; (E) is the best choice.

Winds do rise up and then die, but that analogy is not the best here; it does not seem to relate to the police; and therefore, (A) is not the best answer.

King does not describe the police as turning first one way and then another; (B) is not the best answer.

Since winds are not always easy to protect oneself against, (C) is not the best choice.

A wind, which can be harnessed and used as a windmill, does not seem to be a good analogy here; one does not usually think of harnessing police; thus, (D) is not the best answer.

QUESTION II.2.75

The main theme of this writing is

(A) dissatisfaction.   (D) struggle and defeat.

(B) despair.   (E) faith and hope.

(C) judgment.

ANSWER

(E) Although King is describing great difficulties, the main theme of this writing is faith and hope; (E) is the best answer. King is trying to inspire as he speaks.

There is an element of dissatisfaction (A) with current conditions, but this is not the overriding theme; (A) should not be chosen.

King is not urging his audience to feel despair (B); rather, he is encouraging them with a dream of better times to come.

King is not seeking judgment (C) for those who oppress; (C) should not be chosen. King's speech is one of optimism, faith, and hope—not struggle and defeat (D); therefore, (D) is not the best answer.

■ QUESTION II.2.76

The writer's main feeling toward the Constitution and the Declaration of Independence was

(A) disgust.

(D) faith.

(B) disappointment.

(E) curiosity.

(C) amusement.

ANSWER

(D) The writer's main feeling toward the Constitution and the Declaration of Independence was a feeling of confidence and faith (D); (D) is the correct answer. King never expressed disgust (A) toward the Constitution and Declaration of Independence—only with the way they had been interpreted; (A) is not the right answer. King did not express disappointment (B) with the documents themselves—only with those who used them; thus, (B) is not the correct answer. Nothing in King's speech suggests amusement (C); (C) should not be selected. Nothing in King's speech indicates curiosity (E) about these two documents; therefore (E) should not be selected.

*In this passage, the author highlights events from the Watergate crisis,
which occurred during the Nixon administration.*

1   What became known as the Watergate crisis began during the 1972 presidential campaign. Early on the morning of June 17, James McCord, a security
officer for the Committee for the Re-election of the President (CREEP), and
four other men broke into Democratic headquarters at the Watergate complex
5 in Washington, D.C., and were caught while going through files and installing
electronic eavesdropping devices. On June 22, Nixon announced that the administration was in no way involved in the burglary attempt.

The trial of the burglars began in early 1973, with all but McCord, who was
convicted, pleading guilty. Before sentencing, McCord wrote a letter to Judge
10 John J. Sirica arguing that high Republican officials had known in advance
about the burglary and that perjury had been committed at the trial.

Soon Jeb Stuart Magruder, head of CREEP, and John W. Dean, Nixon's attorney, stated that they had been involved. Dean testified before a Senate Watergate
investigating committee that Nixon had been involved in covering up the inci-
15 dent. Over the next several months, extensive involvement of the administration, including payment of "silence" money to the burglars, destruction of FBI
records, forgery of documents, and wiretapping, was revealed. Dean was fired
and H. R. Haldeman and John Ehrlichman, who headed the White House Staff,
and Attorney General Richard Kleindienst resigned. Nixon claimed that he had
20 not personally been involved in the cover-up but refused, on the grounds of executive privilege, to allow investigation of White House documents.

Under considerable pressure, Nixon agreed to the appointment of a special
prosecutor, Archibald Cox of Harvard Law School. When Cox obtained a subpoena for tape recordings of White House conversations (whose existence had
25 been revealed during the Senate hearings)—and the administration lost an appeal in the appellate court—Nixon ordered Elliot Richardson, now the attorney general, to fire Cox. Both Richardson and his subordinate, William Ruck-
elshaus, resigned, leaving Robert Bork, the solicitor general, to carry out the
order. This "Saturday Night Massacre," which took place on October 20, 1973,
30 aroused a storm of controversy. The House Judiciary Committee, headed by Peter Rodino of New Jersey, began looking into the possibilities of impeachment.
Nixon agreed to turn the tapes over to Judge Sirica and named Leon Jaworski
as the new special prosecutor. But it soon became known that some of the tapes
were missing and that a portion of another had been erased.

35   In March 1974, a grand jury indicted Haldeman, Ehrlichman, former Attorney General John Mitchell, and four other White House aides and named Nixon
an unindicted co-conspirator.

In April, Nixon released edited transcripts of the White House tapes, the contents of which led to further calls for his resignation. Jaworski subpoenaed 64
40 additional tapes, which Nixon refused to turn over, and the case went to the Supreme Court.

Meanwhile, the House Judiciary Committee televised its debate over impeachment, adopting three articles of impeachment. It charged the President with obstructing justice, misusing presidential power, and failing to obey the
45 committee's subpoenas.

Before the House began to debate impeachment, the Supreme Court ordered the President to release the subpoenaed tapes to the special prosecutor. On August 5, Nixon, under pressure from his advisors, released the tape of June 23, 1972, to the public. This tape, recorded less than a week after the break-in, re-
50 vealed that Nixon had used the CIA to keep the FBI from investigating the case. Nixon announced his resignation on August 8, 1974, to take effect at noon the following day. Gerald Ford then became president.

■ QUESTION II.2.77

The idea of impeaching President Nixon arose

(A) out of CREEP, an organization whose acronym proved ironic.

(B) when Archibald Cox subpoenaed White House tapes.

(C) right after John Ehrlichman and Richard Kleindienst resigned.

(D) from a suggestion made by solicitor general Robert Bork.

(E) from the House Judiciary Committee led by Peter Rodino.

ANSWER

(E)   Lines 30–31 overtly broach the subject of impeachment with the sentence, "The House Judiciary Committee, headed by Peter Rodino of New Jersey, began. . . . " (A) is a clear distractor, since CREEP supported President Nixon. (B) is a distractor, because Cox's subpoena led to further doubts concerning the President. (C) and (D) are incorrect, especially as Bork supported Nixon, and the two resignees defended the office of the President.

■ QUESTION II.2.78

The so-called "Saturday Night Massacre" (line 29)

(A) was a media attempt to smear President Nixon as an Al Capone-like gangster.

(B) was a domino effect caused by Nixon's fear of what could be revealed on the White House tapes.

(C) was a label provided by the Democrats to Nixon's appointment of Archibald Cox.

(D) was President Nixon's just policy of firing anyone connected with the Watergate break-in.

(E) revealed the panic in several Presidential appointees who had to carry out unpopular orders.

ANSWER

(B)   President Nixon's attempt to fire Archibald Cox created antagonistic repercussions about a cover-up, during which several officials resigned (see lines 27–30). While the media likely labeled the firings, (A) is a distractor related to the St. Valentine's Day Massacre. (D) is a clear reversal of history's judgment. (E) is partly true, psychologically, but the actions were not due to fear so much as the desire to maintain integrity. (C) is unjustified by the text.

■ QUESTION II.2.79

The final paragraph suggests that President Nixon

(A) suffered deep regrets over the Watergate scandal.

(B) used one government agency against another in order to maintain power.

(C) enjoyed a certain prestige with and immunity from the Supreme Court.

(D) remained indifferent to the advisors that he himself selected.

(E) managed to extend his policies in the administration of Gerald Ford.

ANSWER

(B) The final paragraph states that ". . . Nixon had used the CIA to keep the FBI from investigating the case." President Nixon abused his power in order to destroy opposition (see lines 49–50). The Watergate scandal disabused (C), since the President was not above the law. (A) may be true in retrospect, but the text does not discuss regret per se. President Nixon's relation to his advisors (D) is undiscussed. Gerald Ford's administration (E) is likewise undiscussed.

■ QUESTION II.2.80

President Nixon's first line of defense against his being investigated was

(A) his disassociation from Jeb Stuart Magruder and John W. Dean.

(B) his confirmation that James McCord had masterminded the Watergate operation.

(C) his naming of Leon Jaworski as special prosecutor.

(D) his permitting the hearings to be televised.

(E) his claim of executive privileges.

ANSWER

(E)   Lines 19–21 explicitly state "Nixon . . . refused, on grounds of executive privilege, to allow investigation . . ." The claim of executive privilege (line 21) was supposed to insulate President Nixon from investigation, negating (A) and (B), since the President did not have to answer for his underlings. Both (C) and (D) ironically aggravated the President's situation (see lines 32–33).

▪ QUESTION II.2.81

The payment of "silence" money (line 16)

(A) was part of a major conspiracy to cover up White House involvement.

(B) meant that the media would not mention President Nixon's involvement.

(C) managed to satisfy the Democrats that little damage had been done to their campaign.

(D) reduced the original charges to simply burglary and bribery.

(E) created a major financial drain on CREEP.

ANSWER

(A)   Lines 16–17 list a host of cover-up activities used to mask administration involvement. Both (B) and (E) are clear misreadings, because (B) the media was never silenced and (E) a financial drain is not mentioned. (C) is never addressed. (D) is possibly implied, but it represents a false conclusion.

▪ QUESTION II.2.82

The ramifications of James McCord's testimony

(A) centered around his claim that perjury had occurred.

(B) were nullified because of the use of illegal wire-tapping.

(C) immediately implicated H. R. Haldeman.

(D) led him to destroy FBI records.

(E) vindicated the Republican party of further blame.

ANSWER

(A)   McCord's letter is described in lines 10–14, which say that " . . . high Republican officials had known . . . about the burglary and that perjury had been committed at the trial." McCord's letter implicated higher-ups in the GOP. (B), (D), and (E) are clear misreadings, because none of these things happened. (C) is an indirect—rather than a direct—result of his letter to Judge Sirica.

■ QUESTION II.2.83

The actual process of "impeachment" (line 31) means

(A) that the President is immediately dismissed from office.

(B) that the Senate assumes the executive leadership of government.

(C) that executive power is diverted to the Supreme Court.

(D) that the President is formally accused of wrongdoing.

(E) that the House of Representatives replaces the Cabinet.

ANSWER

(D)   "Impeachment" merely means accusation, not (A), dismissal. (B), (C), and (E) exploit the misuse of the term.

■ QUESTION II.2.84

The House Judiciary Committee felt that

(A) its subpoenas had no power to compel a President to act.

(B) the White House tapes should be protected in the interest of national security.

(C) media publicity would prove detrimental to the office of the President.

(D) no executive privilege put a President above the law.

(E) a definition of "misuse of power" could not be achieved.

ANSWER

(D) Lines 42–45 state that the House Judiciary Committee adopted three articles of impeachment, which clearly proves that they believed that (D) "no executive privilege put a President above the law." They believed, therefore, that their subpoenas did have power over the President (A). Since they did act, they must not have been paralyzed by a fear for "national security" or of "media publicity;" (B) and (C) are, therefore, incorrect. Since one of the charges was "misusing presidential power," they must have reached a definition of this phrase (E).

Communicable illness and disease were often rampant in the ancient world, incapacitating and killing hundreds on a daily basis. The following passage describes the effects of the Athenian plague on history.

(From *Rats, Lice, and History* by Hans Zinsser. Copyright © 1934, 1935, 1963 by Hans Zinsser. Reprinted by permission of Little, Brown and Company.)

1 The oldest recorded epidemic, often regarded as an outbreak of typhus, is the Athenian plague of the Peloponnesian Wars, which is described in the Second Book of the *History* of Thucydides.

In trying to make the diagnosis of epidemics from ancient descriptions, when
5 the differentiation of simultaneously occurring diseases was impossible, it is important to remember that in any great outbreak, while the large majority of cases may represent a single type of infection, there is usually a coincident increase of other forms of contagious diseases; for the circumstances which favor the spread of one infectious agent often create opportunities for the trans-
10 mission of others. Very rarely is there a pure transmission of a single malady. It is not unlikely that the description of Thucydides is confused by the fact that a number of diseases were epidemic in Athens at the time of the great plague. The conditions were ripe for it. Early in the summer of 430 B.C. large armies were camped in Attica. The country population swarmed into Athens, which
15 became very much overcrowded. The disease seems to have started in Ethiopia . . . thence traveled through Egypt and Libya, and at length reached the seaport of Piraeus. It spread rapidly. Patients were seized suddenly, out of a clear sky. The first symptoms were severe headache and redness of the eyes. These were followed by inflammation of the tongue and pharynx, accompanied by sneez-
20 ing, hoarseness, and cough. Soon after this, there was acute intestinal involvement, with vomiting, diarrhea, and excessive thirst. Delirium was common. The patients that perished usually died between the seventh and ninth days. Many of those who survived the acute stage suffered from extreme weakness and a continued diarrhea that yielded to no treatment. At the height of the fever, the body
25 became covered with reddish spots . . . some of which ulcerated. When one of the severe cases recovered, convalescence was often accompanied by necrosis

of the fingers and the toes. Some lost their eyesight. In many there was complete loss of memory. Those who recovered were immune, so that they could nurse the sick without further danger. None of those who, not thoroughly immunized,
30 had it for the second time died of it. Thucydides himself had the disease. After subsiding for a while, when the winter began, the disease reappeared and seriously diminished the strength of the Athenian state.

The plague of Athens, whatever it may have been, had a profound effect upon historical events. It was one of the main reasons why the Athenian armies,
35 on the advice of Pericles, did not attempt to expel the Lacedaemonians, who were raiding Attica. Athenian life was completely demoralized, and a spirit of extreme lawlessness resulted. . . . There was no fear of the laws of God or man. Piety and impiety came to be the same thing, and no one expected that he would live to be called to account. Finally, the Peloponnesians left Attica in a hurry,
40 not for fear of the Athenians, who were locked up in their cities, but because they were afraid of the disease.

■ QUESTION II.2.85

The point of this passage is to demonstrate

(A) that "pure" outbreaks of disease were common in the ancient world.

(B) that treatments of epidemic diseases remain relatively ineffective.

(C) the relation that exists between infectious disease and historical events.

(D) the relatively poor health conditions in ancient Athens.

(E) the wisdom of Pericles in dealing with foreign invaders.

ANSWER

(C)   The first sentence of the final paragraph states, "The plague of Athens . . . had a profound effect upon historical events." The point of this passage is to demonstrate the relation between infectious disease and historical events (C).

(A) is incorrect because it is made clear that epidemics were complex affairs in lines 10–13. (B) is not correct because the current level of treatment is not discussed in this passage.

The level of medical prevention in ancient Athens (D) is also incorrect because, although it may have been mentioned, it is not the main point.

(E) is not correct because Pericles is not discussed in great detail and is in fact only mentioned once.

QUESTION II.2.86

One of the results of extended sickness in Athens was

(A) to put their democratic constitution in danger.

(B) to produce a moral nihilism, where death negated ethical life.

(C) to invite the Peloponnesians for a prolonged occupation of the city.

(D) to increase general belief in supernatural powers.

(E) to clarify the exact cause of the outbreak.

ANSWER

(B)   Lines 37–39 state that " . . . There was no fear of the laws of God or man . . . no one expected he would live to be called to account." Men's morals are neutralized by the continuous presence of death; therefore, (B) is the correct answer. (A) and (D) are both incorrect because they are not justified by the text. (C) is incorrect because the Peloponnesians fled for fear of infection. (E) is also incorrect because the author discusses the lack of certainty in the cause of the epidemic.

QUESTION II.2.87

The symptom "necrosis" (line 26) probably indicates

(A) tissue death.

(B) that victims suffered more at night.

(C) that patients could not be moved.

(D) the incompetence of doctors at that time.

(E) the incredible speed at which victims died.

ANSWER

(A)   Lines 26–27 state that "convalescence was often accompanied by necrosis of the fingers and the toes." Judging from this context, we can infer that necrosis means (A) "tissue death."

Fingers and toes have no relation to night and day (B). Anything that would affect fingers and toes would not make the patient difficult to move (C). The passage never mentions the incompetence of doctors (D). If "necrosis" happened during "convalescence" (recovery), it would not relate to the speed at which the victims died (E).

■ QUESTION II.2.88

Two of the factors exacerbating the spread of the plague were

(A) low standards of medical practice and poor army discipline.

(B) severe overpopulation and outbreaks of several maladies.

(C) poor political judgment and failure to enforce housing codes.

(D) an influx of Ethiopians and the departure of the Lacedaemonians.

(E) the failure to identify the disease and poor nutrition.

ANSWER

(B)   Lines 11–15 identify the two causes of outbreak as overcrowding and coincident epidemics. (A) is incorrect because poor army discipline is not given as a factor in spreading the plague. (C) is also incorrect because housing codes are not mentioned in this passage. An influx of Ethiopians (D) would be a misreading of the author's statement that it seems the disease started in Ethiopia. Poor nutrition is not mentioned as a cause for the outbreak (E).

◼ QUESTION II.2.89

The word "convalescence" in line 26 can most nearly be defined as

(A) languish.   (D) recuperation.

(B) innocuous.   (E) deterioration.

(C) contamination.

ANSWER

(D)   The correct answer is (D). The context clue here is "recover." "Recuperation" and "convalescence" both mean the process of becoming well after an illness, growing strong again. (A) means the opposite; (B) "innocuous" means "innocent or harmless." (C) is incorrect because it means "a process of contaminating, soiling, corrupting, or infecting." (E) is wrong because it means "to weaken" and is the opposite of "convalescence."

The age of Ancient Greece saw many different philosophies come to light. The following passage looks at the ideas and beliefs of Epicurus, Zeno, and Carneades of Cyrene.

1   The Hellenistic Age produced two major and two minor additions to the history of philosophy. Epicureanism and Stoicism represented the period's dominant philosophical movements. Skepticism and Cynicism found limited support among those unwilling to accept the Epicureans' and Stoics' confidence in rea-
5   son. Hellenistic philosophy marked a turning point in the Western intellectual tradition. The classical Greek philosophers linked the individual's happiness to the community's well-being. The philosophers of the Hellenistic period focused on the individual. The goal of philosophy shifted from the pursuit of knowledge for its own sake to that of the individual's peace of mind and personal happi-
10 ness.

        Epicurus (ca. 342–270 B.C.) founded a school in Athens and based his metaphysics on Democritus's atomic theory. Epicurus taught that the goal of philosophy should be to help the individual find happiness. Unlike Socrates and Plato, he did not make citizenship in a polis the basis of happiness. Epicurus argued
15 that a wise man eschewed public affairs and sought self-sufficiency. Later critics accused Epicurus and his followers of advocating a life based on pursuing the pleasures of the flesh. To Epicurus, however, the highest pleasure was to be found in contemplation.

Zeno (ca. 335–263 B.C.) established a rival philosophical school under the
20 *Stoa Poikile* (painted porch) of the Athenian *Agora* (marketplace). There are
a number of similarities between Stoicism and Epicureanism. Like Epicurus,
Zeno emphasized the importance of the individual. Moreover, both schools
were based on a materialistic metaphysics and claimed universal validity for
25 their teachings. There were, however, significant differences between the two
philosophical outlooks. Zeno taught that the cosmos was a unified whole which
was based on a universal order (Logos or Fire). Every man carried a spark of
this Logos in his reason. At death this spark returned to its origin. The Stoics
taught that each person should strive to discover the natural law governing the
30 universe and live in accordance with it.

The Skeptics attacked the Epicureans and the Stoics. Carneades of Cyrene
(ca. 213–129 B.C.) argued that all knowledge was relative. The sensory impres-
sions which we receive from the external world are flawed. Individuals should
abandon the quest for knowledge because nothing can be known for certain.
35 The safest course is to doubt everything. Indifference is the only philosophi-
cally defensible position.

Diogenes of Sinope (d. 323 B.C.) was the most famous cynic. His goal was
to prepare the individual for any disaster. He lived as a beggar and was famous
for his outspoken condemnation of sham and hypocrisy. One story has it that
40 when he met Alexander the Great and the world-conqueror asked him what he
wanted, Diogenes replied that Alexander should get out of his light.

■ QUESTION II.2.90

The saying, "I am trying to find myself and my happiness," might
be employed by a follower of

(A) Diogenes.   (D) Stoics.

(B) Zeno.   (E) Epicurus.

(C) Hellen.

ANSWER

(C)   Lines 7–8 state that "The philosophers of the Hellenistic period focused
on the individual;" therefore, the saying, "I am trying to find myself and my
happiness," might be employed by a follower of (C) Hellen.

Diogenes (A) was the most famous cynic; his goal was to prepare the individual for disaster, so happiness would not have been a part of his philosophy.

Zeno (B) taught that the cosmos was a unified whole that was based on a universal order, so the happiness of the individual would not have been that important to him.

(D) The Stoics taught that each person should strive to discover the natural law governing the universe and live in accordance with it.

(E) Epicurus founded a school and taught that individual happiness was the goal.

■ QUESTION II.2.91

The word "polis" in line 14 most nearly means

(A) a group.

(B) in a certain way.

(C) a place of one's own; a place of solitude.

(D) a tradition.

(E) a philosophical outlook.

ANSWER

(A)   Within the context of the passage, the word "polis," in line 14, most nearly means (A) a group. In a certain way, (B) has nothing to do with the meaning of "polis." Polis (C) does not refer to a place of one's own or a place of solitude. A (D) tradition is not the best meaning for "polis." Polis is not a philosophical outlook (E); therefore, (E) should not be selected.

◼ QUESTION II.2.92

The author focused on the classical Greek philosophers in order to

(A) show similarities with the Jurassic Age.

(B) contrast them with Oriental thinkers.

(C) show their relation to the earlier philosophers of the Hellenistic Age.

(D) contrast them with those of the Hellenistic Age.

(E) show his scorn of the past.

ANSWER

(D)   The author focused on the classical Greek philosophers in order to (D) contrast them with those of the Hellenistic Age. The purpose of the focus is not to contrast the age with a much earlier time; (A) is not the correct choice. No mention is made of the Oriental thinkers; so answer (B) is not the correct choice. Since the Hellenistic Age followed the classical Greek Age, the purpose was not to show their relation to the earlier philosophers of the Hellenistic Period; (C) should not be chosen. The author exhibits no scorn of the past in his writing; (E) is, therefore, not an appropriate answer.

◼ QUESTION II.2.93

The most important element of Stoic thought was

(A) its similarity to Epicureanism.

(B) the universal validity of its teaching.

(C) the idea that each person carried a spark of Logos in his reason.

(D) its establishment under the painted porch of the Athenian marketplace.

(E) its emphasis on the individual.

ANSWER

(E)   The most important element of Stoic thought was its emphasis on the individual—not on the group, as earlier schools of thought had emphasized. The Stoic taught that each person carried a spark of Logos in his reason, but (C) is not the best choice because this was not the most important element of the philosophy. (D) is also a true statement, but it has little to do with "thought." (A) Stoic thought was similar to Epicurus's thought, but that was not the most important element of Stoic thought. The writing claims universal validity, but since this has not been proven, (B) is not the best choice.

■ QUESTION II.2.94

Carneades taught that

(A) all knowledge was relative.

(B) the goal of philosophy should be to help the individual find happiness.

(C) a wise man eschewed public affairs and sought self-sufficiency.

(D) the individual should be prepared for any disaster.

(E) the highest pleasure was to be found in contemplation.

ANSWER

(A)   Carneades taught that all knowledge was relative; (A) is the correct answer. It was Epicurus (B) who taught that the goal of philosophy should be to help the individual find happiness and that (C) a wise man eschewed public affairs and sought self-sufficiency. He also stated that the highest pleasure was to be found in contemplation (E). Diogenes taught that the individual should be prepared for any disaster; (D) is not the correct answer.

In the following passage, Thomas Henry Huxley argues that science is an integral part of culture and should be studied along with traditional courses, which include the classics and other liberal arts.

1   How often have we not been told that the study of physical science is incompetent to confer culture; that it touches none of the higher problems of life; and, what is worse, that the continual devotion to scientific studies tends to generate a narrow and bigoted belief in the applicability of scientific methods to the
5   search after truth of all kinds? How frequently one has reason to observe that no reply to a troublesome argument tells so well as calling its author a "mere scientific specialist." And, as I am afraid it is not permissible to speak of this form of opposition to scientific education in the past tense; may we not expect to be told that this, not only omission, but prohibition, of "mere literary instruction
10   and education" is a patent example of scientific narrow-mindedness?

I am not acquainted with Sir Josiah Mason's reasons for the action which he has taken; but if, as I apprehend is the case, he refers to the ordinary classical course of our schools and universities by the name of "mere literary instruction and education," I venture to offer sundry reasons of my own in support of that
15   action.

For I hold very strongly by two convictions: The first is, that neither the discipline nor the subject-matter of classical education is of such direct value to the student of physical science as to justify the expenditure of valuable time upon either; and the second is, that for the purpose of attaining real culture, an
20   exclusively scientific education is at least as effectual as an exclusively literary education.

I need hardly point out to you that these opinions, especially the latter, are diametrically opposed to those of the great majority of educated Englishmen, influenced as they are by school and university traditions. In their belief, culture
25   is obtainable only by a liberal education; and a liberal education is synonymous, not merely with education and instruction in literature, but in one particular form of literature, namely, that of Greek and Roman antiquity. They hold that the man who has learned Latin and Greek, however little, is educated; while he who is versed in other branches of knowledge, however deeply, is a more or less
30   respectable specialist, not admissible into the cultured caste. The stamp of the educated man, the University degree, is not for him.

I am too well acquainted with the generous catholicity of spirit, the true sympathy with scientific thought, which pervades the writings of our chief apostle of culture to identify him with these opinions; and yet one may cull from one
35   and another of those epistles to the Philistines, which so much delight all who do not answer to that name, sentences which lend them some support.

Mr. Arnold tells us that the meaning of culture is "to know the best that has been thought and said in the world." It is the criticism of life contained in literature. That criticism regards "Europe as being, for intellectual and spiritual
40 purposes, one great confederation, bound to a joint action and working to a common result; and whose members have, for their common outfit, a knowledge of Greek, Roman, and Eastern antiquity, and of one another. Special, local, and temporary advantages being put out of account, that modern nation will in the intellectual and spiritual sphere make most progress, which most thor-
45 oughly carries out this programme. And what is that but saying that we too, all of us, as individuals, the more thoroughly we carry it out, shall make the more progress?"

We have here to deal with two distinct propositions. The first, that a criticism of life is the essence of culture; the second, that literature contains the materials
50 which suffice for the construction of such criticism.

I think that we must all assent to the first proposition. For culture certainly means something quite different from learning or technical skill. It implies the possession of an ideal, and the habit of critically estimating the value of things by comparison with a theoretic standard. Perfect culture should supply a com-
55 plete theory of life, based upon a clear knowledge alike of its possibilities and of its limitations.

But we may agree to all this, and yet strongly dissent from the assumption that literature alone is competent to supply this knowledge. After having learnt all that Greek, Roman, and Eastern antiquity have thought and said, and all that
60 modern literatures have to tell us, it is not self-evident that we have laid a sufficiently broad and deep foundation for that criticism of life, which constitutes culture.

Indeed, to anyone acquainted with the scope of physical science, it is not at all evident. Considering progress only in the "intellectual and spiritual sphere,"
65 I find myself wholly unable to admit that either nations or individuals will really advance, if their common outfit draws nothing from the stores of physical science. I should say that an army, without weapons of precision and with no particular base of operations, might more hopefully enter upon a campaign on the Rhine, than a man, devoid of a knowledge of what physical science has done
70 in the last century, upon a criticism of life.

■ QUESTION II.2.95

Which best describes what the author is doing in the sentence, "And, as I am afraid . . . narrow-mindedness" (lines 7–10)?

(A) Stating the terms of his argument

(B) Arguing for scientific training

(C) Stating common beliefs of his opponents

(D) Redefining the term "culture"

(E) Establishing the central analogy of the passage

ANSWER

(C) He is actually exaggerating his opponents' views through conventional irony. The argument per se (A) is not developed here. The section occurs within (B) the broader plea for scientific training. Culture is taken up much later in the passage (D). There is no central analogy in this passage (E).

■ QUESTION II.2.96

From the first four paragraphs, we can infer that the college has decided to

(A) include classical studies in its curriculum.

(B) exclude classical studies from its curriculum.

(C) establish Latin and Greek as required subjects.

(D) define university education as exclusively scientific.

(E) incorporate scientific studies within the curriculum.

ANSWER

(E) From the displeasure of Huxley's opponents, we can infer that scientific studies have gained some ground. Classical studies have long been within the curriculum (A). There is no suggestion of their abolition (B). Classical studies continue to be (C) required subjects, though Huxley questions their utility in

scientific education. Despite his opponents' fears, exclusively scientific education (D) hardly appears possible.

◼ QUESTION II.2.97

In line 14, the term "sundry" most nearly means

(A) significant.   (D) related.

(B) various.   (E) dependent.

(C) convincing.

ANSWER

(B) The term has the neutral meaning of number, with a slight connotation of offhandedness. It does not include connotations of significance (A). His
views are not *necessarily* convincing arguments (C). There is no necessary relationship among them (D). Further, the specific relation of dependence is not
contained in the word "sundry."

◼ QUESTION II.2.98

The author's use of the term "cultured caste" (line 30) suggests

(A) distinctive merit.   (D) superiority of the wealthy.

(B) exclusion of merit.   (E) inclusion of the poor.

(C) social inequity.

ANSWER

(B) Huxley is referring to an unfair system of intellectual judgment in which
only those with a knowledge of Latin and Greek (which Huxley regards as
fairly useless) are considered "cultured." Understanding of this term depends
upon appreciation of Huxley's subtle irony. Many with distinctive merit, but
little knowledge of Greek, are excluded from the "caste" (A). The question
of social—as opposed to educational—inequality does not arise here (C). The
"caste" includes only those with classical educations, which probably—but not
necessarily—includes the wealthy. (D). Huxley does not address class consid-
erations in this passage (E).

■ QUESTION II.2.99

In the sentence, "I am too well acquainted . . . some support" (lines 32–36), the author argues that "our chief apostle"

(A) unintentionally reinforces prejudices.

(B) has contributed valuable insights.

(C) holds views contrary to those of the author.

(D) does not deserve his current reputation.

(E) is a valuable supporter of the author.

ANSWER

(A) Cited out of context, Arnold, the "chief apostle," lends support to those with biases against science. He *may* well have contributed insights (B); Huxley makes no explicit comment. Arnold probably holds some views contrary to those of the author (C), but this point is not made explicitly in the paragraph. Huxley implies that Arnold certainly deserves his current reputation (D), even if he is not a valuable ally of the author (E).

■ QUESTION II.2.100

The word "outfit" in line 41 most nearly means

(A) company.   (D) tools.

(B) uniform.   (E) beliefs.

(C) gathering.

ANSWER

(B) Huxley is using a metaphor in which his opponents' clothing is made up of their areas of knowledge. Here the word means regalia or costuming. Huxley later (line 66) modifies it to suggest weaponry. The company again forms a gathering that means the uniform, but is not itself the uniform (C). The idea of "tools" might be conceivable in the later usage (line 66) (D), but does not fit here. Beliefs are only one element in the group's common uniform (E).

APPENDIX A

PREFIXES, ROOTS, AND SUFFIXES

Prefix	Meaning	Example
ab –, a –, abs –	away, without, from	absent – away, not present apathy – without interest abstain – keep from doing, refrain
ad –	to, toward	adjacent – next to address – to direct toward
ante –	before	antecedent – going before in time anterior – occurring before
anti –	against	antidote – remedy to act against an evil antibiotic – substance that fights against bacteria
be –	over, thoroughly	bemoan – to mourn over belabor – to exert much labor upon
bi –	two	bisect – to divide biennial – happening every two years
cata –, cat –, cath –	down	catacombs – underground passageways catalogue – descriptive list catheter – tubular medical device
circum –	around	circumscribe – to draw a circle around circumspect – watchful on all sides
com –	with	combine – to join together communication – to have dealings with
contra –	against	contrary – opposed contrast – to stand in opposition
de –	down, from	decline – to bend downward decontrol – to release from government control
di –	two	dichotomy – cutting in two diarchy – system of government with two authorities
dis –, di–	apart, away	discern – to distinguish as separate dismiss – to send away digress – to turn aside

Prefix	Meaning	Example
epi –, ep –, eph –	upon, among	epidemic – happening among many people
		epicycle – circle whose center moves around in the circumference of a greater circle
		epaulet – decoration worn to ornament or protect the shoulder
		ephedra – any of a large genus of desert shrubs
ex –, e –	from, out	exceed – go beyond the limit
		emit – to send forth
extra –	outside, beyond	extraordinary – beyond or out of the common method
		extrasensory – beyond the senses
hyper –	beyond, over	hyperactive – over the normal activity level
		hypercritic – one who is critical beyond measure
hypo –	beneath, lower	hypodermic – parts beneath the skin
		hypocrisy – to be under a pretense of goodness
in –, il –, im –, ir –	not	inactive – not active
		illogical – not logical
		imperfect – not perfect
		irreversible – not reversible
in –, il –, im –, ir –	in, on, into	instill – to put in slowly
		illation – action of bringing in
		impose – to lay on
		irrupt – to break in
inter –	among, between	intercom – to exchange conversations between people
		interlude – performance given between parts in a play
intra –	within	intravenous – within a vein
		intramural – within a single college or its students

Prefix	Meaning	Example
meta –	beyond, over, along with	metamorphosis – change over in form or nature metatarsus – part of foot beyond the flat of the foot
mis –	badly, wrongly	misconstrue – to interpret wrongly misappropriate – to use wrongly
mono –	one	monogamy – to be married to one person at a time monotone – a single, unvaried tone
multi –	many	multiple – of many parts multitude – a great number
non –	no, not	nonsense – lack of sense nonentity – not existing
ob –	against	obscene – offensive to modesty obstruct – to hinder the passage of
para –, par –	beside	parallel – continuously at equal distance apart parenthesis – sentence inserted within a passage
per –	through	persevere – to maintain an effort permeate – to pass through
poly –	many	polygon – a plane figure with many sides or angles polytheism – belief in the existence of many gods
post –	after	posterior – coming after postpone – to put off until a future time
pre –	before	premature – ready before the proper time premonition – a previous warning
pro –	in favor of, forward	prolific – bringing forth offspring project – throw or cast forward
re –	back, against	reimburse – to pay back retract – to draw back
semi –	half	semicircle – half a circle semiannual – half-yearly

Prefix	Meaning	Example
sub –	under	subdue – to bring under one's power submarine – to travel under the surface of the sea
super –	above	supersonic – above the speed of sound superior – higher in place or position
tele –, tel –	across	telecast – transmit across a distance telepathy – communication between mind and mind at a distance
trans –	across	transpose – to change the position of two things transmit – to send from one person to another
ultra –	beyond	ultraviolet – beyond the limit of visibility ultramarine – beyond the sea
un –	not	undeclared – not declared unbelievable – not believable
uni –	one	unity – state of oneness unison – sounding together
with –	away, against	withhold – to hold back withdraw – to take away

Root	Meaning	Example
act, ag	do, act, drive	activate – to make active agile – having quick motion
alt	high	altitude – height alto – high singing voice
alter, altr	other, change	alternative – choice between two things altruism – living for the good of others
am, ami	love, friend	amiable – worthy of affection amity – friendship
anim	mind, spirit	animated – spirited animosity – violent hatred
annu, enni	year	annual – every year centennial – every hundred years

Root	Meaning	Example
aqua	water	aquarium – tank for water animals and plants aquamarine – semiprecious stone of sea-green color
arch	first, ruler	archenemy – chief enemy archetype – original pattern from which things are copied
aud, audit	hear	audible – capable of being heard audience – assembly of hearers audition – the power or act of hearing
auto	self	automatic – self-acting autobiography – story about a person who also wrote it
bell	war	belligerent – a party taking part in a war bellicose – warlike
ben, bene	good	benign – kindly disposition beneficial – advantageous
bio	life	biotic – relating to life biology – the science of life
brev	short	abbreviate – make shorter brevity – shortness
cad, cas	fall	cadence – fall in voice casualty – loss caused by death
capit, cap	head	captain – the head or chief decapitate – to cut off the head
cede, ceed, cess	to go, to yield	recede – to move or fall back proceed – to move onward recessive – tending to go back
cent	hundred	century – hundred years centipede – insect with a hundred legs
chron	time	chronology – science dealing with historical dates chronicle – register of events in order of time
cide, cis	to kill, to cut	homicide – one who kills; planned killing of a person incision – a cut

Root	Meaning	Example
clam, claim	to shout	acclaim – receive with applause proclamation – announce publicly
cogn	to know	recognize – to know again cognition – awareness
corp	body	incorporate – combine into one body corpse – dead body
cred	to trust, to believe	incredible – unbelievable credulous – too prone to believe
cur, curr, curs	to run	current – flowing body of air or water excursion – short trip
dem	people	democracy – government formed for the people epidemic – affecting all people
dic, dict	to say	dictate – to read aloud for another to transcribe verdict – decision of a jury
doc, doct	to teach	docile – easily instructed indoctrinate – to instruct
domin	to rule	dominate – to rule dominion – territory of rule
duc, duct	to lead	conduct – act of guiding induce – to overcome by persuasion
eu	well, good	eulogy – speech or writing in praise euphony – pleasantness or smoothness of sound
fac, fact, fect, fic	to do, to make	facilitate – to make easier factory – location of production confect – to put together fiction – something invented or imagined
fer	to bear, to carry	transfer – to move from one place to another refer – to direct to
fin	end, limit	infinity – unlimited finite – limited in quantity
flect, flex	to bend	flexible – easily bent reflect – to throw back

Root	Meaning	Example
fort	luck	fortunate – lucky fortuitous – happening by chance
fort	strong	fortify – strengthen fortress – stronghold
frag, fract	break	fragile – easily broken fracture – break
fug	flee	fugitive – fleeing refugee – one who flees to a place of safety
gen	class, race	engender – to breed generic – of a general nature in regard to all members
grad, gress	to go, to step	regress – to go back graduate – to divide into regular steps
graph	writing	telegraph – message sent by telegraph autograph – person's own handwriting or signature
ject	to throw	projectile – capable of being thrown reject – to throw away
leg	law	legitimate – lawful legal – defined by law
leg, lig, lect	to choose, gather, read	illegible – incapable of being read ligature – something that binds election – the act of choosing
liber	free	liberal – favoring freedom of ideals liberty – freedom from restraint
log	study, speech	archaeology – study of human antiquities prologue – address spoken before a performance
luc, lum	light	translucent – slightly transparent illuminate – to light up
magn	large, great	magnify – to make larger magnificent – great
mal, male	bad, wrong	malfunction – to operate incorrectly malevolent – evil

Root	Meaning	Example
mar	sea	marine – pertaining to the sea submarine – below the surface of the sea
mater, matr	mother	maternal – motherly matriarchy – government by mothers or women
mit, miss	to send	transmit – to send from one person or place to another mission – the act of sending
morph	shape	metamorphosis – a changing in shape anthropomorphic – having a human shape
mut	change	mutable – subject to change mutate – to change a vowel
nat	born	innate – inborn native – a person born in a place
neg	deny	negative – expressing denial renege – to deny
nom	name	nominate – to put forward a name nomenclature – process of naming
nov	new	novel – new renovate – to make as good as new
omni	all	omnipotent – all powerful omnipresent – all present
oper	to work	operate – to work on something cooperate – to work with others
pass, path	to feel	pathetic – affecting the tender emotions passionate – moved by strong emotion
pater, patr	father	paternal – fatherly patriarchy – government by fathers or men
ped, pod	foot	pedestrian – one who travels on foot podiatrist – foot doctor
pel, puls	to drive, to push	impel – to drive forward compulsion – irresistible force

Root	Meaning	Example
phil	love	philharmonic – loving harmony or music philanthropist – one who loves and seeks to do good for others
port	carry	export – to carry out of the country portable – able to be carried
psych	mind	psychology – study of the mind psychiatrist – specialist in mental disorders
quer, ques, quir, quis	to ask	querist – one who inquires inquiry – to ask about question – that which is asked inquisitive – inclined to ask questions
rid, ris	to laugh	ridiculous – laughable derision – to mock
rupt	to break	interrupt – to break in upon erupt – to break through
sci	to know	science – systematic knowledge of physical or natural phenomena conscious – having inward knowledge
scrib, script	to write	transcribe – to write over again script – text of words
sent, sens	to feel, to think	sentimental – feel great emotion sensitive – easily affected by changes
sequ, secut	to follow	sequence – connected series consecutive – following one another in unbroken order
solv, solu, solut	to loosen	dissolve – to break up absolute – without restraint
spect	to look at	spectator – one who watches inspect – to look at closely
spir	to breathe	inspire – to breathe in respiration – process of breathing
string, strict	to bind	stringent – binding strongly restrict – to restrain within bounds

Root	Meaning	Example
stru, struct	to build	strut – a structural piece designed to resist pressure construct – to build
tang, ting, tact, tig	to touch	tactile – perceptible by touching tangent – touching, but not intersecting contact – touching contiguous – to touch along a boundary
ten, tent, tain	to hold	tenure – holding of office contain – to hold
term	to end	terminate – to end terminal – having an end
terr	earth	terrain – tract of land terrestrial – existing on earth
therm	heat	thermal – pertaining to heat thermometer – instrument for measuring temperature
tort, tors	to twist	contortionist – one who twists violently torsion – act of turning or twisting
tract	to pull, to draw	attract – draw toward distract – to draw away
vac	empty	vacant – empty evacuate – to empty out
ven, vent	to come	prevent – to stop from coming intervene – to come between
ver	true	verify – to prove to be true veracious – truthful
verb	word	verbose – use of excess words verbatim – word for word
vid, vis	to see	video – picture phase of television vision – act of seeing external objects
vinc, vict, vanq	to conquer	invincible – unconquerable victory – defeat of enemy vanquish – to defeat
viv, vit	life	vital – necessary to life vivacious – lively

Root	Meaning	Example
voc	to call	vocation – a summons to a course of action vocal – uttered by voice
vol	to wish, to will	involuntary – outside the control of will volition – the act of willing or choosing

Suffix	Meaning	Example
–able, –ble	capable of	believable – capable of believing legible – capable of being read
–acious, –icious, –ous	full of	vivacious – full of life delicious – full of pleasurable smell or taste wondrous – full of wonder
–ant, –ent	full of	eloquent – full of eloquence expectant – full of expectation
–ary	connected with	honorary – for the sake of honor disciplinary – relating to a field of study
–ate	to make	ventilate – to make public consecrate – to dedicate
–fy	to make	magnify – to make larger testify – to make witness
–ile	pertaining to, capable of	docile – capable of being managed easily infantile – pertaining to infancy
–ism	belief, ideal	conservationism – ideal of keeping safe sensationalism – matter, language designed to excite
–ist	doer	artist – one who creates art pianist – one who plays the piano
–ose	full of	verbose – full of words grandiose – striking, imposing
–osis	condition	neurosis – nervous condition psychosis – psychological condition
–tude	state	magnitude – state of greatness multitude – state of quantity

DRILLS

DRILL: PREFIXES

DIRECTIONS: Provide a definition for each prefix.

1. pro– _____
2. com–_____
3. epi–_____
4. ob– _____
5. ad– _____

DIRECTIONS: Identify the prefix in each word.

6. efface _____
7. hypothetical _____
8. permeate_____
9. contrast_____
10. inevitable _____

DRILL: ROOTS

DIRECTIONS: Provide a definition for each root.

1. cede _____
2. fact _____
3. path_____
4. ject _____
5. ver _____

DIRECTIONS: Identify the root in each word.

6. acclaim_____
7. verbatim _____

8. benefactor_____

9. relegate_____

10. tension _____

DRILL: SUFFIXES

DIRECTIONS: Provide a definition for each suffix.

1. –ant, –ent _____

2. –tude_____

3. –ile _____

4. –fy _____

5. –ary _____

DIRECTIONS: Identify the suffix in each word.

6. audacious _____

7. expedient _____

8. gullible _____

9. grandiose _____

10. antagonism_____

ANSWER KEY

DRILL: PREFIXES

1. forward
2. with
3. upon, among
4. against
5. to, toward

6. ef–
7. hypo–
8. per–
9. con–
10. in–

DRILL: ROOTS

1. to go, to yield
2. to do, to make
3. to feel
4. to throw
5. true

6. claim
7. verb
8. ben(e)
9. leg
10. ten

DRILL: SUFFIXES

1. full of
2. state
3. pertaining to, capable of
4. to make
5. connected with

6. (a)cious
7. ent
8. ible
9. ose
10. ism

APPENDIX B
ESSENTIAL VOCABULARY

VOCABULARY LIST

abaft – *adv.* – on or toward the rear of a ship

abandon – 1. *v.* – to leave behind; 2. *v.* – to give something up

abase – *v.* – to degrade; humiliate; disgrace

abbreviate – *v.* – to shorten; compress; diminish

abdicate – *v.* – to reject, denounce, or abandon

aberrant – *adj.* – abnormal

aberration – *n.* – departure from what is right, true, correct

abeyance – *n.* – a state of temporary suspension

abhor – *v.* – to hate

abjure – *v.* – to renounce upon oath

abnegation – *n.* – a denial

abominate – *v.* – to loathe; to hate

abridge – *v.* – 1. to shorten; 2. to limit; to take away

abscond – *v.* – to go away hastily or secretly; to hide

absolve – *v.* – to forgive; to acquit

abstemious – *adj.* – sparingly used or used with temperance

abstinence – *n.* – the act or practice of voluntarily refraining from any action

abstract – *adj.* – not easy to understand; theoretical

abstruse – *adj.* – 1. hidden, concealed; 2. difficult to be comprehended

abysmal – *adj.* – bottomless; immeasurable

accede – *v.* – to comply with; to consent to

acclaim – *n.* – loud approval; applause

accolade – *n.* – approving or praising mention

accomplice – *n.* – co-conspirator; a partner; partner-in-crime

accretion – *n.* – growth in size by addition or accumulation

accrue – *v.* – collect; build up

acerbity – *n.* – harshness or bitterness

acquiesce – *v.* – agree or consent to an opinion

acrid – *adj.* – sharp; bitter; foul smelling

acrimony – *n.* – sharpness

adamant – *adj.* – not yielding; firm

addle – *adj.* – barren; confused

adept – *adj.* – skilled; practiced

adjure – *v.* – to entreat earnestly and solemnly

adulation – *n.* – praise in excess

adulterate – *v.* – to corrupt, debase, or make impure

adverse – *adj.* – negative; hostile; antagonistic; inimical

adversary – *n.* – an enemy; foe

advocate – 1. *v.* – to plead in favor of; 2. *n.* – supporter; defender

aesthetic – *adj.* – showing good taste; artistic

affable – *adj.* – friendly; amiable; good-natured

aghast – *adj.* – 1. astonished; amazed; 2. horrified; terrified; appalled

agrarian – *adj.* – relating to land and the equal divisions of land

alacrity – *n.* – 1. enthusiasm; fervor; 2. liveliness; sprightliness

alchemy – *n.* – any imaginary power of transmitting one thing into another

allegory – *n.* – symbolic narration or description

allure – *v.* – 1. to attract; entice; 2. *n.* – attraction; temptation; glamour

alleviate – *v.* – to lessen or make easier

allocate – *v.* – set aside; designate; assign

allusion – *n.* – an indirect reference to something

aloof – *adj.* – distant in interest; reserved; cool

altercation – *n.* – controversy; dispute

altruistic – *adj.* – unselfish

amass – *v.* – to collect together; accumulate

amiss – 1. *adj.* – wrong; awry; 2. *adv.* – wrongly; mistakenly

ambiguous – *adj.* – not clear; uncertain; vague

ambivalent – *adj.* – undecided

ameliorate – *v.* – to make better; to improve

amiable – *adj.* – friendly

amorphous – *adj.* – having no determinate form

anachronism – *n.* – representation of something existing at other than its proper time

analogy – *n.* – similarity; correlation; parallelism; simile; metaphor

anarchist – *n.* – one who believes that a formal government is unnecessary

annihilate – *v.* – to reduce to nothing

anoint – *v.* – 1. to crown; ordain; 2. to smear with oil

anomaly – *n.* – abnormality; irregularity; deviation from the regular arrangement

anonymous – *adj.* – nameless; unidentified

antagonism – *n.* – hostility; opposition

antipathy – *n.* – inherent aversion or antagonism of feeling

antiseptic – *adj.* – preventing infection or decay

apathy – *n.* – lack of emotion or interest

apocalyptic – *adj.* – pertaining to revelation or discovery

appease – *v.* – to make quiet; to calm

apprehensive – *adj.* – fearful; aware; conscious

arbiter – *n.* – one who is authorized to judge or decide

arbitrary – *adj.* – based on one's preference or judgment

arduous – *adj.* – difficult; laborious

arid – *adj.* – 1. dry; parched; 2. barren; 3. uninteresting; dull

arrogant – *adj.* – acting superior to others; conceited

arrogate – *v.* – to claim or demand unduly

articulate – 1. *v.* – to speak distinctly; 2. *adj.* – eloquent; fluent; 3. *adj.* – capable of speech; 4. *v.* – to hinge; to connect; 5. *v.* – to convey; to express effectively

artifice – *n.* – skill; ingenuity; craft

askance – *adv.* – sideways; out of one corner of the eye

assay – *n.* – the determination of any quantity of a metal in an ore or alloy

assess – *v.* – to estimate the value of

astute – *adj.* – cunning; sly; crafty

atrophy – *v.* – to waste away through lack of nutrition

attenuate – *v.* – 1. to make thin or slender; 2. to lessen or weaken

audacious – *adj.* – fearless; bold

avarice – *n.* – inordinate desire of gaining and possessing wealth

augment – *v.* – to increase or add to; to make larger

auspicious – *adj.* – 1. having omens of success; 2. prosperous; 3. favorable; kind

austere – *v.* – harsh; severe; strict

authentic – *adj.* – real; genuine; trustworthy

authoritarian – *n.* – acting as a dictator; demanding obedience

awry – *adv.* – 1. crooked(ly); uneven(ly); 2. *adj.* – wrong, askew

axiom – *n.* – an established principle or statement accepted as true

azure – *n.* – the clear blue color of the sky

baleful – *adj.* – sinister; threatening; evil; deadly

banal – *adj.* – common; petty; ordinary

baroque – *adj.* – extravagant; ornate

batten – *v.* – to grow fat; to thrive

bauble – *n.* – 1. that which is gay or showy; 2. a baby's toy

beget – *v.* – to produce, as an effect

beholden – *adj.* – obliged; indebted

behoove – *v.* – to be advantageous; to be necessary

belittle – *v.* – to make small; to think lightly of

bellicose – *adj.* – warlike; disposed to quarrel or fight

benefactor – *n.* – one who helps others; a donor

beneficent – *adj.* – doing good

benevolent – *adj.* – kind; generous

benign – *adj.* – mild; harmless

berate – *v.* – scold; reprove; reproach; criticize

bereave – *v.* – to deprive

bereft – *adj.* – deprived; left sad because of someone's death

beseech – *v.* – 1. to ask or pray with urgency; 2. to beg eagerly for

besmirch – *v.* – to soil or discolor

bestial – *adj.* – having the qualities of a beast

betroth – *v.* – to promise or pledge in marriage

biased – *adj.* – prejudiced; influenced; not neutral

biennial – *adj.* – 1. happening every two years; 2. *n.* – a plant which blooms
every two years

blasphemous – *adj.* – irreligious, away from acceptable standards

blatant – *adj.* – 1. obvious; unmistakable; 2. crude; vulgar

blighted – *adj.* – destroyed; frustrated

blithe – *adj.* – happy; cheery, merry

bode – *v.* – to foreshow something

bombastic – *adj.* – pompous; wordy; turgid

boorish – *adj.* – rude; ill-mannered

brevity – *n.* – briefness; shortness

brindled – *adj.* – streaked or spotted with a darker color

broach – *v.* – 1. to pierce; 2. to introduce into conversation

brusque – *adj.* – abrupt, blunt, or short in manner or speech

bucolic – *adj.* – pastoral

bumptious – *adj.* – impertinent; conceited

burlesque – *v.* – to imitate comically

burly – *adj.* – strong; bulky; stocky

burnish – *v.* – to make or become smooth, bright, and glossy

cabal – *v.* – to intrigue or plot; usually in a small group

cache – *n.* – 1. stockpile; store; heap; 2. hiding place for goods

cacophony – *n.* – a jarring or disagreeable sound of words

cadaver – *n.* – a dead body

cajole – *v.* – to flatter; to coax

calamity – *n.* – disaster

caliber – *n.* – 1. the diameter of a bullet or shell; 2. quality

callow – *adj.* – immature

calumny – *n.* – slander

canard – *n.* – a false statement or rumor

candid – *adj.* – honest; truthful; sincere

capricious – *adj.* – changeable; fickle

captious – *adj.* – disposed to find fault

carnage – *n.* – slaughter

carte blanche – *n.* – unlimited power to decide

cascade – *n.* – 1. waterfall; 2. *v.* – pour; rush; fall

castigate – *v.* – to chastise

cataclysm – *n.* – 1. an overflowing of water; 2. an extraordinary change

catalyst – *n.* – anything which creates a situation in which change can occur

catharsis – *n.* – purgation

caustic – *adj.* – burning; sarcastic; harsh

cavil – *v.* – to find fault without good reason

celibate – *adj.* – unmarried, single; chaste

censor – *v.* – to examine and delete objectionable material

censure – *v.* – to criticize or disapprove of

cessation – *n.* – a ceasing; a stop

chafe – *v.* – to rage; to fret

chaffing – *n.* – banter

chagrin – *n.* – mortification or disappointment

charisma – *n.* – appeal; magnetism; presence

charlatan – *n.* – an imposter; fake

chaste – *adj.* – virtuous; free from obscenity

chastise – *v.* – punish; discipline; admonish; rebuke

choleric – *adj.* – cranky; cantankerous

chronology – *n.* – the arrangement of events, dates, etc. in a certain order of occurrence

circumlocution – *n.* – an indirect or lengthy way of expressing something

circumvent – *v.* – to go around

clandestine – *adj.* – secret; private; hidden

coalesce – *v.* – to combine; come together

coda – *n.* – a musical passage which brings a composition to its definite close

cogent – *adj.* – urgent; compelling; convincing

cognizant – *adj.* – being informed or aware

cohesion – *n.* – the act of holding together

cohort – *n.* – a group; a band

collaborate – *v.* – to work together; cooperate

colloquial – *adj.* – casual; common; conversational; idiomatic

collusion – *n.* – secret agreement for a fraudulent or illegal purpose

compatible – *adj.* – in agreement with; harmonious

complacent – *adj.* – content; self-satisfied; smug

compliant – *adj.* – yielding; obedient

comprehensive – *adj.* – all-inclusive; complete; thorough

comport – *v.* – to agree; to accord

compromise – *v.* – to settle by mutual adjustment

concede – 1. *v.* – to acknowledge; admit; 2. to surrender; to abandon one's position

conciliatory – *adj.* – tending to make peace between persons at variance

concise – *adj.* – in few words; brief; condensed

conclave – *n.* – any private meeting or close assembly

condescend – *v.* – to come down from one's position or dignity

condone – *v.* – to overlook; to forgive

conglomeration – *n.* – mixture; collection

conjoin – *v.* – to unite; to combine

conjure – *v.* – 1. to call upon or appeal to; 2. to cause to be, appear, come

connivance – *n.* – passive co-operation

connoisseur – *n.* – expert; authority (usually refers to a wine or food expert)

consecrate – *v.* – to sanctify; make sacred; immortalize

consensus – *n.* – unanimity; agreement

consort – *n.* -1. a companion; 2. *v.* – to be in harmony or agreement

conspicuous – *adj.* – easy to see; noticeable

consternation – *n.* – amazement or terror that causes confusion consummation – *n.* – the completion; finish

contemporary – *adj.* – living or happening at the same time; modern

contempt – *n.* – scorn; disrespect

contentious – *adj.* – argumentative; quarrelsome

contravene – *v.* – to go against; to oppose

contrite – *adj.* – regretful; sorrowful

contumacious – *adj.* – insubordinate; rebellious; disobedient

contusion – *n.* – a bruise; an injury where the skin is not broken

conundrum – *n.* – any question or thing of a perplexing nature

conventional – *adj.* – traditional; common; routine

copious – *adj.* – abundant; in great quantities

correlate – *v.* – to bring one thing into mutual relation with another thing

corroborate – *v.* – 1. to strengthen; 2. to confirm; to make more certain

covenant – *n.* – a binding and solemn agreement

cower – *v.* – crouch down in fear or shame

coy – *adj.* – 1. modest; bashful; 2. pretending shyness to attract

crass – *adj.* – gross; thick; coarse

craven – *adj.* – cowardly; fearful

culpable – *adj.* – blameworthy

cursory – *adj.* – hasty; slight

cynic – *n.* – one who believes that others are motivated entirely by selfishness

dais – *n.* – a raised platform in a room where tables for honored guests are placed

dally – *v.* – to delay; to put off

dank – *adj.* – disagreeably damp or humid

dauntless – *adj.* – fearless; not discouraged

dearth – *n.* – scarcity; shortage

debacle – *n.* – disaster; ruination

debauchery – *n.* – extreme indulgence of one's appetites, especially for sensual pleasure

debilitate – *v.* – deprive of strength

debonair – *adj.* – having an affable manner; courteous

decadence – *n.* – a decline in force or quality

deciduous – *adj.* – falling off at a particular season or stage of growth

decorous – *adj.* – characterized by good taste

decry – *v.* – to denounce or condemn openly

defamation – *n.* – the malicious uttering of falsehood respecting another

deference – *adj.* – yielding to the opinion of another, *n.* – a yielding in opinion to another

defunct – *adj.* – no longer living or existing

deliquesce – *v.* – to melt away

delusion – *n.* – a false statement or opinion

deign – *v.* – condescend

deleterious – *adj.* – harmful to health, well-being

deliberate 1. – *v.* – to consider carefully; weigh in the mind; 2. *adj.* – intentional

delineate – *v.* – to outline; to describe

demur – *v.* – to object, to take issue

denounce – *v.* – to speak out against; condemn

depict – *v.* – to portray in words; present a visual image

deplete – *v.* – to reduce; to empty

deposition – *n.* – 1. a removal from a position or power; 2. a testimony

depravity – *n.* – moral corruption; badness

depredation – *n.* – a plundering or laying waste

deride – *v.* – to ridicule; laugh at with scorn

derision – *n.* – ridicule; mockery

derogatory – *adj.* – belittling; uncomplimentary

descant – *v.* – to talk at length

desecrate – *v.* – to violate a holy place or sanctuary

desiccate – *v.* – to dry completely

despoil – *v.* – to strip; to rob

despotism – *n.* – 1. tyranny; 2. absolute power or influence

destitute – *adj.* – poor; poverty-stricken

desultory – *adj.* – without order or natural connection

detached – *adj.* – separated; not interested; standing alone

deter – *v.* – to prevent; to discourage; hinder

devoid – *adj.* – lacking; empty

dexterous – *adj.* – having or showing mental skill

dichotomy – *n.* – division of things by pairs

didactic – *adj.* – 1. instructive; 2. dogmatic; preachy

diffidence – *n.* – 1. lack of self-confidence; 2. distrust

digress – *v.* – stray from the subject; wander from topic

dilapidated – *n.* – falling to pieces or into disrepair

dilettante – *n.* – an admirer of the fine arts; a dabbler

diligence – *n.* – hard work

dint – *n.* – a blow; a stroke

disarray – *n.* – 1. disorder; confusion; 2. incomplete or disorderly attire

disavow – *v.* – to deny; to refuse

discerning – *adj.* – distinguishing one thing from another

discomfit – *v.* – 1. to overthrow the plans or expectations of; 2. to confuse

discord – *n.* – disagreement; lack of harmony

discourse – *n.* – a communication of thoughts by words

discriminating – 1. *v.* – distinguishing one thing from another; 2. *v.* – demonstrating bias; 3. *adj.* – able to distingush

disdain – 1. *n.* – intense dislike; 2. *v.* – look down upon; scorn

disheartened – *adj.* – discouraged; depressed

disinterested – *adj.* – impartial; unbiased

disparage – *v.* – to belittle; undervalue

disparity – *n.* – difference in form, character, or degree

dispassionate – *adj.* – lack of feeling; impartial

disperse – *v.* – to scatter; separate

disseminate – *v.* – to circulate; scatter

dissent – *v.* – to disagree; differ in opinion

dissonance – *n.* – harsh contradiction

diverge – *v.* – separate; split

diverse – *adj.* – different; dissimilar

divulge – *v.* – to become public; to become known

docile – *adj.* – manageable; obedient

document – 1. *n.* – official paper containing information; 2. *v.* – to support; substantiate; verify

doggerel – *adj.* – trivial; inartistic

dogmatic – *adj.* – stubborn; biased, opinionated

dormant – *adj.* – as if asleep

doting – *adj.* – excessively fond

doughty – *adj.* – brave; valiant

dowdy – *adj.* – drab; shabby

dregs – *n.* – waste or worthless manner

dubious – *adj.* – doubtful; uncertain; skeptical; suspicious

duress – *n.* – force; constraint

earthy – *adj.* – 1. not refined; coarse; 2. simple and natural ebullient – *adj.* – showing excitement

eccentric – *adj.* – odd; peculiar; strange

ecclesiastic – *adj.* – pertaining or relating to a church

eclectic – *adj.* – choosing or selecting from various sources

economical – *adj.* – not wasteful

edify – *v.* – 1. to build or establish; 2. to instruct and improve the mind

educe – *v.* – draw forth

efface – *v.* – wipe out; erase

effeminate – *adj.* – having qualities generally attributed to a woman

effervescence – *n.* -1. liveliness; spirit; enthusiasm; 2. bubbliness

effigy – *n.* – the image or likeness of a person

effluvium – *n.* – an outflow in the form of a vapor

effrontery – *n.* – impudence; assurance

effusive – *adj.* – pouring out or forth; overflowing

egocentric – *adj.* – self-centered

egregious – *adj.* – eminent; remarkable

egress – *v.* – to depart; to go out

elaboration – *n.* – act of clarifying; adding details

elegy – *n.* – a poem of lament and praise for the dead

eloquence – *n.* – the ability to speak well

elucidate – *v.* – to make clear or manifest; to explain

elusive – *adj.* – hard to catch; difficult to understand

emanate – *v.* – to send forth; to emit

embellish – *v.* – to improve the appearance of

eminence – *n.* – 1. high or lofty place; 2. superiority in position or rank

emulate – *v.* – to imitate; copy; mimic

enamored – *adj.* – filled with love and desire

encroach – *v.* – to trespass or intrude

encumber – *v.* – to hold back; to hinder

endorse – *v.* – support; to approve of; recommend

endue – *v.* – to put on; to cover

engender – *v.* – to create; bring about

enhance – *v.* – to improve; complement; make more attractive

enigma- *n.* – mystery; secret; perplexity

ennui – *n.* – boredom; apathy

enrapture – *v.* – to fill with pleasure

ephemeral – *adj.* – temporary; brief; short-lived

epilogue – *n.* – closing section of a play or novel providing further comment

epiphany – *n.* – an appearance of a supernatural being

epitaph – *n.* – an inscription on a monument, in honor or memory of a dead person

epitome – *n.* – model; typification; representation

equinox – *n.* – precise time when the day and night everywhere is of equal length

equivocal – *adj.* – doubtful; uncertain

equivocate – *v.* – to be purposely ambiguous

errant – *adj.* – wandering

erratic – *adj.* – unpredictable; strange

erroneous – *adj.* – untrue; inaccurate; not correct

erudite – *adj.* – having extensive knowledge; learned

eschew – *v.* – to escape from; to avoid

esoteric – *adj.* – incomprehensible; obscure

estranged – *adj.* – kept at a distance; alienated

ethereal – *adj.* – 1. very light; airy; 2. heavenly; not earthly

ethnic – *adj.* – native; racial; cultural

euphemism – *n.* – the use of a word or phrase in place of one that is distasteful

euphony – *n.* – pleasant sound

euphoria – *n.* – a feeling of well-being

evanescent – *adj.* – vanishing; fleeting

evoke – *v.* – call forth; provoke

exculpate – *v.* – to declare or prove guiltless

execute – *v.* – 1. put to death; kill; 2. to carry out; fulfill

exemplary – *adj.* – serving as an example; outstanding

exhaustive – *adj.* – thorough; complete

exhume – *v.* – to unearth; to reveal

exigent – *n.* – an urgent occasion

exonerate – *v.* – to unload; to release from burden

exorbitant – *adj.* – going beyond what is reasonable; excessive

exotic – *adj.* – unusual; striking

expedient – *adj.* – helpful; practical; worthwhile

expedite – *v.* – speed up

explicit – *adj.* – specific; definite

exposition – *n.* – a setting forth of facts or ideas

expunge – *v.* – to blot out; to delete

extol – *v.* – praise; commend

extraneous – *adj.* – irrelevant; not related; not essential

exuberant – *adj.* – overflowing; lavish; superabundant

exude – *v.* – to flow slowly or ooze in drops

facade – *n.* – front view; false appearance

facetious – *adj.* – lightly joking

facilitate – *v.* – make easier; simplify

facsimile – *n.* – copy; reproduction; replica

faction – *n.* – a number of people in an organization having a common end view

fallacious – *adj.* – misleading

fallible – *adj.* – liable to be mistaken or erroneous

fanatic – *n.* – enthusiast; extremist

fastidious – *adj.* – fussy; hard to please

fathom – *v.* – comprehend; uncover

fatuous – *adj.* – silly; inane; unreal

fealty – *n.* – fidelity; loyalty

feasible – *adj.* – reasonable; practical

fecund – *adj.* – fruitful in children; productive

feign – *v.* – to invent or imagine

ferment – *v.* – to excite or agitate

ferret – *v.* – drive or hunt out of hiding

fervent – *adj.* – passionate; intense

fervid – *adj.* – very hot; burning

fervor – *n.* – passion; intensity

fester – *v.* – to become more and more virulent and fixed

fetish – *n.* – anything to which one gives excessive devotion or blind adoration

fickle – *adj.* – changeable; unpredictable

fidelity – *n.* – faithfulness; honesty

figment – *n.* – product; creation

finesse – *n.* – the ability to handle situations with skill and diplomacy

finite – *adj.* – measurable; limited; not everlasting

fissure – *n.* – a dividing or breaking into parts

flag – *v.* – 1. to send a message by signaling; 2. to become limp

flaccid – *adj.* – 1. hanging in loose folds or wrinkles; 2. lacking force; weak flamboyant – *adj.* – ornate; too showy

fledgling – *n.* – inexperienced person; beginner

flinch – *v.* – wince; draw back; retreat

flippant – *adj.* – 1. speaking with ease and rapidity; 2. impertinent

flout – *v.* – to mock; to sneer

fluency – *n.* – smoothness of speech

flux – *n.* – current; continuous change

foible – *n.* – a slight frailty in character

foist – *v.* – to put in slyly or stealthily

foray – *v.* – to raid for spoils, plunder

forbearance – *n.* – patience; self-restraint

forensic – *adj.* – pertaining to legal or public argument

fortitude – *n.* – firm courage; strength

fortuitous – *adj.* – accidental; happening by chance; lucky

foster – *v.* – encourage; nurture; support

fractious – *adj.* – rebellious; apt to quarrel

frenetic – *adj.* – frantic; frenzied

frivolity – *adj.* – giddiness; lack of seriousness

fraught – *adj.* – loaded; charged

froward – *adj.* – not willing to yield or comply with what is reasonable

frugality – *n.* – thrift

fulminate – *v.* – to explode with sudden violence

fulsome – *adj.* – offensive, especially because of excess

fundamental – *adj.* – basic; necessary

furtive – *adj.* – secretive; sly

fustian – *n.* – an inflated style of talking or writing

futile – *adj.* – worthless; unprofitable

gaffe – *n.* – a blunder

gainsay – *v.* – to deny or contradict

galvanize – *v.* – to stimulate as if by electric shock; startle; excite

gamut – *n.* – 1. a complete range; 2. any complete musical scale

garbled – *adj.* – mixed up

garish – *adj.* – gaudy; showy

garner – *v.* – to accumulate

garrulous – *adj.* – talking much about unimportant things

gauche – *adj.* – awkward; lacking grace

gauntlet – *n.* – a long glove with a flaring cuff covering the lower part of the arm

generic – *adj.* – common; general; universal

genial – *adj.* – 1. contributing to life and growth; 2. amiable; cordial

genre – *n.* – a kind, sort, or type

germane – *adj.* – pertinent; related; to the point

gerrymander – *v.* – to manipulate unfairly

gibber – *v.* – speak foolishly

glib – *adj.* – smooth and slippery; speaking or spoken in a smooth manner

gloat – *v.* – brag; glory over

glutton – *n.* – overeater

gnarled – *adj.* – full of knots

goad – *v.* – to arouse or incite

gormand – *n.* – a greedy or ravenous eater; glutton

grandiose – *adj.* – extravagant; flamboyant

gravity – *n.* – seriousness

gregarious – *adj.* – fond of the company of others

grisly – *adj.* – frightful; horrible

guffaw – *n.* – a loud, coarse burst of laughter

guile – *n.* – slyness; deceit

guise – *n.* – 1. customary behavior; 2. manner of dress; 3. false appearance

gullible – *adj.* – easily fooled

hackneyed – *adj.* – commonplace; trite

haggard – *adj.* – tired-looking; fatigued

halcyon – *adj.* – calm; quiet; peaceful

hamper – *v.* – interfere with; hinder

haphazard – *adj.* – disorganized; random

hapless – *adj.* – unlucky; unfortunate

harangue – *v.* – to speak in an impassioned and forcible manner

haughty – *adj.* – proud and disdainful

hedonistic – *adj.* – pleasure seeking

heed – *v.* – obey; yield to

heresy – *n.* – opinion contrary to popular belief

heretic – *n.* – one who holds opinion contrary to that which is generally accepted

hiatus – *n.* – interval; break; period of rest

hierarchy – *n.* – body of people, things, or concepts divided into ranks

hindrance – *n.* – blockage; obstacle

hoary – *adj.* – very aged; ancient

homage – *n.* – honor; respect

homeostasis – *n.* – the maintenance of stability or equilibrium

hone – *v.* – sharpen

homily – *n.* – discourse or sermon read to an audience

hubris – *n.* – arrogance

humility – *n.* – lack of pride; modesty

hybrid – *n.* – anything of mixed origin

hypocritical – *adj.* – two-faced; deceptive

hypothetical – *adj.* – assumed; uncertain

iconoclast – *n.* – a breaker or destroyer of images

ideology – *n.* – set of beliefs; principles

idiosyncrasy – *n.* – any personal peculiarity, mannerism, etc.

idyllic – *adj.* – pleasing and simple

igneous – *adj.* – having the nature of fire

ignoble – *adj.* – shameful; dishonorable

ignominious – *adj.* – 1. contemptible; 2. degrading

illuminate – *v.* – make understandable

illusory – *adj.* – unreal; false; deceptive

imbue – *v.* – inspire; arouse

immaculate – *adj.* – 1. perfectly clean; perfectly correct; 2. pure

imminent – *adj.* – appearing as if about to happen

immune – *adj.* – protected; unthreatened by

immutable – *adj.* – unchangeable; permanent

impale – *v.* – fix on a stake; stick; pierce

impartial – *adj.* – unbiased; fair

impasse – *n.* – a situation that has no solution or escape

impede – *v.* – to stop in progress

impenitent – *adj.* – without regret, shame, or remorse

imperious – *adj.* – authoritative

impervious – *adj.* – 1. incapable of being penetrated; 2. not affected or influenced by

impetuous – *adj.* – 1. rash; impulsive; 2. forcible; violent

impiety – *n.* – 1. irreverence toward God; 2. lack of respect implement – *v.* – to carry into effect

implication – *n.* – suggestion; inference

implicit – *adj.* – to be understood though not fully expressed

impolitic – *adj.* – unwise; imprudent

imprecate – *v.* – to pray for evil; to invoke a curse

impromptu – *adj.* – without preparation

improvident – *adj.* – lacking foresight and thrift

impudent – *adj.* – shameless; immodest

impugn – *v.* – to contradict

imputation – *n.* – attribution

inadvertent – *adj.* – not on purpose; unintentional

inarticulate – *adj.* – speechless; unable to speak clearly

incarcerate – *v.* – to imprison or confine

incessant – *adj.* – constant; continual

inchoate – *adj.* – existing in elementary or beginning form

incidental – *adj.* – extraneous; unexpected

incisive – *adj.* – cutting into

inclined – 1. *adj.* – apt to; likely to; 2. angled

incognito – *adj.* – unidentified; disguised; concealed

incoherent – *adj.* – illogical; rambling

incommodious – *adj.* – uncomfortable; troublesome

incompatible – *adj.* – disagreeing; disharmonious

incorporeal – *adj.* – not consisting of matter

incorrigible – *adj.* – not capable of correction or improvement

incredulous – *adj.* – unwilling to believe; skeptical

incubate – *v.* – to sit on and hatch (eggs)

inculcate – *v.* – to impress upon the mind by frequent repetition or urging incursion – *n.* – 1. a running in; 2. invasion; raid

indemnify – *v.* – to protect against or keep free from loss

indict – *v.* – charge with a crime

indifferent – *adj.* – unconcerned

indigenous – *adj.* – innate; inherent; inborn

indignant – *adj.* – to consider as unworthy or improper

indolent – *adj.* – lazy; inactive

indomitable – *adj.* – not easily discouraged or defeated

indubitably – *adv.* – unquestionably; surely

indulgent – *adj.* – lenient: patient

ineluctable – *adj.* – not to be avoided or escaped

inept – *adj.* – incompetent; unskilled

inert – *adj.* – without power to move or to resist an opposite force

inevitable – *adj.* – sure to happen; unavoidable

infamous – *adj.* – having a bad reputation; notorious

infer- *v.* – form an opinion; conclude

ingenious – *adj.* – gifted with genius; innate or natural quality

inherent – *adj.* – innate; basic; inborn

inimical – *adj.* – unfriendly; adverse

iniquitous – *adj.* – unjust; wicked

initiate – 1. *v.* – begin; admit into a group; 2. *n.* – a person who is in the process of being admitted into a group

innate – *adj.* – natural; inborn

innocuous – *adj.* – harmless; innocent

innovate – *v.* – introduce a change; depart from the old

innuendo – *n.* – an indirect remark, gesture or reference

inordinate – *adj.* – not regulated; excessive

insipid – *adj.* – uninteresting; bland

insolvent – *adj.* – bankrupt; not able to pay debts

instigate – *v.* – start; provoke

intangible – *adj.* – incapable of being touched; immaterial

intermittent – 1. *adj.* – stopping and starting again at intervals; 2. *n.* – a disease which entirely subsides or ceases at certain intervals

intransigent – *adj.* – refusing to compromise

intrepid – *adj.* – fearless; brave

inured – *adj.* – accustomed

invective – *n.* – a violent verbal attack

invoke – *v.* – ask for; call upon

irascible – *adj.* – easily provoked or inflamed to anger

ironic – *adj.* – contradictory; inconsistent; sarcastic

irrational – *adj.* – not logical

irreparable – *adj.* – that which cannot be repaired or regained

itinerary – *n.* – travel plan; schedule; course

jaded – *adj.* – 1. tired or worn-out; 2. dulled

jeopardy – *n.* – danger

jettison – *n.* – a throwing overboard of goods to lighten a vehicle in an emergency

jocund – *adj.* – merry; gay; cheerful

jovial – *adj.* – cheery; jolly; playful

judicious – *adj.* – possessing sound judgement

juncture – *n.* – critical point; meeting

juxtapose – *v.* – place side-by-side

ken – *n.* – range of knowledge

kindle – *v.* – ignite; arouse

kinship – *n.* – family relationship

kith – *n.* – acquaintances and relations

knavery – *n.* – dishonesty

knead – *v.* – mix; massage

labyrinth – *n.* – maze

laconic – *n.* – a brief, pithy expression

lacerate – *v.* – 1. to tear or mangle; 2. to wound or hurt

laggard – *n.* – a lazy person; one who lags behind

lambent – *adj.* – giving off a soft radiance

lament – *v.* – to mourn or grieve

languid – *adj.* – weak; fatigued

larceny – *n.* – theft; stealing

lascivious – *adj.* – indecent; immoral

lassitude – *n.* – a state or feeling of being tired or weak

latency – *n.* – the condition of being hidden or undeveloped

laud – *v.* – praise

lax – *adj.* – careless; irresponsible

lecherous – *adj.* – impure in thought and act

lethal – *adj.* – deadly

lethargic – *adj.* – lazy; passive

levee – *n.* – the act or time of rising

levity – *n.* – silliness; lack of seriousness

lewd – *adj.* – lustful; wicked

liaison – *n.* – connection; link

libertine – *n.* – one who indulges his desires without restraint

licentious – *adj.* – disregarding accepted rules and standards

ligneous – *adj.* – consisting of or resembling wood

limber – *adj.* – flexible; pliant

lithe – *adj.* – easily bent; pliable

litigate – *v.* – to contest in a lawsuit

livid – *adj.* – 1. black-and-blue; discolored; 2. enraged; irate

loquacious – *adj.* – talkative

lucent – *adj.* – shining; translucent

lucid – *adj.* -1. shining; 2. easily understood

lucrative – *adj.* – profitable; gainful

lugubrious – *adj.* – mournful; very sad

luminous – *adj.* – giving off light; bright

lurid – *adj.* – ghastly pale; gloomy

lustrous – *adj.* – bright; radiant

macerate – *v.* – 1. to soften by soaking; 2. to cause to waste away; 3. to torment

magnanimous – *adj.* – forgiving; unselfish

magnate – *n.* – a very influential person in any field of activity

malediction – *n.* – curse; evil spell

malefactor – *n.* – one who commits a crime

malicious – *adj.* – spiteful; vindictive

malign – *v.* – to defame; speak evil of

malleable – *adj.* – that which can be pounded without breaking; adaptable

mandate – *n.* – order; charge

mandatory – *adj.* – authoritatively commanded or required

manifest – *adj.* – obvious; clear

marauder – *n.* – a rover in search of booty or plunder

marred – *adj.* – damaged

maudlin – *adj.* – foolishly and tearfully sentimental

maverick – *n.* – person who acts independent of a group

meander – *v.* – wind on a course; go aimlessly

melancholy – *n.* – depression; gloom

mellifluous – *adj.* – flowing sweetly and smoothly

mendacious – *adj.* – addicted to deception

mentor – *n.* – teacher

mercenary – *n.* – working or done for payment only

mercurial – *adj.* – quick, volatile; changeable

meretricious – *adj.* – alluring by false, showy charms; fleshy

mesmerize – *v.* – hypnotize

metamorphosis – *n.* – change of form

meticulous – *adj.* – exacting; precise

mettle – *n.* – high quality of character

mien – *n.* – manner; external appearance

mimicry – *n.* – imitation

minute – *adj.* – extremely small; tiny

misanthropy – *n.* – hatred of mankind

miser – *n.* – penny pincher; stingy person

mite – *n.* – 1. very small sum of money; 2. very small creature

mitigate – *v.* – alleviate; lessen; soothe

modulate – *v.* – 1. to regulate or adjust; 2. to vary the pitch of the voice

mollify – *v.* – to soften; to make less intense

molten – *adj.* – melted

moot – *adj.* – subject to or open for discussion or debate

mordant – *adj.* – biting. cutting, or caustic

morose – *adj.* – moody; despondent

motif – *n.* – theme

motility – *n.* – the quality of exhibiting spontaneous motion

mundane – *adj.* – ordinary; commonplace

munificent – *adj.* – very generous in giving; lavish

mutinous – *adj.* – inclined to revolt

myriad – *adj.* – innumerable; countless

narcissistic – *adj.* – egotistical; self-centered

nautical – *adj.* – of the sea

nebulous – *adj.* – 1. cloudy; hazy; 2. unclear; vague

nefarious – *adj.* – very wicked; abominable

negligence – *n.* – carelessness

nemesis – *n.* – just punishment; retribution

neophyte – *n.* – beginner; newcomer

nettle – *v.* – annoy; irritate

neutral – *adj.* – impartial; unbiased

nexus – *n.* – a connection

nostalgic – *adj.* – longing for the past; filled with bittersweet memories

nostrum – *n.* – a quack medicine

notorious – *adj.* – infamous; renowned

novel – *adj.* – new

noxious – *adj.* – harmful to health or morals

nugatory – *adj.* – trifling; futile; insignificant

nullify – *v.* – cancel; invalidate

oaf – *n.* – 1. a misshapen child; 2. a stupid, clumsy fellow

obdurate – *adj.* – stubborn; inflexible

obeisance – *n.* – a gesture of respect or reverence

obfuscate – *v.* – to darken; to confuse

objective – 1. *adj.* – open-minded; impartial; 2. *n.* – goal

objurgate – *v.* – to chide vehemently

obligatory – *adj.* – mandatory; necessary

obliterate – *v.* – destroy completely

obloquy – *n.* – verbal abuse of a person or thing

obscure – *adj.* – not easily understood; dark

obsequious – *adj.* – slavishly attentive; servile

obsolete – *adj.* – out of date; passé

obstinate – *adj.* – stubborn

obtrude – *v.* – to thrust forward; to eject

occult – *adj.* – mystical; mysterious

odious – *adj.* – hateful; disgusting

oligarchy – *n.* – form of government in which the supreme power is placed in
    the hands of a small exclusive group

ominous – *adj.* – threatening

omniscient – *adj.* – having universal knowledge

opalescent – *adj.* – iridescent

opaque – *adj.* – dull; cloudy; nontransparent

opprobrious – *adj.* – reproachful or contemptuous

optimist – *n.* – person who hopes for the best; sees the good side

opulence – *n.* – wealth; fortune

ornate – *adj.* – elaborate; lavish; decorated

orthodox – *adj.* – traditional; accepted

oscillate – *v.* – 1. to swing to and fro; 2. to be indecisive; to fluctuate

ossify – *v.* – to settle or fix rigidly in a practice, custom, attitude, etc.

ostensible – *adj.* – 1. proper to be shown; 2. apparent; declared

ostracize – *v.* – to cast out or banish

oust – *v.* – drive out; eject

pagan – 1. n – polytheist; 2. *adj.* – polytheistic

painstaking – *adj.* – thorough; careful; precise

palatial – *adj.* – large and ornate, like a palace

palindrome – *n.* – a word, verse or sentence that is the same when read backward or forward

palliate – *v.* – 1. to alleviate or ease; 2. to make appear less serious

pallid – *adj.* – sallow; colorless

palpable – *adj.* – tangible; apparent

paltry – *adj.* – worthless; trifling

pandemonium – *n.* – a place of wild disorder, noise, or confusion

panegyric – *n.* – a formal speech written in praise of a distinguished person

paradigm – *n.* – model; example

paradox – *n.* – 1. a statement that seems contradictory but that may actually be true in fact; 2. something inconsistent with common experience

parallel – *adj.* – extending in the same direction and at the same distance apart at every point

parapet – *n.* – a wall or railing to protect people from falling

paraphernalia – *n.* – equipment; accessories

pariah – *n.* – an outcast; someone despised by others

parity – *n.* – state of being the same in power, value, or rank

parley – *v.* – to speak with another; to discourse

parochial – *adj.* – religious; narrow-minded

parry – *v.* – to ward off; to avoid

parsimonious – *adj.* – miserly; stingy

partisan – 1. n. – supporter; follower; 2. *adj.* – biased; one-sided

passive – *adj.* – submissive; unassertive

pathology – *n.* – part of medicine dealing with the nature of diseases, their causes and symptoms, and the structural and functional changes

paucity – *n.* – scarcity; small number

peculate – *v.* – to embezzle

pecuniary – *adj.* – relating to money

pedagogue – *n.* – a dogmatic teacher

pedestrian – *adj.* – mediocre; ordinary

pellucid – *adj.* – transparent

penchant – *n.* – a strong liking or fondness

pensive – *adj.* – reflective; contemplative

penury – *n.* – lack of money or property

perceptive – *adj.* – full of insight; aware

perdition – *n.* – complete and irreparable loss

peremptory – *adj.* – 1. barring future action; 2. that cannot be denied, changed, etc.

perfidious – *adj.* – violating good faith or vows

percussion – *n.* – the striking of one object against another

peripheral – *adj.* – marginal; outer

perjury – *n.* – the practice of lying

permeable – *adj.* – porous; allowing to pass through

pernicious – *adj.* – dangerous; harmful

perpetual – *adj.* – enduring for all time

perquisite – *n.* – a fee, profit, etc. in addition to the stated income of one's employment

pertinent – *adj.* – related to the matter at hand

peruse – *v.* – to read carefully and thoroughly

pervade – *v.* – to occupy the whole of

pessimism – *n.* – seeing only the gloomy side; hopelessness

petty – *adj.* – unimportant; of subordinate standing

petulant – *adj.* – 1. forward; immodest; 2. impatient or irritable

phenomenon – *n.* – 1. miracle; 2. occurrence

philanthropy – *n.*- charity; unselfishness

phlegmatic – *adj.* – without emotion or interest

phobia – *n.* – morbid fear

pied – *adj.* – spotted

pinioned – *adj.* – 1. having wings; 2. having wings or arms bound or confined

pinnacle – *n.* – 1. a small turret that rises above the roof of a building; 2. the highest point

pious – *adj.* – religious; devout; dedicated

piquant – *adj.* – 1. agreeably pungent or stimulating to the taste; 2. exciting interest or curiosity

pittance – *n.* – small allowance

placate – *v.* – pacify

placid – *adj.* – serene; tranquil

platonic – *adj.* – 1. idealistic or impractical; 2. not amorous or sensual

plausible – *adj.* – probable; feasible

plenary – *adj.* – full; entire; complete

plethora – *n.* – condition of going beyond what is needed; excess; overabundance

plumb – *v.* – 1. to fall or sink straight down; 2. to hang vertically

polemic – *adj.* – controversial; argumentative

pommel – *n.* – the rounded, upward-projecting front of a saddle

portend – *v.* – to foreshadow

potable – *adj.* – drinkable

potent – *adj.* – having great power or physical strength

pragmatic – *adj.* – matter-of-fact; practical

prate – *v.* – to talk much and foolishly

prattle – *v.* – to speak in a childish manner; babble

precept – *n.* – a rule or direction of moral conduct

precipitate – *v.* – 1. to throw headlong; 2. to cause to happen

preclude – *v.* – inhibit; make impossible

precocious – *adj.* – developed or matured earlier than usual

predecessor – *n.* – one who has occupied an office before another

prefatory – *adj.* – introductory

preponderate – *adj.* – to outweigh

prerogative – *n.* – a prior or exclusive right or privilege

prevaricate – *v.* – to evade the truth

pristine – *adj.* – still pure or untouched

privy – *adj.* – private; confidential

probity – *n.* – true virtue or integrity; complete honesty

problematic – *adj.* – uncertain

prodigal – *adj.* – wasteful; lavish

prodigious – *adj.* – exceptional; tremendous

prodigy – *n.* – 1. an extraordinary happening; 2. something so extraordinary as
   to inspire wonder

profound – *adj.* – deep; knowledgeable; thorough

profusion – *n.* – great amount; abundance

progeny – *n.* – children; offspring

prognosis – *n.* – a forecast, especially in medicine

prolific – *adj.* – fruitful

propagate – *v.* – to reproduce or multiply

propinquity – *n.* – nearness in time or place, relationship, or nature

propitiate – *v.* – to win the good will of

prosaic – *adj.* – tiresome; ordinary

proselytize – *v.* – to make a convert of

protocol – *n.* – an original draft or record of a document

provident – *adj.* – prudent; economical

provincial – *adj.* – regional; unsophisticated

proviso – *n.* – conditional stipulation to an agreement

provocative – *adj.* – 1. tempting; 2. irritating

provoke – *v.* – to stir action or feeling; arouse

prudent – *adj.* – wise; careful; prepared

pseudonym – *n.* – a borrowed or fictitious name

puerile – *adj.* – childish; immature

pundit – *n.* – a person of great learning

pungent – *adj.* – sharp; stinging

purloin – *v.* – to steal

purview – *n.* – the range of control, activity, or understanding

quaff – *v.* – to drink or swallow in large quantities

quagmire – *n.* – a difficult position, as if on shaky ground

quaint – *adj.* – old-fashioned; unusual; odd

qualified – *adj.* – experienced; indefinite

qualify – *v.* – 1. to render fit; 2. to furnish with legal power; 3. to modify

qualm – *n.* – sudden feeling of uneasiness or doubt

quandary – *n.* – dilemma

quarantine – *n.* – isolation of a person to prevent spread of disease

quiescent – *adj.* – inactive; at rest

quintessence – *n.* – 1. the ultimate substance; 2. the pure essence of anything

quirk – *n.* – peculiar behavior; startling twist

quixotic – *adj.* – extravagantly chivalrous

quizzical – *adj.* – odd; comical

rabid – *adj.* – furious; with extreme anger

ramification – *n.* – the arrangement of branches; consequence

rampant – *adj.* – violent and uncontrollable action

rampart – *n.* – 1. anything that protects or defends; 2. an embankment of earth that surrounds a fort or castle

rancid – *adj.* – having a bad odor

rancor – *n.* – a continuing and bitter hate or ill will

rant – *v.* – to speak in a loud, pompous manner; rave

ratify – *v.* – to make valid; confirm

rationalize – *v.* – to offer reasons for; account for

raucous – *adj.* – disagreeable to the sense of hearing; harsh

raze – *v.* – 1. to destroy to the gound; 2. to scrape or shave off

realm – *n.* – an area; sphere of activity

rebuff – *n.* – an abrupt, blunt refusal

rebuttal – *n.* – refutation

recalcitrant – *adj.* – refusing to obey authority

recession – *n.* – withdrawal; depression

reciprocal – *adj.* – mutual; having the same relationship to each other

recidivism – *n.* – habitual or chronic relapse

recluse – *n.* – solitary and shut off from society

recondite – *adj.* – beyond the grasp of ordinary understanding

rectify – *v.* – correct

recumbent – *adj.* – leaning or reclining

recusant – *adj.* – disobedient of authority

redolent – *adj.* – sweet-smelling; fragrant

redundant – *adj.* – repetitious; unnecessary

refurbish – *v.* – to make new

refute – *v.* – challenge; disprove

regal – *adj.* – royal; grand

reminiscence – *n.* – a remembering

reiterate – *v.* – repeat; to state again

relegate – *v.* – banish; put to a lower position

relevant – *adj.* – of concern; significant

relinquish – *v.* – to let go; abandon

remonstrate – *v.* – to exhibit strong reasons against an act

remorse – *n.* – guilt; sorrow

renascence – *n.* – a new birth; revival

render – *v.* – deliver; provide; to give up a possession

rendition – *n.* – a performance or interpretation

repertoire – *n.* – stock of plays that can be readily performed by a company

replica – *n.* – copy; representation

reprehend – *v.* – to reprimand; to find fault with

reprehensible – *adj.* – wicked; disgraceful

reprieve – *v.* – to give temporary relief

reprobate – 1. *adj.* – vicious; unprincipled; 2. *v.* – to disapprove with detestation

repudiate – *v.* – reject; cancel

repugnant – *adj.* – inclined to disobey or oppose

rescind – *v.* – retract; discard

resignation – *n.* – 1. quitting; 2. submission

resilient – *adj.* – flexible; capable of withstanding stress

resonant – *adj.* – resounding; re-echoing

resplendent – *adj.* – dazzling; splendid

resolution – *n.* – proposal; promise; determination

respite – *n.* – recess; rest period

resurgent – *adj.* – rising or tending to rise again

reticent – *adj.* – silent; reserved; shy

retroaction – *n.* – an action elicited by a stimulus

reverent – *adj.* – respectful

reverie – *n.* – the condition of being unaware of one's surroundings; trance

revile – *v.* – to be abusive in speech

rhetorical – *adj.* – having to do with verbal communication

ribald – *adj.* – characterized by coarse joking or mocking

rigor- *n.* – severity

risible – *adj.* – able or inclined to laugh

rivet – *v.* – to fasten, fix, or hold firmly

roseate – *adj.* – bright, cheerful, or optimistic

rote – *n.* – a fixed, mechanical way of doing something

rotundity – *n.* – condition of being rounded out or plump

rudimentary – *adj.* – elementary

ruminate – *v.* – to muse on

rummage – *v.* – search thoroughly

rustic – *adj.* – plain and unsophisticated; homely

saga – *n.* – a legend; story

sagacious – *adj.* – wise; cunning

salient – *adj.* – noticeable; prominent

salubrious – *adj.* – favorable to health

salutatory – *adj.* – of or containing greetings

salvage – *v.* – rescue from loss

sanction – *n.* – 1. support; encouragement; 2. something which makes a rule binding

sanguine – *adj.* – 1. optimistic; cheerful; 2. red

sapid – *adj.* – having a pleasant taste

sarcasm – *n.* – irony; bitter humor designed to wound

sardonic – *adj.* – bitterly ironical

satire – *n.* – a novel or play that uses humor or irony to expose folly

satiric – *adj.* – indulging in the use of ridicule or sarcasm to expose or attack vice, folly, etc.

saturate – *v.* – soak thoroughly; drench

saturnine – *adj.* – heavy; grave; gloomy

saunter – *v.* – walk at a leisurely pace; stroll

savant – *n.* – a learned person

savor – *v.* – to receive pleasure from; enjoy

scanty – *adj.* – inadequate; sparse

schism – *n.* – a division in an organized group

scourge – *v.* – to whip severely

scurrilous – *adj.* – using low and indecent language

scrupulous – *adj.* – honorable; exact

scrutinize – *v.* – examine closely; study

sedentary – *adj.* – 1. characterized by sitting; 2. remaining in one locality

seethe – *v.* – to be in a state of emotional turmoil; to become angry

serendipity – *n.* – an apparent aptitude for making fortunate discoveries accidentally

serrated – *adj.* – having a sawtoothed edge

servile – *adj.* – slavish, groveling

shoal – *n.* – a great quantity

shoddy – *adj.* – of inferior quality; cheap

sinuous – *adj.* – winding; crooked

sloth – *n.* – disinclination to action or labor

slovenly – *adv.* – careless in habits. behavior, etc.; untidy

skeptic – *n.* – doubter

skrumble – *v.* – to toss about haphazardly

skulk – *v.* – to move secretly

slander – *v.* – defame; maliciously misrepresent

sojourn – *n.* – temporary stay; visit

solace – *n.* – hope; comfort during a time of grief

solemnity – *n.* – seriousness

solicit – *v.* – ask; seek

soliloquy – *n.* – a talk one has with oneself (esp. on stage)

somber – *adj.* – dark and depressing; gloomy

sordid – *adj.* – filthy; base; vile

specious – *adj.* – appearing just and fair without really being so

spelunker – *n.* – one who explores caves

spendthrift – *n.* – one who spends money carelessly or wastefully

splenetic – *adj.* – bad-tempered; irritable

sporadic – *adj.* – rarely occurring or appearing; intermittent

spurious – *adj.* – false; counterfeit

squalid – *adj.* – foul; filthy

stagnant – *adj.* – motionless; uncirculating

staid – *adj.* – sober; sedate

stamina – *n.* – endurance

stanch – *v.* – to stop or check the flow of blood

stanza – *n.* – group of lines in a poem having a definite pattern

static – *adj.* – inactive; changeless

steadfast – *adj.* – loyal

sterile – *adj.* – 1. incapable of producing others; 2. lacking in interest or vitality;
3. free from living microorganisms

stigma – *n.* – a mark of disgrace

stigmatize – *v.* – to characterize or make as disgraceful

stipend – *n.* – payment for work done

stoic – *adj.* – detached; unruffled; calm

stolid – *adj.* – unexcitable; dull

striated – *adj.* – marked with fine parallel lines

strident – *adj.* – creaking; harsh; grating

stupor – *n.* – a stunned or bewildered condition

stymie – *n.* – 1. to hinder or obstruct; 2. in golf, an opponent's ball lying in direct line between the player's ball and the hole

suave – *adj.* – effortlessly gracious

subsidiary – *adj.* – subordinate

substantive – *adj.* – 1. existing independently; 2. having a real existence

subtlety – *n.* – 1. understatement; 2. propensity for understatement; 3. sophistication; 4. cunning

succinct – *adj.* – consisting of few words; concise

succor – *n.* – aid; assistance

succumb – *v.* – give in; yield; collapse

suffuse – *v.* – to overspread

sullen – *adj.* – 1. showing resentment; 2. gloomy; dismal

sumptuous – *adj.* – involving great expense

sunder – *v.* – break; split in two

sundry – *adj.* – 1. various; miscellaneous; 2. separate; distinct

superficial – *adj.* – on the surface; narrow-minded; lacking depth

superfluous – *adj.* – unnecessary; extra

supplant – *v.* – to take the place of

suppliant – *adj.* – asking earnestly and submissively

suppress – *v.* – to bring to an end; hold back

surmise – *v.* – draw an inference; guess

surfeit – *v.* – to feed or supply in excess

surpass – *v.* – go beyond; outdo

surreptitious – *adj.* – done without proper authority

susceptible – *adj.* – easily imposed; inclined

swathe – *v.* – to wrap around something; envelop

sycophant – 1. *adj.* – flatterer; 2. *n.* – a person who seeks favor by flattering people of wealth or influence

syllogism – *n.* – reasoning from the general to the particular

symmetry – *n.* – correspondence of parts; harmony; equal in form on either side of a dividing line

synthesis – *n.* – 1. the putting together of two or more things; 2. a whole made up of parts put together

tacit – *adj.* – not voiced or expressed

taciturn – *adj.* – reserved; quiet; secretive

tantalize – *v.* – to tempt; to torment

tarry – *v.* – to go or move slowly; delay

taut – *adj.* – 1. stretched tightly; 2. tense

tawdry – *n.* – a gaudy ornament

tedious – *adj.* – time-consuming; burdensome; uninteresting

teem – *v.* – 1. to be stocked to overflowing; 2. to pour out; to empty

temerity – *n.* – foolish boldness

temper – *v.* – soften; pacify; compose

temperament – *n.* – 1. a middle course reached by mutual concession; 2. frame of mind

tenacious – *adj.* – persistently holding to something

tenet – *n.* – any principle, doctrine, etc. which a person, school, etc. believes or maintains

tentative – *adj.* – not confirmed; indefinite

tepid – *adj.* – lacking warmth, interest, enthusiasm; lukewarm

termagant – *n.* – a boisterous, scolding woman; a shrew

terrestrial – *adj.* – pertaining to the earth

terse – *adj.* – concise; abrupt

tether – *n.* – the range or limit of one's abilities

thrall – *n.* – a slave

thrifty – *adj.* – economical; pennywise

throe – *v.* – to put in agony

thwart – *v.* – prevent from accomplishing a purpose; frustrate

timbre – *n.* – the degree of resonance of a voiced sound

timorous – *adj.* – fearful

torpid – *adj.* – lacking alertness and activity; lethargic

tortuous – *adj.* – pertaining to or involving excruciating pain

toxic – *adj.* – poisonous

tractable – *adj.* – easily led or managed

traduce – *v.* – 1. to exhibit; 2. to slander

tranquility – *n.* – peace; stillness; harmony

transitory – *adj.* – of a passing nature; speedily vanishing

transmute – *v.* – to transform

transpire – *v.* – to take place; come about

traumatic – *adj.* – causing a violent injury

travail – *v.* – to harass; to torment

travesty – *n.* – a crude and ridiculous representation

trek – *v.* – to make a journey

trenchant – *adj.* – 1. keen; penetrating; 2. clear-cut; distinct

trepidation – *n.* – apprehension; uneasiness

tribunal – *n.* – the seat of judgment

tribute – *n.* – expression of admiration

trite – *adj.* – commonplace; overused

trivial – *adj.* – unimportant; small; worthless

troth – *n.* – belief; faith; fidelity

truculent – *adj.* – aggressive; eager to fight

tumid – *adj.* – swollen; inflated

tumult – *n.* – great commotion or agitation

turbid – *adj.* – 1. thick; dense; 2. confused; perplexed

turbulence – *n.* – condition of being physically agitated; disturbance

turmoil – *n.* – unrest; agitation

turpitude – *n.* – shameful wickedness

tutelage – *n.* – the condition of being under a guardian or a tutor

tycoon – *n.* – wealthy leader

tyranny – *n.* – absolute power; autocracy

ubiquitous – *adj.* – ever present in all places; universal

ulterior – *adj.* – buried; concealed

umbrage – *n.* – shade; shadow

uncanny – *adj.* – of a strange nature; weird

uncouth – *adj.* – uncultured; crude

undermine – *v.* – weaken; ruin

unequivocal – *adj.* – clear; definite

unfeigned – *adj.* – genuine; real; sincere

uniform – *adj.* – consistent; unvaried; unchanging

unique – *adj.* – without equal; incomparable

universal – *adj.* – concerning everyone; existing everywhere

unobtrusive – *adj.* – inconspicuous; reserved

unprecedented – *adj.* – unheard of; exceptional

unpretentious – *adj.* – simple; plain; modest

unruly – *adj.* – not submitting to discipline; disobedient

untoward – *adj.* – 1. hard to manage or deal with; 2. inconvenient

unwonted – *adj.* – not ordinary; unusual

urbane – *adj.* – cultured; suave

usurpation – *n.* – act of taking something for oneself; seizure

usury – *n.* – the act of lending money at illegal rates of interest

utopia – *n.* – imaginary land with perfect social and political systems

uxoricide – *n.* – the murder of a wife by her husband

vacillation – *n.* – fluctuation

vacuous – *adj.* – containing nothing; empty

vagabond – *n.* – wanderer; one without a fixed place

vagary – *n.* – 1. an odd action or idea; 2. a wandering

vagrant – 1. *n.* – homeless person; 2. *adj.* – rambling; wandering; transient

valance – *n.* – short drapery hanging over the window frame

valid – *adj.* – acceptable; legal

valor – *n.* – bravery

vantage – *n.* – position giving an advantage

vaunt – *v.* – to brag or boast

vaunted – *v.* – boasted of

vehement – *adj.* – intense; excited; enthusiastic

velocity – *n.* – speed

venal – *adj.* – that can be readily bribed or corrupted

vendetta – *n.* – feud

veneer – 1. *n.* – a thin surface layer; 2. any attractive but superficial appearance

venerate – *v.* – revere

venue – *n.* – location

veracious – *adj.* – conforming to fact; accurate

veracity – *n.* – 1. honesty; 2. accuracy of statement

verbatim – *adj.* – employing the same words as another; literal

verbiage – *n.* – wordiness

verbose – *adj.* – wordy; talkative

verity – *n.* – truthfulness

versatile – *adj.* – having many uses; multifaceted

vertigo – *n.* – dizziness

vestige – *n.* – a trace of something that no longer exists

vex – *v.* – to trouble the nerves; annoy

viable – *adj.* – 1. capable of maintaining life; 2. possible; attainable

vicarious – *adj.* – taking the place of another person or thing

vicissitude – *n.* – charges or variation occurring irregularly in the course of something

vigilance – *n.* – watchfulness

vigor – *n.* – energy; forcefulness

vigorous – *adj.* – energetic; strong

vilify – *v.* – slander

vindicate – *v.* – to free from charge; clear

virile – *adj.* – manly, masculine

virtuoso – *n.* – highly skilled artist

virulent- *adj.* – deadly; harmful; malicious

visage – *n.* – appearance

viscous – *adj.* – thick, syrupy, and sticky

visionary – *adj.* – 1. characterized by impractical ideas; 2. not real

vital – *adj.* – important; spirited

vitriolic – *adj.* – extremely biting or caustic

vivacious – *adj.* – animated; gay

vociferous – *adj.* – making a loud outcry

vogue – *n.* – modern fashion

volatile – *adj.* – changeable; undependable

volition – *n.* – the act of willing

voluble – *adj.* – fluent

voracious – *adj.* – greedy in eating

vouchsafe – *v.* – 1. to be gracious enough to grant; 2. to guarantee as safe

vulnerable – *adj.* – open to attack; unprotected

waft – *v.* – move gently by wind or breeze

waive – *v.* – to give up possession or right

wan – *adj.* – pale; pallid

wane – *v.* – grow gradually smaller

wanton – *adj.* – unruly; excessive

warrant – *v.* – justify; authorize

welter – *v.* – 1. to roll about or wallow; 2. to rise and fall

wheedle – *v.* – try to persuade; coax

whet – *v.* – sharpen

whimsical – *adj.*- fanciful; amusing

wily – *adj.* – cunning; sly

winsome – *adj.* – agreeable; charming; delightful

wither – *v.* – wilt; shrivel; humiliate; cut down

wizened – *adj.* – withered; shrunken

wrath – *n.* – violent or unrestrained anger; fury

wreak – *v.* – to give vent or free play

wrest – *v.* – 1. to turn or twist; 2. usurp; 3. to distort or change the true meaning of

wry – *adj.* – mocking; cynical

xenophobia – *n.* – fear of foreigners

yoke – *n.* – harness; collar; bond

yore – *n.* – former period of time

zealot – *n.* – believer, enthusiast; fan

zenith – *n.* – point directly overhead in the sky

zephyr – *n.* – a gentle wind; breeze

DRILL 1

DIRECTIONS: Match each word in the left column with the word in the right column that is most opposite in meaning.

Word	Match
1. _____ articulate	A. hostile
2. _____ apathy	B. concrete
3. _____ amiable	C. selfish
4. _____ altruistic	D. reasoned
5. _____ ambivalent	E. ally
6. _____ abstract	F. disperse
7. _____ acquiesce	G. enthusiasm
8. _____ arbitrary	H. certain
9. _____ amass	I. resist
10. _____ adversary	J. incoherent
11. _____ audacious	K. fragrant
12. _____ aberration	L. conformity
13. _____ acrid	M. unadventurous

DIRECTIONS: Match each word in the left column with the word in the right column that is most similar in meaning.

Word	Match
14. ____ adamant	A. afraid
15. ____ aesthetic	B. disagreement
16. ____ apprehensive	C. tasteful
17. ____ antagonism	D. insistent
18. ____ altercation	E. hostility

DRILL 2

DIRECTIONS: Match each word in the left column with the word in the right column that is most opposite in meaning.

Word	Match
1. ____ augment	A. permit
2. ____ biased	B. heroine
3. ____ banal	C. praise
4. ____ benevolent	D. diminish
5. ____ censor	E. dishonest
6. ____ authentic	F. malicious
7. ____ candid	G. neutral
8. ____ belittle	H. mournful
9. ____ charlatan	I. unusual
10. ____ blithe	J. fake
11. ____ bombastic	K. directness
12. ____ circumlocution	L. modest

DIRECTIONS: Match each word in the left column with the word in the right column that is most similar in meaning.

Word	Match
13. ____ collaborate	A. harmless
14. ____ benign	B. cunning
15. ____ astute	C. changeable
16. ____ censure	D. cooperate
17. ____ capricious	E. criticize
18. ____ baleful	F. reprimand
19. ____ berate	G. ominous

DRILL 3

DIRECTIONS: Match each word in the left column with the word in the right column that is most opposite in meaning.

Word	Match
1. ____ deplete	A. unintentional
2. ____ contemporary	B. disapprove
3. ____ concise	C. invisible
4. ____ deliberate	D. respect
5. ____ depravity	E. fill
6. ____ condone	F. support
7. ____ conspicuous	G. beginning
8. ____ consummation	H. ancient
9. ____ denounce	I. virtue
10. ____ contempt	J. verbose
11. ____ colloquial	K. submissive
12. ____ contumacious	L. innocent

13. _____ culpable   M. success

14. _____ demur   N. agree

15. _____ debacle   O. sophisticated

DIRECTIONS: Match each word in the left column with the word in the right column that is most similar in meaning.

Word	Match
16. _____ compatible	A. portray
17. _____ depict	B. content
18. _____ conventional	C. harmonious
19. _____ comprehensive	D. thorough
20. _____ complacent	E. common

DRILL 4

DIRECTIONS: Match each word in the left column with the word in the right column that is most opposite in meaning.

Word	Match
1. _____ detached	A. agree
2. _____ deter	B. certain
3. _____ dissent	C. lethargy
4. _____ discord	D. connected
5. _____ efface	E. assist
6. _____ dubious	F. respect
7. _____ diligence	G. compliment
8. _____ disdain	H. sanctify
9. _____ desecrate	I. harmony
10. _____ disparage	J. restore
11. _____ dowdy	K. excitement

12. _____ erudite   L. acknowledge

13. _____ ennui   M. chic

14. _____ evanescent   N. uninformed

15. _____ disheartened   O. wild

16. _____ disavow   P. appearing

17. _____ docile   Q. uplifted

DIRECTIONS: Match each word in the left column with the word in the right column that is most similar in meaning.

Word	Match

18. _____ effervescence   A. stubborn

19. _____ dogmatic   B. distribute

20. _____ disseminate   C. substantiate

21. _____ document   D. liveliness

22. _____ eccentric   E. odd

23. _____ ethnic   F. native

24. _____ discomfit   G. confuse

DRILL 5

DIRECTIONS: Match each word in the left column with the word in the right column that is most opposite in meaning.

Word	Match

1. _____ extraneous   A. incomplete

2. _____ ephemeral   B. delay

3. _____ exhaustive   C. dependable

4. _____ expedite   D. comprehensible

5. _____ erroneous   E. dissonance

6. _____ erratic   F. eternal

7. _____ explicit   G. condemn

8. _____ euphony   H. relevant

9. _____ elusive   I. indefinite

10. _____ extol   J. accurate

11. _____ facetious   K. combat

12. _____ extol   L. considerate

13. _____ foster   M. rude

14. _____ fastidious   N. quiet

15. _____ flippant   O. denounce

16. _____ germane   P. calm

17. _____ garrulous   Q. solemn

18. _____ genial   R. immaterial

19. _____ frenetic   S. neglectful

DIRECTIONS: Match each word in the left column with the word in the right column that is most similar in meaning.

Word	**Match**
20. _____ endorse	A. enable
21. _____ expedient	B. recommend
22. _____ facilitate	C. create
23. _____ fallacious	D. worthwhile
24. _____ engender	E. deceptive
25. _____ furtive	F. stealthy
26. _____ fickle	G. unpredictable

DRILL 6

DIRECTIONS: Match each word in the left column with the word in the right column that is most opposite in meaning.

Word	Match
1. ____ heresy	A. predictable
2. ____ fickle	B. dispassionate
3. ____ illusory	C. simple
4. ____ frivolity	D. extraneous
5. ____ grandiose	E. real
6. ____ fervent	F. beneficial
7. ____ fundamental	G. orthodoxy
8. ____ furtive	H. organized
9. ____ futile	I. candid
10. ____ haphazard	J. seriousness
11. ____ ignoble	K. vigorous
12. ____ haggard	L. cynical
13. ____ gloat	M. deter
14. ____ hedonist	N. belittle
15. ____ gullible	O. admirable
16. ____ goad	P. puritan

DIRECTIONS: Match each word in the left column with the word in the right column that is most similar in meaning.

Word	Match
17. ____ glutton	A. hinder
18. ____ heed	B. obstacle
19. ____ goad	C. trite

20. ____ hackneyed   D. overeater

21. ____ hindrance   E. obey

22. ____ impale   F. principles

23. ____ ideology   G. transfix

DRILL 7

DIRECTIONS: Match each word in the left column with the word in the right column that is most opposite in meaning.

Word	Match
1. ____ innate	A. proper
2. ____ incredulous	B. injurious
3. ____ inevitable	C. responsible
4. ____ intangible	D. honor
5. ____ lamentable	E. blissful
6. ____ livid	F. encouraging
7. ____ lascivious	G. compromising
8. ____ innocuous	H. prudish
9. ____ lecherous	I. gravity
10. ____ levity	J. resentful
11. ____ lax	K. gullible
12. ____ intransigent	L. material
13. ____ invective	M. avoidable
14. ____ magnanimous	N. learned

DIRECTIONS: Match each word in the left column with the word in the right column that is most similar in meaning.

Word	Match
15. _____ infer	A. bewail
16. _____ instigate	B. radiant
17. _____ luminous	C. fatigued
18. _____ knave	D. alliance
19. _____ liaison	E. rogue
20. _____ languid	F. provoke
21. _____ lament	G. conclude

DRILL 8

DIRECTIONS: Match each word in the left column with the word in the right column that is most opposite in meaning.

Word	Match
1. _____ ostensible	A. aversion
2. _____ obsolete	B. flexible
3. _____ nebulous	C. unnoticeable
4. _____ penchant	D. actual
5. _____ neophyte	E. opponent
6. _____ partisan	F. domineering
7. _____ obdurate	G. distinct
8. _____ obsequious	H. assertive
9. _____ palpable	I. modern
10. _____ passive	J. veteran
11. _____ meticulous	K. jovial
12. _____ morose	L. sloppy

13. ____ minute   M. huge

14. ____ novel   N. stale

DIRECTIONS: Match each word in the left column with the word in the right column that is most similar in meaning.

Word	Match
15. ____ nullify	A. invalidate
16. ____ ominous	B. irritate
17. ____ nettle	C. dull
18. ____ palliate	D. threatening
19. ____ opaque	E. alleviate
20. ____ marred	F. lessen
21. ____ mitigate	G. damaged
22. ____ negligence	H. carelessness

DRILL 9

DIRECTIONS: Match each word in the left column with the word in the right column that is most opposite in meaning.

Word	Match
1. ____ pristine	A. inexperienced
2. ____ phlegmatic	B. anger
3. ____ profound	C. central
4. ____ qualified	D. cheerful
5. ____ placid	E. shallow
6. ____ placate	F. joyous
7. ____ pensive	G. extraordinary
8. ____ peripheral	H. contaminated
9. ____ petulant	I. excited

10. ____ prosaic   J. turbulent

11. ____ placate   K. dearth

12. ____ profusion   L. facilitate

13. ____ peripheral   M. superficial

14. ____ plausible   N. improbable

15. ____ preclude   O. minute

16. ____ prodigious   P. anger

17. ____ profound   Q. central

DIRECTIONS: Match each word in the left column with the word in the right column that is most similar in meaning.

Word   **Match**

18. ____ provocative   A. nearness

19. ____ pungent   B. tempting

20. ____ propinquity   C. reverent

21. ____ pious   D. flavorsome

22. ____ pragmatic   E. practical

23. ____ pernicious   F. lavish

24. ____ prodigal   G. harmful

DRILL 10

DIRECTIONS: Match each word in the left column with the word in the right column that is most opposite in meaning.

Word   **Match**

1. ____ salient   A. forward

2. ____ reticent   B. promote

3. ____ raucous   C. pleasant

4. ____ redundant   D. minor

5. ____ relegate

6. ____ repugnant

7. ____ repudiate

8. ____ rebuff

9. ____ scrupulous

10. ____ sanguine

11. ____ reticent

12. ____ prudent

13. ____ relegate

14. ____ remorse

15. ____ repudiate

16. ____ sanguine

17. ____ relevant

E. affirm

F. unprincipled

G. necessary

H. pleasant

I. welcome

J. pessimistic

K. joy

L. pessimistic

M. unrelated

N. careless

O. affirm

P. forward

Q. promote

DIRECTIONS: Match each word in the left column with the word in the right column that is most similar in meaning.

Word	Match
18. ____ rescind	A. deliver
19. ____ reprehensible	B. blameworthy
20. ____ render	C. retract
21. ____ sagacious	D. drench
22. ____ saturate	E. wise
23. ____ rigor	F. drench
24. ____ saturate	G. retract
25. ____ rescind	H. severity
26. ____ reprehensible	I. disgraceful

DRILL 11

DIRECTIONS: Match each word in the left column with the word in the right column that is most opposite in meaning.

Word	Match
1. ____ scrutinize	A. frivolity
2. ____ skeptic	B. enjoyable
3. ____ solemnity	C. prodigal
4. ____ static	D. chaos
5. ____ tedious	E. give
6. ____ tentative	F. skim
7. ____ thrifty	G. turbulent
8. ____ tranquility	H. active
9. ____ solicit	I. believer
10. ____ stagnant	J. confirmed

DIRECTIONS: Match each word in the left column with the word in the right column that is most similar in meaning.

Word	Match
11. ____ symmetry	A. understated
12. ____ superfluous	B. unnecessary
13. ____ sycophant	C. balance
14. ____ subtle	D. fear
15. ____ trepidation	E. flatterer

DRILL 12

DIRECTIONS: Match each word in the left column with the word in the right column that is most opposite in meaning.

Word	Match
1. ____ uniform	A. amateur
2. ____ virtuoso	B. trivial
3. ____ vital	C. visible
4. ____ wane	D. placid
5. ____ unobtrusive	E. unacceptable
6. ____ vigor	F. support
7. ____ volatile	G. constancy
8. ____ vacillation	H. lethargy
9. ____ undermine	I. wax
10. ____ valid	J. varied

DIRECTIONS: Match each word in the left column with the word in the right column that is most similar in meaning.

Word	Match
11. ____ wither	A. intense
12. ____ whimsical	B. deadly
13. ____ viable	C. amusing
14. ____ vehement	D. possible
15. ____ virulent	E. shrivel

ANSWER KEY

DRILL 1

1.	(J)	6.	(B)	11.	(M)	16.	(A)
2.	(G)	7.	(I)	12.	(L)	17.	(E)
3.	(A)	8.	(D)	13.	(K)	18.	(B)
4.	(C)	9.	(F)	14.	(D)		
5.	(H)	10.	(E)	15.	(C)		

DRILL 2

1.	(D)	6.	(J)	11.	(L)	16.	(E)
2.	(G)	7.	(E)	12.	(K)	17.	(C)
3.	(I)	8.	(C)	13.	(D)	18.	(G)
4.	(F)	9.	(B)	14.	(A)	19.	(F)
5.	(A)	10.	(H)	15.	(B)		

DRILL 3

1.	(E)	6.	(B)	11.	(O)	16.	(C)
2.	(H)	7.	(C)	12.	(K)	17.	(A)
3.	(J)	8.	(G)	13.	(L)	18.	(E)
4.	(A)	9.	(F)	14.	(N)	19.	(D)
5.	(I)	10.	(D)	15.	(M)	20.	(B)

DRILL 4

1.	(D)	7.	(C)	13.	(K)	19.	(A)
2.	(E)	8.	(F)	14.	(P)	20.	(B)
3.	(A)	9.	(H)	15.	(Q)	21.	(C)
4.	(I)	10.	(G)	16.	(L)	22.	(E)
5.	(J)	11.	(M)	17.	(O)	23.	(F)
6.	(B)	12.	(N)	18.	(D)	24.	(B)

DRILL 5

1.	(H)	8.	(E)	15.	(L)	22.	(A)
2.	(F)	9.	(D)	16.	(R)	23.	(E)
3.	(A)	10.	(G)	17.	(N)	24.	(C)
4.	(B)	11.	(Q)	18.	(M)	25.	(F)
5.	(J)	12.	(O)	19.	(P)	26.	(G)
6.	(C)	13.	(K)	20.	(B)		
7.	(I)	14.	(S)	21.	(D)		

DRILL 6

1.	(G)	7.	(D)	13.	(N)	19.	(A)
2.	(A)	8.	(I)	14.	(P)	20.	(C)
3.	(E)	9.	(F)	15.	(L)	21.	(B)
4.	(J)	10.	(H)	16.	(M)	22.	(G)
5.	(C)	11.	(O)	17.	(D)	23.	(F)
6.	(B)	12.	(K)	18.	(E)		

DRILL 7

1.	(N)	7.	(A)	13.	(D)	19.	(D)
2.	(K)	8.	(B)	14.	(J)	20.	(C)
3.	(M)	9.	(H)	15.	(G)	21.	(A)
4.	(L)	10.	(I)	16.	(F)		
5.	(F)	11.	(C)	17.	(B)		
6.	(E)	12.	(G)	18.	(E)		

DRILL 8

1.	(D)	7.	(B)	13.	(M)	19.	(C)
2.	(I)	8.	(F)	14.	(N)	20.	(G)
3.	(G)	9.	(C)	15.	(A)	21.	(F)
4.	(A)	10.	(H)	16.	(D)	22.	(H)
5.	(J)	11.	(L)	17.	(B)		
6.	(E)	12.	(K)	18.	(E)		

DRILL 9

1.	(H)	7.	(F)	13.	(Q)	19.	(D)
2.	(I)	8.	(C)	14.	(N)	20.	(A)
3.	(E)	9.	(D)	15.	(L)	21.	(C)
4.	(A)	10.	(G)	16.	(O)	22.	(E)
5.	(J)	11.	(P)	17.	(M)	23.	(G)
6.	(B)	12.	(K)	18.	(B)	24.	(F)

DRILL 10

1.	(D)	8.	(I)	15.	(O)	22.	(D)
2.	(A)	9.	(F)	16.	(L)	23.	(H)
3.	(H)	10.	(J)	17.	(M)	24.	(F)
4.	(G)	11.	(P)	18.	(C)	25.	(G)
5.	(B)	12.	(N)	19.	(B)	26.	(I)
6.	(C)	13.	(Q)	20.	(A)		
7.	(E)	14.	(K)	21.	(E)		

DRILL 11

1.	(F)	5.	(B)	9.	(E)	13.	(E)
2.	(I)	6.	(J)	10.	(G)	14.	(A)
3.	(A)	7.	(C)	11.	(C)	15.	(D)
4.	(H)	8.	(D)	12.	(B)		

DRILL 12

1.	(J)	5.	(C)	9.	(F)	13.	(D)
2.	(A)	6.	(H)	10.	(E)	14.	(A)
3.	(B)	7.	(D)	11.	(E)	15.	(B)
4.	(I)	8.	(G)	12.	(C)		

INDEX

Numbers on this page refer to **QUESTION NUMBERS**, not page numbers.